TIME

Reaching for Tomorrow

Authentic Readings for Language Development

Articles selected by
Linda Schinke-Llano

National Textbook Company
a division of *NTC Publishing Group* • Lincolnwood, Illinois USA

ACKNOWLEDGMENTS

My sincere appreciation goes to Rebecca Rauff for her invaluable assistance in every stage of the conceptualization and development of this project; to Kathleen Schultz of National Textbook Company for her patience with all the challenges this project entailed; and to Millikin University whose Hardy Professorship granted me time to work on a portion of this text. Once again this book is a gift to my daughter Melissa: Here's a view of your world at age ten!

ABOUT THE AUTHOR

Linda Schinke-Llano is associate professor and Hardy Distinguished Professor of English at Millikin University in Decatur, Illinois. She holds a Ph.D. in Linguistics and an M.A. in TESOL. Specializing in second-language acquisition, English as a second or foreign language, and bilingual education, she also has taught at Northwestern University and the University of Puerto Rico.

Articles from TIME Magazine are republished by permission of Time Inc., the copyright proprietor.

1995 Printing

INTRODUCTION

TIME magazine is read weekly by millions of people around the world and is recognized by millions more. Its up-to-date, informative articles familiarize readers with issues of international interest, as well as with topics of specific concern to Americans and to those interested in life in the United States.

Just as *TIME* offers a unique view of the United States and its people, *TIME: Reaching for Tomorrow* presents a special reading opportunity for students of English. Those already familiar with *TIME: We the People* will be pleased to see that this is an all-new volume consisting of forty-three recently published articles. The articles are organized into seven sections similar to those used in *TIME* magazine: *Lifestyles, Education, Nature and the Environment, Science and Technology, Health and Medicine, Entertainment and Sports,* and *Fads and Fashions.* The articles have been selected to present a broad overview of aspects of life in the United States—both the positive and the negative, the permanent and the transitory. Each article appears in its original form, without abridgment or simplification. Photographs, illustrations, charts, and other graphics accompany the articles.

Although the articles are grouped into subject categories, they are not sequenced by difficulty level and may be read in any order. Each reading is preceded by a "Before You Read" section (consisting of Preview, Getting Started, Culture, Vocabulary, and Culture and Vocabulary Activities) intended to prepare the reader for the article. The Preview is a brief statement that summarizes or introduces the content of the article. Getting Started includes questions and activities that focus on students' prior knowledge of the general topic of the article. The Culture and Vocabulary lists include definitions and phonetic transcriptions of important or unusual words and phrases used in the article. The Culture and Vocabulary Activities allow students to examine particular terms, to link them to already known words and phrases, and to draw conclusions about how English, particularly American English, functions.

Following each article is an "After You Read" section (consisting of Comprehension Questions, Discussion and Analysis Questions, Group Activities, and Individual Work). The Comprehension Questions are factual questions designed to check the reader's understanding of the article. The Discussion and Analysis Questions allow readers to react to the content of the article and to examine how the writer conveys ideas. The Group Activities encourage critical thinking about both the issues presented in the article and the way the English language functions. Finally, the Individual Work offers students the opportunity to develop and practice both oral and written communication skills.

With its combination of authentic contemporary articles and specially designed activities, *TIME: Reaching for Tomorrow* can serve as a bridge to the independent reading of other authentic texts. More specifically, this text has been created with six goals for its readers:

1. to increase comprehension of written English through the use of authentic materials commonly read by native speakers;
2. to improve oral English skills through meaningful communicative activities, both in the classroom and outside of it;
3. to practice written English skills through focused assignments;
4. to develop an understanding of common writing conventions in English;
5. to learn more about how English, particularly American English, functions; and
6. to develop a knowledge of the United States and its people.

It is hoped that all readers will achieve these goals and enjoy the text in the process.

Linda Schinke-Llano

CONTENTS

© JILL SALYARDS

1

PHOTO BY RAY BALTES/COURTESY OF MILLIKIN UNIVERSITY

2

FRANK HOFFMAN—MARTIN MARIETTA ENERGY SYSTEMS

3

NASA

©JILL SALYARDS

ROB BROWN/SAMUEL GOLDWYN COMPANY

©JILL SALYARDS

GUIDE TO PRONUNCIATION

Vowels and Diphthongs

[i]   heed, bead, see
[ɪ]   hid, lid, tin
[e]   shade, played, trade
[ɛ]   head, sled, men
[æ]   had, glad, sad
[u]   shoot, glue, shoe
[ʊ]   put, foot, would
[o]   home, glow, so
[ɔ]   caught, raw, yawn
[ɑ]   odd, clock, wad
[ə]   hut, about, tuna, parade
[ɚ]   hurt, shirt, butter
[ɑɪ]   height, mine, sigh
[ɑʊ]   house, brown, shout
[ɔɪ]   coin, joy, hoist

Consonants

[p]   pipe, top, pie
[b]   boat, job, bone
[t]   town, coat, right
[d]   road, deer, down, water, charity, waiter
[k]   duck, king, cone
[g]   girl, frog, ghost
[f]   friend, fix, phantom
[v]   have, vent, save
[θ]   with, thing, throw
[ð]   this, then, soothe
[s]   miss, soft, mouse
[z]   zoom, buzz, phase
[ʃ]   wish, shave, ship
[ʒ]   measure, azure, pleasure
[h]   house, who, help
[tʃ]   chew, catch, chart
[dʒ]   edge, job, Gene
[m]   room, mother, some
[n]   sun, nest, nurse
[ŋ]   sing, rang, swing
[w]   win, swing, twist
[j]   yellow, you, yes
[l]   will, lip, slick
[r]   red, wrist, tree
[']   precedes syllables with primary stress.
[ˌ]   precedes syllables with secondary stress.
( )   encloses sounds that are sometimes not pronounced.

Note: In American English, when a *t* appears between two vowels and the first vowel is stressed, the *t* is reduced to a flap. In this textbook, the flap is transcribed as a [d]. For example, the word *letter* is pronounced ['lɛdɚ].

Lifestyles

OLD-FASHIONED PLAY—FOR PAY

BEFORE YOU READ

Preview

The newest trend in children's playgrounds is to build them indoors.

Getting Started

1. What was your favorite play activity when you were a child? Where did you play it?
2. Think of a child you know. What is his or her favorite activity?
3. Have children's activities changed over the years? If so, in what ways have they changed? Why do you think such changes have happened?

Culture

beeper ['bipɚ]   a portable device used to call or signal someone. Many doctors carry beepers so that their hospitals can contact them wherever they are.

couch potato ['kaʊtʃ pə,tedo]   a lazy, do-nothing television watcher

day-care facility ['de kɛr fə,sɪləti]   a place where children are cared for while their parents work. Some adult day-care facilities exist for the elderly.

franchise ['fræntʃaɪz]   a business that is associated with a larger corporation. Franchises usually have individual owners.

moonwalk ['munwɔk]   a group of air-filled tubes for children to jump and bounce on. A moonwalk resembles a huge, brightly colored air mattress.

Nintendo [nɪn'tɛndo]   the brand name of a popular series of video games for children

turkey dog ['tɚki ,dɔg]   a hot dog made from turkey meat instead of from pork or beef

Vocabulary

(to) break the (family) bank ['brek ðə (,fæmli) 'bæŋk]   to cost a lot of money; to cause bankruptcy

for-profit [for 'prɑfɪt]   intended to earn money. In contrast, charitable organizations are usually not-for-profit.

(to) get squeezed [gɛt 'skwizd]   to be reduced; to have pressure put on

(to) have a ball [,hæv ə 'bɔl]   to have a really great time; to enjoy oneself

mega- ['mɛgə]   very large; huge

(to) pop up [,pap 'əp]   to appear suddenly

seedy ['sidi]   shabby and dirty; poorly maintained and possibly dangerous

workout ['wɚkaʊt]   a period of exercise

Culture and Vocabulary Activities

1. Choose five words or phrases from the lists above and write a sentence using each one. Recopy the sentences, leaving blanks in place of the Culture and Vocabulary terms. Exchange sentences with a partner and fill in the blanks. Check each other's work.
2. The prefix *mega-* can be added to nouns in English to change their meanings. Invent five to ten English words using *mega-*. What do they mean? For example, a *megacity* is a very large city.

Old-Fashioned Play–for Pay

Parents and kids gather for a few hours of moonwalking, mountain climbing and other activities at the "McPlayland" outside Chicago

As outdoor playgrounds decay, more families are turning to cheery franchises that offer supervised fun for a fee

By ELIZABETH RUDULPH

Kids! come have a ball! or 60,000 of them! There's a new type of business franchise that is popping up in shopping malls and neighborhoods across America. At least two nationwide companies are offering pay-per-use indoor playgrounds, which feature toys, games, supervised fun and a workout that doesn't break the family bank.

As public playgrounds grow increasingly seedy, the for-profit centers offer clean, safe, supervised activity as well as a variety of challenging exercises to develop youngsters' physical fitness, usually for a fee of around $5 an hour. "Playgrounds are dirty, not supervised," says Dick Guggenheimer, owner of the two-month-old Discovery Zone in Yonkers, N.Y., part of a Kansas City–based chain. "We're indoors; we're padded; parents can feel their child is safe."

Discovery Zone has sold 120 outlets in the past 14 months, boasting sandboxes full of brightly colored plastic spheres, mazes, mats to bounce on, obstacle courses, moonwalks, slides and mountains to climb. Now mega-franchiser McDonald's is getting into the act. The burger giant is test-marketing a new playground, Leaps & Bounds, in Naperville, Ill. Phys Kids of Wichita has opened one center and has plans to expand.

American parents are rightly worried about their kids' leisure life, built around Saturday-morning cartoons and Nintendo. There are 36 million children in the U.S. ages 2 to 11; they watch an average of 24 hours of TV a week and devote less and less energy to active recreation. Nationwide cutbacks in education budgets are making the problem worse, as gym classes and after-hours sports time get squeezed. Says Discovery Zone president Jack Gunion: "We have raised a couple of generations of pure couch potatoes."

In an attempt to soup up that life-style, the new facilities cater to the concerns of two-earner families, staying open in the evenings, long after traditional public playgrounds have grown dark and unusable. At Naperville's Leaps & Bounds, families can play together for $4.95 per child, parents free. Fresh-faced "counselors," dressed in colorful sport pants and shirts, guide youngsters to appropriate play areas for differing age groups. Three-year-olds and younger can learn spatial concepts—in and out, over and around—

by crawling in a padded plastic turtle shell or sinking into a quicksand of colorful balls and learning to control the multicolored plastic objects. Kids ages 4 to 6 climb a padded "Swiss-cheese mountain" or creep through a maze of blue, fuchsia and yellow tunnels. Youngsters up to 12 balance on a rope walk or on a webbed "bean field," a bouncy surface with punching bags that hang above it within a child's grasp. A nearby concession offers turkey dogs, pizza, and carrot and celery sticks.

These new playgrounds are not meant to be day-care facilities; parents are expected to stay and play with their kids rather than drop them off. But several also provide high-tech baby-sitting services. At some of the Discovery Zones, parents can register their children in special supervised programs, then leave them and slip away for a couple of hours to enjoy a movie or dinner. If there is a problem, Mom and Dad are paged by beeper.

The most fun of all, though, is getting to do what parents used to do in the days before two-career families and two-hour commutes: play with their kids. That, at least, is old-fashioned, even at per-hour rates. —*With reporting by Elizabeth Taylor/Chicago*

AFTER YOU READ

Comprehension Questions

1. What problems do many outdoor playgrounds have?
2. What are the names of the new playground franchises?
3. How do many American children spend their leisure time? How many hours of television do they watch each week?
4. What are some benefits of the new indoor playgrounds?

Discussion and Analysis Questions

1. Do you think the indoor playgrounds are a good idea? Why or why not? Can you think of any disadvantages?
2. The fifth paragraph mentions foods that are sold at one playground. What is significant about these foods?
3. Both the title and the last sentence of the article refer to the new playgrounds as "old-fashioned." What does the writer mean by this?

Group Activities

1. In groups of three, discuss the names of the playgrounds. What images do these names suggest? Imagine that your group owns an indoor playground. Make up a name for it. Share your name with the class. Explain why you chose it.
2. With the same group, invent an activity or a piece of playground equipment for your playground. Describe it to the class.

Individual Work

Visit a playground and take notes on what you see. For example, how many children are there? What are their approximate ages? How many pieces of equipment are there? What is the condition of the playground? What are the best features of this playground? What are its worst features? Turn in your notes or tell the class about your observations.

2 TIDINGS OF BLACK PRIDE AND JOY

BEFORE YOU READ

Preview

Each year, more and more African Americans celebrate a new holiday called Kwanzaa.

Getting Started

1. What is your favorite holiday? Explain its purpose and tell how it is celebrated in your culture.
2. Has your favorite holiday been celebrated for a very long time, or is it a relatively new holiday?

Culture

black-nationalist [ˌblæk ˈnæʃənəlɪst]   pertaining to a group of African Americans who believe that blacks and whites should have separate, self-governing communities

Hanukkah [ˈhɑnəkə]   an eight-day Jewish holiday that celebrates the rededication of the Temple of Jerusalem

Nehru-style suit [ˈneru stɑɪl ˌsut]   a type of suit worn by the late Indian Prime Minister Nehru. The suit jacket had a stand-up collar and no lapels. Some Americans adopted the style in the 1960s.

Nintendo [nɪnˈtɛndo]   the brand name of a popular series of video games for children

Yule [jul]   Christmas

Vocabulary

ball [bɔl]   a large formal dance

commercial [kəˈmɚʃəl]   emphasizing profit (buying and selling) over purpose

mainstream [ˈmenstrim]   the majority group

radical [ˈrædɪkəl]   extreme; drastic

roots [ruts]   one's origins; one's cultural heritage

(to) surf [sɚf]   to ride the waves on a special board called a surfboard. Surfing is very popular in southern California.

Swahili [swɑˈhili]   a language that is widely spoken in East Africa

tiding [ˈtɑɪdɪŋ]   a bit of news (old-fashioned)

Culture and Vocabulary Activity

Skim the article to find the Swahili words used. How many can you find? What do they mean?

Tidings of Black Pride and Joy

Kwanzaa, the African-American Yule-time celebration, is becoming more popular—and more commercial

By JANICE C. SIMPSON

ADD A NEW SEASONAL GREETING TO YOUR list: *Habari gani.* It is Swahili for "What's new?" and the salutation for millions of African Americans who celebrate Kwanzaa, a seven-day holiday that begins on Dec. 26. Inaugurated 25 years ago as a black-nationalist celebration of familial and social values, the festivities are now being embraced by the black mainstream.

Kwanzaa is patterned after various African agricultural festivals, and the name derives from the Swahili word for first fruit of the harvest. It was created by Maulana Karenga, a black-studies professor at California State University, Long Beach. The purpose of the holiday, he says, is to help black people "rescue and reconstruct our history and culture and shape them in our own image."

Unlike Christmas or Hanukkah, Kwanzaa is not a religious holiday; the festival celebrates seven principles—unity, self-determination, collective work and responsibility, cooperative economics, purpose, creativity and faith—assigned to each of the days. Observers gather each evening to light one of the candles in the *kinara,* a seven-cup candelabrum, and discuss how the principle of the day affects their life. Small gifts are often exchanged.

In the late 1960s, Kwanzaa was celebrated mainly by the more radical members of the black-nationalist community. But now, says the Rev. Willie Wilson, pastor at Union Temple Baptist Church in Washington, "you find a lot of people trying to return to their roots and cultural values." Each year Wilson's church holds nightly Kwanzaa observances that culminate in a ball, which now draws about 1,000 participants. No one knows precisely how many

people observe Kwanzaa, but its biggest boosters are middle-class professionals seeking to give their children a sense of black pride. "My children grew up in a fairly white community, and that motivated me to teach them the value of the African-American heritage," says Vickie Butcher, 50, a lawyer in El Cajon, Calif., who celebrates with her physician husband and their five children. "We sit in a circle, and every person talks about that day's principle," she says. "The creating and sharing is real quality time."

On the final night of the holiday, friends and relatives join the family for a feast

---

THE PRINCIPLES OF KWANZAA

1. **Unity (umoja)**
2. **Self-determination (kujichagulia)**
3. **Collective responsibility (ujima)**
4. **Cooperative economics (ujamaa)**
5. **Purpose (nia)**
6. **Creativity (kuumba)**
7. **Faith (imani)**

Young celebrators perform a holiday play

© BRENT JONES

known as the Karamu. This year a compendium of celebratory recipes has been published in Eric Copage's *Kwanzaa: An African-American Celebration of Culture and Cooking* (Morrow; $25). The book also contains stories about black history and culture, along with suggestions on how to use them to illustrate the seven principles.

Museums and other institutions have begun to adopt the celebrations. Last year more than 8,500 people attended poetry readings, music performances and puppet shows during the sixth annual observance at Manhattan's American Museum of Natural History. The Smithsonian added a program of Kwanzaa activities to its Christmas and Hanukkah celebrations in 1988.

The proximity to Christmas and the fact that gifts are bestowed have led some people to think of Kwanzaa as a Yule alternative, but increasingly, black families observe both. As the black holiday spirit spreads, however, so do problems of creeping commercialism. One black-owned publishing company already markets 21 styles of Kwanzaa cards and a 32-page activity book for children. Future products include a Kwanzaa kit, complete with a *kinara* and instructions for novice celebrators.

Some parents even purchase bicycles and Nintendo sets for Kwanzaa gifts; they rationalize the excess by buying from black-owned businesses. That, they say, is in the spirit of *ujamaa,* or cooperative economics. "This is the U.S., and if anything becomes successful, it almost automatically becomes commercial," says Copage. "Doing otherwise is like trying to surf without getting wet."

What next? Cedric McClester, author of *Kwanzaa: Everything You Always Wanted to Know but Didn't Know Where to Ask,* has created Nia Umoja, "an African answer to Santa Claus." The character, who is supposed to represent an African griot, or wise man, wears a Nehru-style suit and joins hands with youngsters to ask what they have learned about Kwanzaa. Says McClester: "Kwanzaa needed a character because we need to attract younger people and their parents."

Traditionalists disapprove of these developments but say they are a natural part of the evolution of holiday celebrations. "These things are going to happen, just as they have with Christmas, Chinese New Year and Hanukkah," says Tulivu Jadi, an official at the African American Cultural Center in Los Angeles. "But there is still a community—and not a small one—that observes the serious intent of the holiday." This year the center is collecting food and clothing for the homeless, another way to spread the true joys of Kwanzaa. ■

AFTER YOU READ

Comprehension Questions

1. What does the word *Kwanzaa* mean? What is the Kwanzaa celebration patterned after?
2. Who created Kwanzaa? Why did he create it?
3. How is the holiday celebrated?
4. Who originally celebrated Kwanzaa? Who are its biggest supporters now?
5. What do some people criticize about Kwanzaa today?

Discussion and Analysis Questions

1. Do you think it is important for different groups of people to celebrate their own holidays? Why or why not?
2. Think about your favorite holiday. Is it commercialized? Do you think commercialization of holidays is a problem? Why or why not?
3. This article contains many Swahili words. Why do you think the writer used so many non-English words? Do you think they help the article? Why or why not?
4. Do you think the writer explained Kwanzaa well? What other information would you like to know about this holiday?

Group Activity

Form seven groups to discuss the seven principles of Kwanzaa. (Be sure that each group talks about a different principle.) In your group, discuss how the principle affects your lives. Be ready to report your conclusions to the class.

Individual Work

Choose one of the seven principles of Kwanzaa. Write a half-page description of how the principle affects your life.

3 THE STATE OF MANY TONGUES

BEFORE YOU READ

Preview

Speaking many languages can be profitable.

Getting Started

1. What are the individual benefits of being bilingual or multilingual? What are the benefits to the community?
2. What areas of the United States do you think are multilingual?
3. Quickly read the first paragraph, the first sentence in every paragraph, and the last paragraph of the article. Write down any words or phrases that you are unsure of. What do you think they mean? What do you think the main point of the article is?

Culture

missionary ['mɪʃə,nɛri]   a person who goes out to teach other people about a particular religion and to try to convert (change) them to that religion

Tower of Babel ['tɑʊɚ əv 'bæbəl]   according to the Bible, a tower whose construction was interrupted by a confusion of languages

Vocabulary

clientele [,klɑɪən'tɛl]   customers

(to) hawk [hɔk]   to sell

homegrown ['hom'gron]   locally made

landlocked ['lænd'lɑkt]   having no access to water; surrounded by land

like bees in a hive [,lɑɪk 'biz ɪn ə 'hɑɪv]   busily

literate ['lɪdɚət]   well-informed

lured [lurd]   attracted

(to) pay off ['pe 'ɔf]   to succeed

per capita [pɚ 'kæpɪtə]   for each person

savvy ['sævi]   knowledgeable

tongue [təŋ]   language

Culture and Vocabulary Activities

1. Check the list of words and phrases you made for number three in "Getting Started." Do any of your selections appear on the Culture and Vocabulary lists? If so, do their meanings match your guesses?
2. Which two words on the Vocabulary list are *synonyms* (words with approximately the same meaning)?

Instructor Jalene Merkley teaches French to future missionaries in Provo

LIFESTYLES

The State of Many Tongues

Utah's Mormon missionaries make the state America's most linguistically diverse region, and it's paying off

By SALLY B. DONNELLY SALT LAKE CITY

I F THE BUILDERS OF THE LEGENDARY Tower of Babel had hired a work crew from Utah, the massive structure might actually have been completed instead of collapsing in the confusion of the workers' diverse languages. The linguistically savvy Utahans could have worked like bees in a hive. Or at least that is the boast among modern-day locals, who are using their language skills to build the economy of their home state.

Sparsely populated, landlocked and laced with the deserts, mountains and rugged wilderness regions typical of the American West, Utah is an unlikely place to find people who collectively speak 90% of the world's written languages. "I can make one phone call and get a foreign-language speaker in 30 minutes. That's pretty impressive for a state of 2 million," says Fred Ball, head of the local Chamber of Commerce, who frequently is host to foreign executives. Per capita, Utah is the most linguistically diverse region of the U.S.—a feature the state is exploiting to attract foreign businesses and make tourists feel more welcome. The world-class ski resorts at Park City and Deer Valley reflect the clientele by providing signs in both English and Japanese, and the state is hawking its linguistic skills as part of its campaign to be host of the Winter Olympics in 2002.

Much of the multilingual talent is a dividend from the missionary work performed by the Salt Lake City–based Mormon Church, officially known as the Church of Jesus Christ of Latter-day Saints. For decades the church has sent thousands of young men (and a few women) each year on missions to win converts around the world. They spend at least two years in an assigned region, preaching the Mormon message and living side by side with locals. With more than 8 million members worldwide, the church has 44,500 missionaries serving in 95 countries and 26 territories.

Each of those who serves first attends the Missionary Training Center in Provo, which can handle 3,000 students at a time. Part of their studies includes intensive language training for several hours a day, seven days a week. From Armenian to Vietnamese—including such low-demand tongues as Estonian, Tahitian and Icelandic—38 different languages are taught at the center, usually by former missionaries

SPEAKING FREELY

The Missionary Training Center in Provo teaches 38 languages:

Afrikaans, American Sign, Armenian, Bulgarian, Cambodian, Cantonese, Czech, Danish, Dutch, Estonian, English, Finnish, French, German, Greek, Haitian Creole, Hmong, Hungarian, Icelandic, Italian, Japanese, Korean, Lao, Mandarin, Norwegian, Polish, Portuguese, Romanian, Russian, Samoan, Serbo-Croatian, Spanish, Swedish, Tagalog, Tahitian, Thai, Tongan, Vietnamese.

or foreign students from nearby universities. At Mormon-backed Brigham Young University, more than 60% of the 28,000 students acquire extensive foreign-language experience.

Utah's linguistic richness has prompted several international companies to open divisions in the state. Atlanta-based Delta Air Lines, which recently expanded service to 35 cities in Europe and Asia, has set up an international reservations center in Salt Lake City. Agents can take bookings in 13 foreign languages, including Hindi and Swedish. Several years ago, American Express decided to situate its worldwide traveler's check service center in Salt Lake City. On the outside, the four-story glass-and-concrete structure looks like any other modern office building, but inside the atmosphere is more like the Disneyland ride It's a Small World. More than half the 1,600 employees are bilingual; all told, they speak 118 languages. "As any traveler knows, it can be frustrating to deal with a complicated problem if you don't speak the language. We find customers are relieved to find that someone on the other end of the line can understand," says Ronna Draper, an operator and Spanish-language student at the University of Utah.

Homegrown firms have discovered that the local talent pool offers more than enough depth to build global businesses. ALPNET, a translation company B.Y.U. started as a research project in 1980, has developed into a $26 million business with 250 employees in 22 offices around the globe. Because Salt Lake City has become a high-tech center as well, computer-aided translation comes naturally to many local workers. "It is a unique combination: a linguistically and culturally conscious society that is also computer literate," says ALPNET president Thomas Seal. Among the company's clients: Apple Computer, British Petroleum, NATO and Siemens. The U.S. Army recently called on ALPNET to translate 32,000 pages of information on the Bradley Fighting Vehicle into Arabic for the Saudi military.

Officials from the state's Economic Development Corporation, which has branches from Brussels to Tokyo, like to point out that 60% of all public high school students in Utah study a foreign language. And the state has done well by vigorously pushing its language skills as an attraction to potential foreign-transplant factories and offices.

Last year, for example, the Taiwan-based computer firm Compeq Manufacturing chose Utah for its first overseas plant. Compeq's executives were lured by Utah residents who not only spoke Mandarin but also understood the customs and culture of a Taiwanese company—further proof that, in an increasingly global economy, the multilingual abilities of Utahans may speak louder than words. ∎

AFTER YOU READ

Comprehension Questions

1. Why is Utah an unlikely place to find so many multilingual people?
2. What is the main reason that so many people in Utah are multilingual?
3. Why does the Mormon Church want its members to study foreign languages? Where are they trained? How many languages are taught there?
4. What international companies have opened offices in Utah?
5. What is ALPNET?

Discussion and Analysis Questions

1. Have you ever thought of languages as being "good business"? Why or why not?
2. Are you surprised by the emphasis on foreign languages in Utah and in the Mormon Church? What is your opinion of the Mormon Church training its missionaries to speak foreign languages?
3. This article includes many statistics. Find several sentences that contain statistics. What purpose do they serve?
4. This article also includes direct quotations from three different people. Find these quotations. What purpose do they serve?

Group Activities

1. In groups of three or four, look at the list of languages taught at the Missionary Training Center. Make a list of the country or countries in which each language is spoken. How many do you know? Which languages are spoken in more than one country? Which languages have names that are different from the names of the countries in which they are spoken?
2. In groups of three or four, discuss the picture that goes with the article. What do you see? What are your conclusions about the people in the picture and about their language classes? Do you think these are accurate observations? Why or why not?

Individual Work

Take a poll of ten people who are not in your class. Ask them to tell which state in the United States has the most multilingual residents. Did anyone name Utah? Report your results to the class.

4 AMERICA'S HAMBURGER HELPER

BEFORE YOU READ

Preview

Fast-food restaurants have become very popular in the United States. One of the oldest and best-known fast-food chains is McDonald's.

Getting Started

1. When you read or hear the word *McDonald's,* what do you think of?
2. Would you like to work at a McDonald's? Why or why not? How do you think McDonald's treats its employees?
3. Read the brief description of the article. What do you expect to learn about McDonald's from this article?

Culture

affirmative action [əˈfɚmətɪv ˈækʃən]   a policy in government, business, and education that gives opportunities to women and minority group members. Affirmative-action programs began after the civil-rights movement of the 1960s.

franchise [ˈfræntʃaɪz]   the right and power to be part of a corporation; a business that is associated with a larger corporation. Most McDonald's restaurants are franchises with individual owners.

Golden Arches [ˈgoldən ˈartʃəz]   a McDonald's restaurant. The gold colored *M,* which looks like a pair of arches, is a trademark for McDonald's.

Hamburger Helper [ˈhæmbɚgɚ ˈhɛlpɚ]   the brand name of packaged ingredients that are added to ground beef to make a one-dish meal

hamburger stand [ˈhæmbɚgɚ ˈstænd]   a fast-food restaurant that sells hamburgers

inner-city [ˈɪnɚ ˈsɪdi]   belonging to the older, usually poorer, central area of a city. Many inner-city neighborhoods are inhabited by minority groups.

special-ed [ˈspɛʃəl ˈɛd]   in need of special educational services because of mental or physical disabilities

"We do it all for you." [wi du ɪt ˈɔl for ˈju]   an advertising slogan used by McDonald's

Vocabulary

at-risk [æt ˈrɪsk]   in danger of failing in school

cookie-cutter [ˈkʊki ˈkədɚ]   repetitious; identical. This is a negative term that suggests a lack of imagination or creativity.

(to) flip burgers [ˈflɪp ˈbɚgɚz]   to cook hamburgers by turning them on a grill

(to) keep on [ˈkip ˈɔn]   to continue

to boot [tu ˈbut]   in addition; besides

Culture and Vocabulary Activity

Many of the words and phrases listed above use familiar words in new or unexpected ways. Which terms are new to you? Which are used in a different way than you expected? Discuss the relationship between the definitions you expected and the ones that are given.

America's Hamburger Helper

McDonald's gives new meaning to "we do it all for you" by investing in people and their neighborhoods

By **EDWIN M. REINGOLD** LOS ANGELES

McDonald's stands tall for its community-minded activities

WHEN THE SMOKE CLEARED after mobs burned through South Central Los Angeles in April, hundreds of businesses, many of them black owned, had been destroyed. Yet not a single McDonald's restaurant had been torched. Within hours after the curfew was lifted, all South Central's Golden Arches were back up and running, feeding fire fighters, police and National Guard troops as well as burned-out citizens. The St. Thomas Aquinas Elementary School, with 300 hungry students and no utilities, called for lunches and got them free—with delivery to boot.

For Edward H. Rensi, president and CEO of McDonald's U.S.A., the explanation of what happened, or didn't happen, in South Central L.A. was simple: "Our businesses there are owned by African-American entrepreneurs who hired African-American managers who hired African-American employees who served everybody in the community, whether they be Korean, African American or Caucasian."

The $19-billion-a-year company has often been the target of those who disparage everything from its entry-level wage structure to the aesthetic blight of its cookie-cutter proliferation. But the Los Angeles experience was vindication of enlightened social policies begun more than three decades ago. The late Ray Kroc, a crusty but imaginative salesman who forged the chain in 1955, insisted that both franchise buyers and company executives get involved in community af-

fairs. "If you are going to take money out of a community, give something back," Kroc enjoined. "It's only good business."

As a result, McDonald's stands out not only as one of the more socially responsible companies in America but also as one of the nation's few truly effective social engineers. Both its franchise operators, who own 83% of all McDonald's restaurants, and company officials sit on boards of local and national minority service organizations, allowing the company to claim that its total involvement in everything from the Urban League and the N.A.A.C.P. to the U.S. Hispanic Chamber of Commerce may constitute the biggest volunteer program of any business in the nation.

Because their original prosperity came from hamburger stands in middle-class suburbs, McDonald's managers were at

first reluctant to move into inner-city markets. But company executives say their first tentative steps in the '70s showed those fears to be unfounded. The policy practiced in the suburbs, which dictated that McDonald's stores reflect the communities in which they operate, was applied to the new urban markets. As a result, nearly 70% of McDonald's restaurant management and 25% of the company's executives are minorities and women, and so are about half its corporate department heads. This year McDonald's will nearly double its purchases from companies that are minority or female owned, from last year's $157 million to $300 million. Several of the biggest are owned and operated by former McDonald's managers or franchise holders.

The spawning ground for many of the new ideas and programs designed to

GIORGIO PALMISANO

McJobs

Joe King, who has Down syndrome, has been on the job for nine years

integrate the franchises into neighborhoods in which they operate has been the company's moral and intellectual McCenter, Hamburger University, set in its own 80-acre nature preserve near Oak Brook, Ill. Since 1979 the company has held affirmative-action seminars for its executives and managers there, as well as in many of the company's 40 regional offices, on such topics as how to manage the changing work force and handle career development for women, blacks and Hispanics. Each year 3,000 employees complete affirmative action training programs that last 1½ to 3 days. Ideas originated at headquarters and by individual franchisees have led to programs such as McJobs, which takes on mentally and physically impaired employees, and McPride, which keeps students in school and rewards them for academic achievement while they work.

Through a program devised by its store owners, the company has helped establish 153 Ronald McDonald Houses, named for the chain's trademark clown, where families of seriously ill children can stay while the child is undergoing extensive medical treatment, such as chemotherapy or bone-marrow transplants. Each house serves an average of 15 families who pay from $5 to $15 a night, if they can afford it. The local projects are supported by local fund drives, and all the money collected goes directly to the houses; McDonald's pays all administrative costs of the program, which extends to Canada, France, Germany, Holland, Australia and New Zealand.

B UT MCDONALD'S BROADEST IMPACT has been through its basic job-training system. Its 8,800 U.S. restaurants (there are an additional 3,600 overseas from Beijing to Belgrade) train American youth of every ethnic hue. "Sending a kid to the Army used to be the standard way to teach kids values, discipline, respect for authority, to be a member of a team, get to work on time, brush your teeth, comb your hair, clean your fingernails," says Ed Rensi. "Now, somehow, McDonald's has become the new entry-level job-training institution in America. We find ourselves doing things in that role that we would never imagine we would do." Among them: paying kids to study, rewarding them for staying in school, hiring physically and mentally handicapped youngsters and adults and giving sensitivity training to co-workers. In a program called McMasters, older people, usually retirees, are hired to work alongside young crew members to give the workplace a sense of family and to set an example of caring, courtesy and responsibility.

In conjunction with the vocational-rehabilitation services of several states, nearly 7,000 disabled and handicapped people have been trained to function as full McDonald's employees by job coaches drawn from within the company. Before these less fortunate employees take their places, company trainers often put young able-bodied workers in blindfolds, gloves or dark glasses to demonstrate the kind of handicaps their new colleagues have to deal with in doing the same jobs.

At Pat Newbury's McDonald's restaurant in Renton, Wash., some young employees earn an hour's pay not for flipping burgers but for studying an hour before their work shift begins. In a Chicago-area restaurant, Hispanic teenagers are being tutored in English. In Tulsa, a McDonald's crew is studying algebra after work. At a Honolulu restaurant, student workers get an extra hour's pay to study for an hour after closing. In Colorado, Virginia and Massachusetts there are Stay in School programs offering bonus money for employees who receive good grades. Reading-improvement classes frequently take place at restaurants in Kansas and New Jersey.

Despite the initial skepticism of educators, McDonald's programs have managed to allay the fears of many that work and school could not mix. In February the National Association of Secondary School Principals passed a resolution commending the company for "exemplary and motivational efforts to support education, students and assistant principals."

Bob Charles, the owner of a McDonald's in Boulder, has seen some of his employed at-risk students begin to get A's after joining his McPride program, which

limits them to a 14-hour workweek and pays bonuses for improvement and school attendance. Many of them have a very low level of self-esteem, says Charles. But once they come to work as part of a team and gain a sense of confidence, "you'd almost never believe the change in these kids."

Mark Brownstein's company owns 13 restaurants in Orange County, Calif., and hires elderly and handicapped workers aggressively. "They are people who need work, and we need people to work. You wonder why everybody makes a big deal about it," shrugs Brownstein. "Besides, the seniors and the special-ed kids in our stores create a sense of humanity." Owner Jonah Kaufman has 26 handicapped people, mainly with Down syndrome, on the payroll in his 12 Long Island stores.

> ## "If you're going to take money out of a community, give something back."
>
> RAY KROC,
> *McDonald's founder*

One of them, Joe King, trains new employees. Kaufman says the key to his success with the disabled is "to try not to treat them differently." McDonald's has used Braille and its own kind of sign language as aids for impaired employees. At McDonald's Oak Brook headquarters, staff workers are sought from specialized schools, such as Gallaudet University and the Rochester Institute for Technology, which has an educational center for the deaf.

Senior vice president Robert H. Beavers Jr., who gave up plans to become an electrical engineer 19 years ago to stay with McDonald's, says the company's socially minded business practices have made the company stronger: "Our energy level and our understanding of the market today are much better because of the cultural diversity we have." He points out that in the inner city, where he grew up, they say, "If you talk the talk, you better walk the walk."

In Los Angeles, they talked and they walked—and they didn't burn. So Rensi and his team intend to keep on keeping on. After all, it's only good business. ∎

AFTER YOU READ

Comprehension Questions

1. According to Edward H. Rensi, why weren't the McDonald's stores burned during the rioting in Los Angeles?
2. Who was the founder of McDonald's? What advice did he give to franchise buyers and company executives?
3. What are some examples of McDonald's commitment to minorities and women?
4. What is Hamburger University? McPride? McJobs? McMasters? Ronald McDonald House?
5. What are some of the special things that McDonald's stores have done to help their employees?

Discussion and Analysis Questions

1. Do you have a different opinion of McDonald's after reading the article than you had before? If so, explain how your attitude has changed.
2. Do you think corporations have a social responsibility to employ people of various ages, ethnic groups, and abilities? Should they help their employees with academic subjects such as reading, math, and English? Why or why not?
3. The title of the article contains a *double entendre* (a phrase with two meanings). Using your knowledge gained from the article and the Culture section, explain the meanings.
4. Choose one sentence in the article that serves as the *thesis* (the main idea or unifying concept). Do you think the thesis is supported by adequate examples? Why or why not?
5. This article uses two *framing devices* (a phrase or topic used at the beginning of a composition and again at the end). Find the framing devices used in the first and fifteenth paragraphs and in the third and fifteenth paragraphs. How do they help the thesis of the article?

Group Activities

1. The McDonald's corporation uses the prefix *Mc* to form many words, such as *McPride*. In groups of four or five, develop a list of *Mc* words related to McDonald's. Write the definition of each word (for example, *McWork* = employment at McDonald's).
2. In groups of four or five, discuss fast-food restaurants. What do they tell about the lifestyle of a culture? Are there fast-food restaurants in your home culture? Are they beneficial to the culture? Do they harm the culture in any way? Be prepared to report your conclusions to the class.

Individual Work

Visit a McDonald's (or another popular local restaurant). Observe the employees. Is there a variety of ages, races, and abilities? Is there an equal number of males and females? Write a one-paragraph summary of your findings. Be prepared to read it to the class or to tell the class what you observed.

5 RAISE HIGH THE ROOF BEAM

BEFORE YOU READ

Preview

People working together can solve many problems.

Getting Started

1. Do you believe that a group of women could rebuild an entire town? Why or why not?
2. Read the brief description of the article, the photo caption, and the quotation printed in bold. Based on these, do you think the *tone* of the article (the attitude of the writer toward the topic) will be positive, negative, or neutral?

Culture

antebellum [ænti'bɛləm]   prior to the American Civil War (1861–65)

bake sale ['bek 'sel]   a sale of homemade baked goods, such as cakes and cookies. Many organizations hold bake sales to raise money for special causes.

cane curtain ['ken 'kɚtən]   an imaginary line behind which sugarcane is grown. The term comes from the Iron Curtain, which formerly divided Communist and non-Communist areas of Europe.

company store ['kəmpəni 'stor]   a store owned by a firm or plantation. Since the firm or plantation workers couldn't shop anywhere else, company stores often took advantage by charging high prices.

cycle of poverty ['saɪkəl əv 'pavɚdi]   a condition in which several generations of families are poor

Robert's Rules of Order ['rabɚts 'rulz əv 'ordɚ]   a published set of rules for conducting a meeting

sweat equity [ˌswɛt 'ɛkwɪti]   investment in property gained by working instead of by paying money

Vocabulary

backwater ['bæk,wɔdɚ]   an isolated, out-of-the-way place

field hand ['fild ,hænd]   a farmworker

indenture [ɪn'dɛntʃɚ]   a situation in which one person must work for another for a certain length of time

(to) put (people's) heads together [pʊt 'hɛdz tu,gɛðɚ]   to think in a group

rehab ['rihæb]   rehabilitation; reconstruction

(to) shore up ['ʃor 'əp]   to prop up; to support

(to) stand behind ['stænd bi'haɪnd]   to support; to endorse

tab [tæb]   a bill; an account

Culture and Vocabulary Activities

1. Look at the list of Culture terms. Which are directly associated with the history of the southern plantation system?
2. Look at the list of Vocabulary items. Find the two-word verbs. What is their structure?

Raise High The Roof Beam

With sweat equity and private financing, the women of an impoverished backwater are building their own future

By **DANIEL S. LEVY**

JOSEPHINE ROBERSON POSITIONS A CHALK line along the top of a sheet of plywood as Nolan Derouen flicks the taut string and imprints a fuzzy red stripe across the board. They slice the wood to size, carry it into Betty Hines' living room and nail it to the ceiling. Hines works at the back of the room, straining from the rungs of a ladder as she attaches tiles to the plywood with the aid

Derouen and Roberson cutting lumber in Four Corners, Louisiana

"They came with good ideas about what we could do to help ourselves."

of one of Derouen's assistants. Heavy rains, excessive groundwater and years of neglect in southern Louisiana's sugarcane region have led to creeping decay in Hines' home. Now, instead of harsh sunshine peeking through rotting walls, daylight filters through brand-new window frames.

Through a mixture of sweat equity and private financing, the women of Four Corners are replacing old wood with fresh clapboards, drying up stagnant pools and sealing busted pipes. The homes are livable again, and the community has found a new pride and hope for a better future.

"It is a hard job, but together we can do a lot," says Roberson in a soft, raspy voice. "What gives us so much courage and strength is that we have so many people standing behind us helping us build our community."

Roberson, 59, is one of a determined band of women in this small unincorporated hamlet 20 miles east of New Iberia. Most of the 150 houses have antiquated wiring and leaking roofs; few public services reach places like Four Corners. As the cane industry became mechanized, many people lost jobs that their families had held for generations. The average annual family income in this town of 400 is below $10,000.

Life appeared grim until March 1989, when the directors of the Southern Mutual Help Association, a New Iberia-based organization that has been working for 22 years to improve the lives of sugarcane workers, met with 15 of Four Corners' women and offered to help them help themselves. The women founded the Four Corners Self Help Housing Committee and pledged to work together to rebuild

their lives. The five-year project has not only shored up the homes but has also created a sense of accomplishment among the residents. "We held up a mirror to them, so that they could see themselves," says Lorna Bourg, Southern Mutual's assistant executive director. "They are reflecting their sense of self-worth."

Since 1969, Southern Mutual has worked to improve the lives of those who toil in the fields. Back then, many farmworkers lived behind the "cane curtain" in self-contained plantations with names such as the Bottoms, Oxford and Dog Quarters, filled with rented shacks reminiscent of the tarnished side of the antebellum era. The field hands were paid with chits and exchanged the paper for goods at overpriced company stores. Since crops are seasonal, the field hands ran up large tabs, which were then deducted from their pay and resulted in a lifetime of indenture. Those who quit were ordered off the land. Virginia Sutton, 74, a graying yet dapper great-grandmother of 17 and co-chairwoman of the group, once labored in the sugarcane fields for 70¢ a day. "We used to work from can't to can't," she says, recalling the long days. "You go to work, it is so dark you can't see your hand, and when you finish, you still can't see your hand."

Southern Mutual was the first to document the number of farmworkers in Louisiana. It fought for their legal rights and helped them obtain more than $1.25 million in back pay. It established the first farmworkers' medical and dental clinics, gathered oral histories of life on the plantation, founded an adult-literacy program, set up a scholarship fund for the children, documented the use of pesticides and is currently fighting against the spraying of certain chemicals. "Four Corners' new motto is 'From can't to can,'" says Bourg. "From can't do to can do." Sutton now proudly shows off her refurbished home. "Southern Mutual opened up our understanding, so that we could know what we can do and can't do," says Sutton. "They came with good ideas about what we could do to help ourselves."

The organization came to Four Corners with years of rehab experience in other communities. Yet when its members arrived, the initial response of the local women was wariness. Says Mary Matthews, 55, Four Corners' other co-chairwoman: "At first, I didn't think it would work, but we then put our heads together and did it. Soon others heard about us and joined us. Now we don't want to quit. We want to finish."

Southern Mutual arranged for carpenters, plumbers and electricians to work alongside the women and teach them the necessary skills. "We won't get a carpenter or a plumber out here unless he shows the committee members as much as they can and want to learn," says Bourg. Much of the credit for the project's success belongs to the professionals, men like Derouen, 57, who have given more than just their time. Derouen, who just helped complete 11 houses and is ready to begin work on an additional 15, encourages the women, supplies materials at a discount and once even presented Southern Mutual with a laughable $12.50 bill for roof repairs and materials.

Initial work in Four Corners consisted of emergency repairs: some homes were in such poor shape there was no hope of restoration, so new ones were trucked in from nearby communities. Subsequent chores included rewiring, plumbing or simply applying a fresh coat of paint, which is generally done by Four Corners' star painter, Thelma Collins. The women raise money through bake sales, barbecue dinners, fish fries and a TV raffle that netted $1,345. All money is deposited in an account at Iberia Savings Bank, which, along with Southern Mutual and in conjunction with the Federal Affordable Housing Program, has set aside up to $250,000 to make 1% loans to the residents. "The people live in our community, and we have a responsibility to provide them with decent housing," says Larrey Mouton, president of Iberia Savings. "We want to teach them about financial affairs, so that they can pull themselves out of this cycle of poverty."

By year's end, the women hope to complete an additional six homes. They are forming a community-development corporation to rebuild the whole village, not just the housing, and have started to spread the do-it-yourself project to neighboring communities, like Sorrel. The work is not going unnoticed: Louisiana Governor Buddy Roemer declared Oct. 24 Four Corners Community Day to celebrate the spirit of self-help.

M OST DAYS THE NONDESCRIPT, RAIN-soaked community is filled with the sounds of crowing blackbirds, howling dogs and squealing pigs, along with the pounding of hammers and the whining of electric saws. Women and a few men can be seen carrying beams, and newly dug ditches quickly fill with golden ragworts, fire-ant hills and crayfish chimneys. Groups of women gather lumber from demolished houses, stretch the long boards across sawhorses and pry out old nails. After the wood is cleaned, it is sorted and stored in a shed for later use or sale.

Priscilla Loston, 35, the group's feisty treasurer, is one of the nail pullers. She recently received a new home, a former country barroom that was transplanted to Four Corners to replace her tumbledown shack. She did much of the makeover, dividing the interior into separate rooms and installing paneling and electrical boxes. "This is Four Corners Self Help, not sit on your butt and get help," says Loston, as she yanks out a stubborn nail.

At the regular Monday evening planning session, 30 women meet at the local Catholic church and loosely follow *Robert's Rules of Order.* The minutes are read. Loston announces how much is in the bank and what donations have been sent in. The women discuss the work and announce upcoming projects. A few members ask to borrow $500 to $1,000 for paint or supplies. New members sign a pledge to help repair every house in the community, and the lax and lazy are goaded to work harder. When all is done, the women hold hands as Roberson leads them in an impassioned prayer thanking God for his help. They then wish each other good night and head out into the dark, back to their refurbished homes to prepare for another day of work, another day of change. ■

AFTER YOU READ

Comprehension Questions

1. Why were the homes in Four Corners so in need of repair?
2. What is the Southern Mutual Help Association? In what ways has it helped farmworkers in Louisiana?
3. How did Southern Mutual help the women in Four Corners?

Discussion and Analysis Questions

1. Why do you think the Four Corners Self Help Housing Committee has been so successful?
2. What is your attitude toward the women of the committee?
3. Why do you think there are no men on the committee?
4. The women use two phrases to describe the changes in the community: "from can't to can't" and "from can't to can." Explain each phrase.

Group Activity

In groups of three or four, discuss whether you think a similar project would be successful in your town. Does everyone in the group agree? Why or why not?

Individual Work

Imagine that you could interview one of the women from the Four Corners Self Help Housing Committee. Make a list of ten questions that you would ask her.

6 LIFE AT THE END OF THE RAINBOW

BEFORE YOU READ

Preview

Because of state lotteries, millionaires are no longer rare in the United States.

Getting Started

1. Does your home country have legalized gambling? If so, what games are played?
2. What do you think the title of this article means? What do you think the article will be about?

Culture

American work ethic [ə,mɛrəkən ˈwɚk ˌɛθɪk]   the belief that success results from hard work. Supposedly most Americans have this belief.

gold rush [ˈgold rəʃ]   a situation in which many people try to get quickly to a source of wealth. The famous Gold Rush in California began in 1848.

Lightning never strikes twice in the same place. [ˈlaɪtnɪŋ nɛvɚ straɪks ˈtwaɪs ɪn ðə sem ˈples]   the same bad thing never happens two times to the same person (proverb)

major leagues [ˈmedʒɚ ˈligz]   the most important or prominent section of a group. The term comes from baseball, where professionals play in the major leagues.

Me-first [ˈmi ˈfɚst]   characterized by selfishness or attention to oneself. Some people claim that American youth in the 1980s were a me-first generation.

pot of gold [ˌpɑt əv ˈgold]   according to folklore, the treasure found at the end of a rainbow

Vocabulary

(to) hound [ˈhaʊnd]   to continually chase; to bother

(to) keep one's feet on the ground [ˌkip wənz ˈfit ɔn ðə ˌgraʊnd]   to remain firmly established; to stay sensible

lottery [ˈlɑdɚi]   a game of chance in which bettors select combinations of numbers. The more people who play a game, the more unlikely one's chances of winning.

luck of the draw [ˈlək əv ðə ˈdrɔ]   the results of chance; the lack of any choice

-mania [ˈmeniə]   craziness; insanity

one's ship (to) come in [wənz ˈʃɪp ˌkəm ɪn]   one's success or good fortune to arrive

(to) rake in [ˈrek ˈɪn]   to gather something (usually money) in large quantities

(to) strike gold [ˈstraɪk ˈgold]   to win a large amount of money

super- [ˈsupɚ]   very; extremely

Culture and Vocabulary Activities

1. *-mania* is a productive suffix in English. It can be added to nouns to create new nouns, such as *lottomania*. As a class, invent some new English words using *-mania* (for example, *footballmania*).
2. *Super-* is a productive prefix in English. In conversation, people often attach it to an adjective to create a new adjective, such as *superrich*. With your classmates, invent some new words using *super-* (for example, *supertired*).

Life at the End of the Rainbow

As lottomania sweeps the nation, thousands of Americans are becoming sudden millionaires—but pots of gold don't seem to go to their head

By BONNIE ANGELO

IN THE LOS ANGELES SUBURB OF GLENdora, entrepreneur Keith Porchia cheerfully dons a hard hat to check on the progress of the 51-unit apartment complex he is developing. In Winter Springs, Fla., Sheelah Ryan, a retired real estate agent, meets with the board of the Ryan Foundation to map programs for what she calls "the new poor." Somewhere in southern Atlantic waters, Anthony Palermo, formerly of the U.S. Navy, cruises with his family aboard his own yacht, joyfully named *Picked Six.*

When state-run lotteries first became popular in the late 1970s, "instant millionaires" were the isolated stuff of media sensation. Now Porchia, Ryan and Palermo are part of something else entirely: an expanding niche of American society filled with overnight plutocrats. As lottomania has swept the nation, one result is an entirely new social stratum of millionaires, over 3,000 in all, and more are added each month. With some prizes soaring past nine digits (the largest: $118 million in California last April), a few recipients even approach being superrich. But America's pot-of-gold winners are to a surprising degree the opposite of the Me-first cohort of nouveau speculators who bedecked the greedy '80s.

According to the most comprehensive survey, winners are heavily clustered in higher-income brackets. Once they win, they shun spending sprees, pay off debts and, by a big percentage, continue to work or get additional education after their sudden windfall. Only 23% quit their job. Sharon Turner, a U.S. government worker, now has a $7.5 million nest egg but says her husband Darnell stays at his job at a Washington junior high school "because he wants to teach." Last week Don Wittman, 29, of Denver, amazed everybody twice: he won his second $2 million prize—against odds figured at 17 trillion

to 1—and decided to stay at his job as a carpenter. "Sure, I'm going to keep on working," he says. "Otherwise I'd just be bored."

The odds of joining the flourishing ranks of lotto millionaires are still longer than the risk of being struck by lightning. About 90 million players will ring up $20.6 billion in ticket sales this year. So far, 34 states have joined the lottery gold rush, raking in vital revenues for depleted coffers. Charles Clotfelter and Philip Cook, professors of public policy and economics at Duke University, challenge the games of chance as regressive, inefficient means of raising revenue and suggest they prey upon minorities and the poor. The professors also wonder whether the lotteries' get-rich-quick appeal undermines the American work ethic. Arnie Wexler, director of the Council on Compulsive Gambling in New Jersey, another opponent, says almost half the calls for help that come to his organization are from lottery players.

Nonetheless, more and more rainbows continue to end on American doorsteps. Double-digit millions falling into your lap can have a wonderfully life-altering effect, but not necessarily the self-indulgent changes that lottery promotions lead customers to fantasize. Sheelah Ryan, for example: her $55.5 million Florida jackpot in 1988 is the biggest single win yet. She immediately set up a foundation named in honor of her parents, "to help the new poor: single mothers and senior citizens who must live on Social Security and cannot. They need help." In addition, she gives small scholarships to young people because "they are our future, and it's a fun way of doing it."

And, yes, instant fortune changed the lifestyle of this unassuming former businesswoman. "What do I like about it most?" she muses. "Valet parking!" Ryan had her initial indulgences: she bought the Mercury Grand Marquis she had coveted and a handsome house to replace her mobile

home. Otherwise she lives modestly, but with payments of nearly $2.8 million rolling in each year, she knows "I never, never have to worry for the rest of my life."

The luck of the draw can mean freedom to take a different kind of risk. "I'd been trying to build a hotel," says businessman Porchia, who owned several minimarkets. "But the banks weren't interested in financing it." Then he hit California's $10.7 million jackpot in 1987. "Suddenly, financing was available," he says wryly. At 55, he enrolled in Azusa Pacific University to earn a master's degree in business administration "to maximize my investments." His 75-room Comfort Suites Hotel opened three years ago and is being followed by his large apartment development. "Every goal you ever desired is satisfied in one day, so you have to set new goals," Porchia says. "It took me about three years to get used to the idea that if you want something, you just go and do it."

Cautionary tales abound of lottery winners whose bad investments lead them to bankruptcy, but most of America's luckiest people seem to keep their feet on the ground. The fact that they are paid in 20 annual taxable installments helps. (Annual payments also mean a much lower outlay by the lotteries.) Most winners stay in the same neighborhood, keep old friends and continue to look at price tags.

Sharon Barnes, 46, a loan officer who won $16 million in Worthington, Ohio, in 1988, is typical: she took sewing lessons after she struck it rich. "I'm still me," she says. "I was raised that way." She and her husband Eli, a retired Army master sergeant, also set up a $15,000 endowment for black studies at Ohio State University and gave $5,000 to an inner-city health conference. At the University of Akron, Mike Woodford, 31, stayed on as assistant football coach after winning $15 million in 1989. He was going through a divorce at the time and gave half the money to his ex-wife. In Virginia a relatively modest $1.4

million win enabled Old Dominion University student Jeff Berry, 20, to switch from a business major to the career he really wanted: teaching.

America's first big winner, Lou Eisenberg of Brooklyn, whose $5 million ticket made him an overnight celebrity in 1981, hardly ranks in the major leagues anymore. Before his ship came in, he says, "my job was changing light bulbs in an office building, making $225 a week. I had anxiety attacks; I was not functioning. I won the lotto, and the anxiety disappeared." An ebullient Eisenberg still lives in Brooklyn, but with an ocean view. The biggest flyer he takes these days is modest but steady betting at local racetracks.

Often it seems that friends and family have a harder time dealing with the sudden flood of cash than the winners. When Mike Wittkowski of Chicago won $42 million in 1984, he expected, at 26, to keep working as a printing-press foreman. Instead he was hassled by co-workers for holding a job he

didn't need. Dismayed, he bought a liquor store and is now his own boss.

To be sure, the old saga of unexpected wealth, envy and rancor has not been abolished. In Philadelphia last summer, bitter feuding erupted between Danny Hagan, 28, and Margie Moore, 27, co-workers at an engineering company, over Hagan's slice of the $17 million winning ticket he bought for Moore. The battle ended last month in a sealed settlement and a shredded lifetime friendship.

For Boston cafeteria cook William Curry, 37, winning the Massachusetts lottery last year turned out to be his unluckiest bet. Three weeks after winning, he dropped dead of a heart attack, brought on by ceaseless hounding once his $3.6 million win was made public. Curry's is an extreme case, but the business offers, investment schemes and heartrending pleas for help that rain down on winners are a source of widespread worry. A number of states offer basic guidance courses in sur-

viving good luck. They usually counsel winners to get a good tax accountant, an unlisted telephone number and a veneer of skepticism. Virginia's lottery gives each winner an advice video. In it, David Snyder of Lynchburg, a $10.9 million winner in 1990 and a dedicated community worker, offers the sage counsel he received from his pastor: Don't have a guilty conscience abut rejecting pleas. You cannot cure all the world's poverty. But you can help some of the poor. Snyder has made Meals on Wheels a favorite charity.

Even for those who win big, there's always the chance that lightning might just strike twice, as it did five times even before Don Wittman's incredible luck. And then there is George Magalio, 49, owner of an office-supply company in Flemington, N.J. Using his own system to pick winning numbers, he has struck gold in New York, New Jersey and Pennsylvania for a total of $4 million. He has invested his winnings conservatively. And he's still playing. ■

$10.7
MILLION

"Work keeps you going. If you are out of the pattern, you are not part of what life's all about."

Keith Porchia
Glendora, Calif.

AFTER YOU READ

Comprehension Questions

1. How many states have legalized lottery games? What is the purpose of these lotteries?
2. What do most lottery winners do with their money? How many quit their jobs?
3. Why do some people criticize lotteries?
4. What negative things have happened to some winners?

Discussion and Analysis Questions

1. Have you ever played a lottery or any other legal game of chance? Did you ever win? If so, what did you do with the money?
2. Do you think governments should use lotteries to raise money? Should they use other kinds of gambling (for example, horse racing) to raise money? Why or why not?
3. Think about the lottery winners described in this article. Do you think the writer did a good job of presenting a variety of reactions to becoming a millionaire? Explain your answer.

Group Activity

Imagine that you and a partner have purchased a winning lottery ticket worth two million dollars. Decide with your partner how you will use the money. Be prepared to report your decisions to the class.

Individual Work

1. If lottery games are legal where you live, take a poll of twenty people. Ask them:
   - Do you buy lottery tickets?
   - If so, how often?

   Tabulate your results and write a brief summary statement. You may wish to use the following form: "Out of twenty people, X reported playing _____ , Y _____ , and Z _____ ."
2. If lottery games are not legal where you live, take a poll of twenty people. Ask them:
   - Would you buy lottery tickets if they were available here?
   - If so, how often?

   Tabulate your results and write a brief summary statement.

Education

1 IS SCHOOL UNFAIR TO GIRLS?

BEFORE YOU READ

Preview

Some researchers are investigating how and why girls and boys perform differently in school.

Getting Started

1. Do you think that males and females have different academic interests? If so, give some examples.
2. Do you think that males and females have different academic abilities? Why or why not?

Culture

A.A.U.W. ['e 'e 'ju 'dəbəl,ju]   the American Association of University Women, a national organization of female college graduates. The A.A.U.W. is concerned with social, political, and educational issues affecting women.

gender gap ['dʒɛndɚ ,gæp]   the difference between how males and females think and act; the difference between how males and females are treated

grade 12 [gred 'twɛlv]   the final year of secondary school

preschool ['priskul]   pertaining to the years before a child attends kindergarten, often referring to three- to five-year-olds

SAT ['ɛs e 'ti]   the Scholastic Aptitude Test, usually taken by high school juniors. Many U.S. colleges and universities use students' SAT scores to help determine their admission.

standardized test ['stændɚ,dɑɪzd 'tɛst]   a specially prepared achievement test taken by large numbers of students. Standardized test scores often affect students' advancement and placement in schools.

Vocabulary

edge [ɛdʒ]   an advantage

(to) make fun of [,mek 'fən əv]   to ridicule

self-esteem [,sɛlf ɛ'stim]   one's opinion of oneself

(to) stink [stɪŋk]   to be awful

(to) tinker ['tɪŋkɚ]   to work, but not seriously

Culture and Vocabulary Activities

1. As you read the article, decide if the SAT and Advanced Placement tests are standardized tests.
2. As you read the article, find words that mean approximately the same as *to make fun of, self-esteem,* and *to stink.*

JOHN HARDING/TIME MAGAZINE

Is School Unfair to Girls?

The latest research finds that the gender gap goes well beyond boys' persistent edge in math and science

BY RICHARD N. OSTLING

ATHLETIC BUDGETS. READING LISTS. Pronouns in textbooks. All sorts of things have changed since 1972, when Congress outlawed sex discrimination in federally aided schools. But so far, charges the American Association of University Women (A.A.U.W.), reforms have only tinkered with the gender gap. The organization issued a cry of alarm last week, citing "compelling evidence that girls are not receiving the same quality, or even quantity, of education as their brothers." That conclusion was contained in a report compiled by specialists at the Wellesley College Center for Research on Women that synthesized hundreds of studies of girl students from preschool age through Grade 12.

The findings showed that in some ways the American public school classroom is a feminine domain. Nearly three-quarters of teachers are women. Though the sexes do equally well in math and science grades, girls outperform boys overall. In verbal skills, girls move into the lead around Grade 5 or 6 and thereafter do better than boys in writing and, by most measures, reading. Females constitute less than a third of students identified as emotionally disturbed or learning disabled. Despite teen pregnancies, girls are less likely to drop out of high school and more likely to attend college.

So, what's the problem? For one thing, there is a gap in scores on standardized tests, especially in math and science, which the report blames partly on lingering bias in both testing and curriculum. On Advanced Placement tests, which enable students to earn college credit during high school, boys outperform girls in math, physics and biology. On the SAT test, that ubiquitous measure of alleged merit, in 1991 boys beat girls by 8 points in the verbal score and 44 points in math.

Susan Bailey, the report's chief author, says differences persist in math because "girls are still not participating in equal proportion to boys in advanced-level courses." Specifically, 7.6% of boys choose calculus, compared with 4.7% of girls. As for science performance, Bailey says, "the gap may be getting wider." A fourth of high school boys take physics, but only 15% of girls do.

Even girls who take the same math and science courses and do just as well on standardized tests are far less likely to consider technological careers. A study of Rhode Island high school seniors, for instance, found that 64% of boys but only 19% of girls taking physics and calculus planned to pursue science or engineering in college. Last week's report contends that girls' aversion to these fields limits their career options and future income.

One-fourth of boys take physics in high school, in contrast to 15% of girls

Judy Logan teaching science class: new techniques will be needed to foster self-esteem

Seeking to explain these patterns, the report states that school gradually undermines girls' self-esteem. In a 1990 survey, 3,000 youngsters were asked such questions as whether they were "happy the way I am." Predictably, everyone's self-confidence declined during adolescence, but the self-esteem of girls suffered deeper wounds. The pivotal factor in low self-esteem and performance, and the most intriguing aspect of the research, is what actually occurs in the classroom.

Bluntly stated, boys do well by being bad. They are the troublemakers who intimidate girls into silence, monopolize discussions and steal an inordinate amount of teachers' attention. One sixth-grader observed by researchers in Montgomery County, Md., said, "I'm afraid, when I get something wrong, the boys in the classroom might make fun of me because they usually laugh at some people if they get something wrong."

Obviously then, enhancing girls' self-confidence is not simply a matter of including more stories about heroic women in history textbooks. Judy Logan, a teacher at San Francisco's Everett Middle School, is convinced that girls "learn better in noncompetitive, nonhierarchical ways," so she divides her students into small groups. At Pattonville Holman Middle School in suburban St. Louis, computer teacher Jayne Kasten runs a no-boys F.E.M. (Female Electronic Marvels) Club, in which girls work with new software and demonstrate their know-how in classrooms.

The 40 A.A.U.W. proposals offered last week lean toward such predictable remedies as improved teacher training or further studies and avoid bold proposals suggested by the research, such as sex-segregated math and science classes. Diane Ravitch, an Assistant Secretary of Education, complains that much of the report "is just special pleading and, frankly, whining." Opportunities are opening up, she says, and girls should be urged to take advanced courses, not told that they are victims. Chester Finn, director of Vanderbilt University's Educational Excellence Network, thinks disparities simply show that students have different interests and abilities. He considers gender complaints a diversion from the overall weakness of U.S. education: "It stinks. It's dreadful." Ravitch adds that America is indeed biased, not against girls but "against academic achievement." If so, that is still one lesson that girls understand better than boys. —*Reported by Sidney Urquhart/New York*

AFTER YOU READ

Comprehension Questions

1. Why does the writer say that "in some ways the American public school classroom is a feminine domain"?
2. In what ways do boys do better than girls academically?
3. According to the report by the Wellesley College Center on Research for Women, what causes the different academic performance of boys and girls?
4. According to Judy Logan, what is the best way for girls to learn?

Discussion and Analysis Questions

1. Are you surprised by the findings reported in this article? Why or why not?
2. Think of students in your home country. Do you think boys and girls perform differently? Do you think teachers treat them differently?
3. What is Diane Ravitch's opinion of the Wellesley report? Do you agree with her? Explain your answer.
4. Diane Ravitch says that America is biased "against academic achievement." Do you think she is correct? Support your answer.

Group Activity

Form four groups of students. Have each group support one of the following statements:
  a. Males and females have equal abilities in math and science.
  b. Males are more intelligent than females in math and science.
  c. Males and females are treated equally in the classroom.
  d. Males receive more attention than females in the classroom.

Individual Work

In another class that you are taking or in a class that you visit, observe the following:
  a. the number of times that males and females are called on when they volunteer, and
  b. the number of times that males and females are called on when they don't volunteer.
Summarize your findings in a brief report (approximately one-half page). Did you find any differences in the treatment of males and females? Be sure to indicate the total number of males and females in the class and the gender of the instructor. Compare your findings to those of your classmates.

2 「合っていますか」(IS THAT CORRECT?)

BEFORE YOU READ

Preview

An innovative language program uses Japanese to teach content subjects to American students.

Getting Started

1. At what age did you begin to study a foreign language?
2. Was the language taught as a separate subject (for example, English or French), or was it used to teach other subjects (for example, history or math)?

Culture

achievement test [ə'tʃivmənt ˌtɛst]   an examination that tests a student's level of accomplishment in a certain subject. Standardized achievement tests are given in most U.S. schools.

critical thinking ['krɪdəˌkəl 'θɪŋkɪŋ]   an advanced level of thought that involves reasoning and inference. Critical thinking is more complex than memorization.

hiragana [ˌhɪrə'ɡɑnə]   a phonetic system used in writing modern Japanese

partial immersion ['pɑrˌʃəl ɪ'mɚˌʒən]   a type of foreign language program in which the language being learned is used to teach several content subjects

Vocabulary

(to) dive into the deep water ['daɪv ɪntu ðə ˌdip 'wɔdɚ]   to bravely try something difficult

open-minded [ˌopən 'maɪndəd]   willing to think about new ideas

spillover ['spɪlˌovɚ]   extra; additional

(to) spot [spɑt]   to see; to recognize

stream [strim]   a constant supply; a continuous flow

(to) stretch [strɛtʃ]   to expand; to develop

Culture and Vocabulary Activity

Which four of the Culture and Vocabulary items have literal meanings associated with water? What are those literal meanings? Can you think of other English words or phrases whose original meanings are related to water?

「合っていますか」
(Is That Correct?)

In a handful of American schools, first-graders are discovering math and science—in Japanese

By **DAVID AIKMAN** WASHINGTON

"YON-BUN NO SAN" (THREE-FOURTHS), says the eager second-grader as he holds up a card with the fraction spelled out in Japanese hiragana script and numerals. Then a classmate selects a segmented triangle that illustrates the fraction. *"Atte imasuka?"* (Is that correct?) asks the teacher from Tokyo. *"Hai,"* says the class in unison as little hands go up to answer the next question.

This is a perfectly normal morning math class for 31 seven- and eight-year-olds in a room filled with typical Japanese elementary school wall charts. The only odd thing is, it's not in Tokyo. It's in Great Falls, Va., just outside Washington, and all of the children are American.

The second-graders are part of a program adopted three years ago by Virginia's Fairfax County to introduce elementary school children to foreign languages in a new way. With a small amount of federal funding, the county instituted "partial-immersion" language programs in eight schools in Japanese, Spanish and French. Similar experiments in partial immersion can be spotted around the country in such cities as Eugene and Portland, Ore., and Anchorage. The idea is that children's minds are stretched and their skills enhanced when they are introduced to any foreign language. By being taught math and science in Japanese, the students unconsciously acquire the language. "Learning another language opens new pathways of connections in the brain, basically connecting new things with things you know," explains Clifford Walker, director of the Anchorage program.

Such findings should be of special interest to school districts that are struggling to allocate precious resources. Only 17% of U.S. elementary schools offer foreign-language programs, and nearly all of them teach their students the old-fashioned way. Yet results from partial-immersion programs suggest that students gain more than language skills and a taste for a foreign culture. The mental muscles they build from concentrating hard in their Japanese-taught classes make them stronger in other subjects as well. Some of the most enthusiastic proponents are the English-language teachers exposed to the Japanese-taught students. Says Great Falls third-grade teacher Roberta Sherman: "It's a class from heaven. They go beyond what I expect."

A first-grader illustrates "symmetrical"

The hard evidence is in the test scores: Japanese-taught children at Great Falls scored at the same level in math and science tests as other children from similar backgrounds. But in English-taught subjects, the immersion children scored 8 percentile points higher on a standard achievement test. The advantages show up in subtler ways as well. "The kids are more flexible in their analysis and their critical thinking," says Great Falls principal Gina Ross, an ardent advocate of the program. "They are more open-minded."

The teachers are quick to note other factors that could account for the students' successes. Second-language students may be especially motivated, more willing to take chances and accept challenges. In most partial-immersion schools, half the day is taught in English and half in Japanese. This means that students study math and science in Japanese and other subjects in English. The high verbal concentration required for Japanese clearly has a beneficial spillover effect in the English subjects.

Still, it takes a brave student to dive into the deep water of a complicated subject. "For the first couple of weeks, I couldn't understand anything," recalls Great Falls second-grader Courtney Pilka. "But after I got used to it, I started liking it a lot. I learned the alphabet and the numbers. Now it's part of my life." For many students, this is true outside the classroom as well, as they are inspired to explore Japanese restaurants, art and music. "I think the cultural experience is every bit as important as the language," says Jill McKee, a college teacher whose son Robert is in second grade. "He's exposed to another way of doing things." Tokyo-born Sumiko Limbocker, the second-grade teacher, adds with a laugh, "When the children meet me in the supermarket, they bow and say, '*Konnichi-wa*' [Hello]."

The benefits of bilingual study may also apply to students who learn English as a second language. According to Alma Flor Ada, a multicultural language expert at the University of San Francisco, many students, particularly Asians, who study English in immersion programs back home or upon arrival in the U.S. have the same learning patterns and achievement characteristics. That might account for the steady stream of visitors to Great Falls elementary, especially from Japan. Now that country has paid the young students of its own language the ultimate compliment: Japan wants to establish similar partial-immersion programs in elementary schools—using English.

—With reporting by Miko Yim/Portland

AFTER YOU READ

Comprehension Questions

1. What portion of elementary schools in the United States teach foreign languages?
2. How does a partial-immersion program operate?
3. How do the children in Great Falls perform in math and science classes taught in Japanese? How do they perform in subjects taught in English?
4. What factors could account for the students' success?

Discussion and Analysis Questions

1. Would you like to study in a partial-immersion program? Why or why not?
2. Can you think of any possible problems with the type of language program described? Explain your answer.
3. The writer uses several Japanese phrases in the article. Do you think they are essential to the article? Do you think they benefit the article at all?
4. The writer also uses quotes from teachers, a parent, and a student. Are these quotes important to the article? Explain your answer.

Group Activities

1. Pretend that you are a school administrator. Your school will offer a new partial-immersion program. In groups of three or four "administrators," decide what information you will use to explain the program to the parents. Be prepared to present your information to the class.
2. Pretend that you are a teacher. In groups of three or four "teachers," plan how you will introduce the new partial-immersion program to your students. Be prepared to present your ideas to the class.

Individual Work

Write a one-page description of your foreign language learning experiences. Tell what language(s) you studied, where you studied them, your age at the time, and how well you learned them. Which experiences helped your learning the most? the least? Why?

3 WHY 180 DAYS AREN'T ENOUGH

BEFORE YOU READ

Preview

American elementary and secondary students do not perform as well academically as students in many other countries. The length of the school year may be one reason.

Getting Started

1. How long is the school year in your home country? Do you know how its length was decided?
2. Look at the table. Where does the United States rank in comparison with the other countries listed? How much shorter is the U.S. school year than the Japanese school year?

Culture

dropout rate ['drɑpɑʊt ˌret]   the percentage of students who leave school before graduating

inner-city [ˌɪnɚ 'sɪdi]   belonging to the older, usually poorer, central area of a city. Many inner-city neighborhoods are inhabited by minority groups.

litmus test ['lɪtməs ˌtɛst]   an issue used to determine a person's level of commitment or position on a subject

private sector ['prɑɪvət 'sɛktɚ]   businesses and industries that are privately owned and operated. Government agencies belong to the *public sector.*

school board ['skul bord]   an elected group of people who make financial and policy decisions for a school district

Vocabulary

caveat ['kæviˌɑt]   a warning

head start [hɛd 'stɑrt]   an early beginning that places one ahead of others; an advantage

meat [mit]   substance; the important part of something

Culture and Vocabulary Activity

Skim the article to find five of the Culture and Vocabulary items. Study the context and the definition for each item. Then create a new sentence for each one.

Why 180 Days Aren't Enough

The U.S. has one of the shortest school years in the industrialized world: it's time for a change

220 Days: At Lockett elementary school in New Orleans, students work on reading and math, meeting needs that are particularly acute in the inner cities, where family ties are weak and dropout rates are high

By SAM ALLIS NEW ORLEANS

ALL ACROSS THE U.S., KIDS TROOP back to school each year in late August or early September. However, for youngsters at the Robert Russa Moton and Johnson C. Lockett elementary schools in New Orleans, summer ended this year on July 10. On that date, the 1,450 youngsters returned for the third year of an experimental program that adds 40 extra days to the usual 180-day school year. They were breaking a long-standing American tradition of summer vacations—dating back to a time when family labor was vital to the late-summer harvest—that give the U.S. one of the shortest school years in the industrialized world. There is surely a connection, a growing number of reformers argue, between that distinction and the dismal academic performances of American students, compared with their peers elsewhere.

Increasingly, many of those critics urge that what is good for the kids at Moton and Lockett might be good for the entire U.S.: an extended academic year for everybody. The case for that radical change, says Ernest L. Boyer, president of the Carnegie Foundation for the Advancement of teaching, is "absolutely compelling."

A growing number of ordinary Americans support the idea. The Gallup Organization, which has been polling on the subject since 1958, found last week for the first time that a majority (51%) of its sample favored a longer year. "If I spend more time at the piano, I get better at it," argues Dwight McKenna, the New Orleans school-board member who initiated the Moton and Lockett experiment.

PUTTING IN THE SCHOOL DAYS	
Japan	243
West Germany	210
Soviet Union	210
Thailand	200
The Netherlands	200
England	192
Finland	190
France	185
Sweden	180
U.S.	180

Source: Education Commission of the States

The case for the longer school year is particularly acute in the inner cities, where family ties are weak, at-home support for education is often minimal and dropout rates are high. Summertime spent on the hot ghetto streets is hardly as culturally enriching as the time middle-class students devote to camps, exotic vacations and highly organized sports. Moton and Lockett, for example, are located near New Orleans' notorious Florida and Desire housing projects, where children sometimes skip rope within the sound of gunfire. "This has nothing to do with competition with the Japanese and everything to do with urban reality," says McKenna. "This is eight hours when the drug addicts can't get at these kids."

Teachers get them instead. Attired in trim khaki-and-white uniforms, Moton youngsters between the ages of four and 11 work through reading and mathematics exercises and then at recess stampede out of the air-conditioned, cinder-block building to become blurs in the steamy 100° heat. They are candid about their options. "If I was home, I'd just sit around," says fifth-grader Alkima Thomas.

So far, the educational results of the New Orleans experiment are mixed. Teachers at Moton and Lockett find that the extra-long year at a minimum gives them a head start on the traditional weeks of review work at the beginning of the new school term. "Come September, I'm ready to get into the meat of reading," says Juanita Smith, a second-grade teacher at Lockett. "Normally, I can't do that until the end of October." But students at both schools test far below the state average in reading, and their scores since the 220-day year began have improved only marginally. "My kids can't read the way they ought to," says Ellenese Brooks-Simms, the principal of Moton school. Brooks-Simms and her counterpart at Lockett, Wilbert Dunn, are trying to put even more emphasis on reading instruction by cutting time spent on gym, music and other activities.

The major obstacle to the extended year in New Orleans, as it is across the country, is money. The Moton and Lockett experiment cost about $870,000 last year. More than $500,000 came from the Federal Government, while the school board anted up the remainder. But the future of the program after this year is dim because the board claims it can no longer afford to contribute its share. Thus far, there have been no appeals to the private sector for funding to continue the project. Financially hard-pressed state and local governments across the U.S. would find it extremely tough to assume the burden of such a program. In California, for example, a move to a 220-day program from kindergarten through high school would cost $121 million a day, according to Charles Ballinger, executive director of the National Association for Year-Round Education.

But most parents at Moton and Lockett strongly support the longer school session and worry about a return to the old system. "My kids are learning more, and I know they're safe," says Dwan Greene, who has two children at Moton. Even the kids appear enthusiastic about days spent near a teacher instead of a television set. Teachers at the two schools also seem pleased, despite the extra work. Among other things, they like the additional money they earn, which is prorated into their regular salaries.

The glowing recommendations for a wider adoption of the longer school year are based on the premise that the added time would in all cases be put to good use. This assumes a lot. Many inner-city schools labor under appalling conditions that produce poor education and endless disciplinary problems. "More of the same isn't any better if the same isn't good enough to begin with," says Norman Morgan, whose Polk County, N.C., school board in 1985 stopped an experimental program that had suddenly lifted the school year from 180 days to 200. Lockett principal Dunn agrees, "The simple fact of more time spent on tasks does not change anything. It must be coupled with something extra."

Even with that caveat, it is clear that the time for a hard look at the longer school year has come. "It's a litmus test on how serious we are about education," says the Carnegie Foundation's Boyer. The state of Oregon evidently agrees: a comprehensive education bill enacted in July will add 40 days to the school year over the next two decades. The Federal Government and corporate America would also do well to support the change, at least on an experimental basis. The summertime harvest that America needs to reap these days is not down on the farm, but up in the mind. ■

AFTER YOU READ

Comprehension Questions

1. What is the historical reason for U.S. schools having a 180-day school year?
2. What is the main reason that many people recommend having a longer school year?
3. Why do many inner-city educators and parents want an extended school year?
4. What is the main obstacle to a longer school year?
5. Why did the Polk County, North Carolina, schools stop their lengthened school year?

Discussion and Analysis Questions

1. Based on the information in this article, do you think U.S. schools should lengthen their year? Support your answer.
2. Do you think the benefits of an extended year are worth the expense?
3. Do you think the writer presents a balanced view of an extended school year? In other words, does he present both advantages and disadvantages?
4. Can you infer the writer's position on this subject? Find the sentence that best suggests his opinion.

Group Activity

Imagine that you are the parent of a child whose school year will be increased from 180 to 240 days. Meet in groups of six "parents" to discuss the advantages and disadvantages of the change. Try to think of some that weren't mentioned in the article. Be prepared to share your ideas with the class.

Individual Work

In one page, write what you think are the three most important factors in being a successful elementary or secondary student. Be prepared to share your ideas with classmates.

4 DO THE POOR DESERVE BAD SCHOOLS?

BEFORE YOU READ

Preview

There are great differences between the education received by poor children and that received by rich children in the United States.

Getting Started

1. How are public schools funded in your home country?
2. Who controls public education in your home country?
3. What is your perception of elementary and secondary education in the United States?

Culture

Bunsen burner ['bɒnsən ˌbɚnɚ]   a gas burner used in laboratories to produce a very hot flame. It was named after the German chemist Robert Bunsen.

caste system ['kæst ˌsɪstəm]   a division of society into different ranks of people. The caste system is usually associated with the Hindu religion in India.

inner-city [ˌɪnɚ 'sɪdi]   belonging to the older, usually poorer, central area of a city. Many inner-city neighborhoods are inhabited by minority groups.

Pledge of Allegiance ['plɛdʒ əv ə'lidʒəns]   a spoken oath of loyalty to the United States and its flag

popcorn popper ['pɑpkorn 'pɑpɚ]   a device used to cook popcorn

Robin Hood ['rɑbɪn ˌhʊd]   a legendary Englishman who took money from the rich and gave it to the poor

tug-of-war ['təg əv 'wor]   a conflict. Tug-of-war is a game in which two teams pull at opposite ends of a rope to determine which team is stronger.

Vocabulary

(to) backpedal ['bæk,pɛdəl]   to reverse a promise; to change direction or go backward

disparity [dɪs'pɛrɪti]   a difference; a dissimilarity

(to) dole out ['dol 'aʊt]   to distribute; to allocate

gadfly ['gædflaɪ]   an annoying person; someone who tries to disturb others

gulf [gəlf]   a very large gap

(to) juxtapose ['dʒəkstə,poz]   to put one thing beside another

(to) overhaul [ˌovɚ'hɔl]   to make major repairs; to change greatly

patchwork ['pætʃwɚk]   consisting of many different parts. A patchwork quilt is made of many pieces of cloth sewn together.

Culture and Vocabulary Activities

1. Which three of the Culture items come from other countries?
2. As you read the article, find other words that have approximately the same meaning as *disparity* and *gulf.*

Do the Poor Deserve Bad Schools?

Of course not. Equal opportunity is what America is all about. That is why there is growing criticism of the shameful disparities in funding.

By EMILY MITCHELL

BEFORE STARTING THEIR MORNING LESsons, children in public schools across the U.S. recite the Pledge of Allegiance. The familiar words echo in immaculate suburban buildings with bright, airy classrooms and labs where children study art and languages, learn on the latest computers and play sports in well-equipped gyms. They also ring out in overcrowded, eroding, inner-city schools where sewage backs up into bathroom plumbing and where students share used textbooks and practice typing on handmade, fake keyboards. Whatever the setting, the pledge ends the same: "with liberty and justice for all."

The notion of equal opportunity is central to the American ideal. For that goal to have any meaning, it must be rooted in an education system that gives every child a chance to succeed. But for decades, a gulf has been widening between the quality of public schooling for children of privilege and that for those born into poverty. By relying on local property taxes as a crucial source of funds, the U.S. has created a caste system of public education that is increasingly separate and unequal.

As these disparities have become too glaring and shameful to ignore, a reform movement has grown that seeks to play Robin Hood by taking funds from richer districts to help pay for schools in poorer ones. Since the 1970s, 10 states have decided—or been forced by courts—to overhaul their methods of funding some of their school districts. In the process, tempers are flaring in a manner reminiscent of the disagreements that once raged over school busing. "It is a tug-of-war between equity and excellence," says Tony Rollins, executive director of the Colorado Education Association, a state teachers' union that has been active in the funding wars.

The forces of equity have now been joined by a powerful voice: that of education gadfly Jonathan Kozol, author of a galvanizing new book, *Savage Inequalities* (Crown; $20). After two years of research, Kozol has written a searing exposé of the extremes of wealth and poverty in America's school system and the blighting effect on poor children, especially those in cities.

From San Antonio to New York City's South Bronx, Kozol observes, inner-city schools are bleak fortresses with rotting classrooms and few amenities to inspire or motivate the young. A history teacher at East St. Louis' Martin Luther King Jr. High School, he notes, has 110 students in four classes, and only 26 books. Every year, says a teacher in a nearby school, "there's one more toilet that doesn't flush, one more drinking fountain that doesn't work, one more classroom without texts."

In painful detail, Kozol describes such inner-city schools as Morris High in the

RYE HIGH SCHOOL, RYE, N.Y.
ANNUAL EXPENDITURE PER STUDENT: $12,570
NUMBER OF STUDENTS: 536; TEACHERS: 73

ARMEN KACHATURIAN/TIME MAGAZINE

South Bronx, where water cascades down the stairways when it rains, and Chicago's Du Sable High, where the chemistry teacher uses a popcorn popper as a Bunsen burner. Kozol juxtaposes these im-

ages with descriptions of the luxurious facilities in nearby wealthy suburbs like Winnetka, north of Chicago. Its New Trier High has, among other things, seven gyms, rooms for fencing, wrestling and dance instruction, and an Olympic-size pool.

For Kozol and many activist reformers, the chief villain of the education tragedy is "local control," America's decentralized system of school administration and its heavy reliance on property taxation. Everything from pencils to teachers' salaries is paid for through a patchwork process that varies from state to state. But

in most cases, about 6% of the money in any district comes from Washington, 47% from the state government and 47% from locally generated property taxes. Kozol believes the best way to improve schools—

all schools—would be to do away completely with the property tax as a source of revenue. In its place he suggests a progressive income tax to raise money that would then be distributed fairly among districts.

There is no denying the key role that property levies have played in creating the vast educational gap between rich and poor. School trustees in the affluent Texas district of Glen Rose, for example, annually dole out $9,326 per pupil—three times as much as the per-student allocation in the Rio Grande Valley's bleak Roma district. For reformers, the chief ally has been state courts, which have ruled in many cases—Kentucky, Texas, New Jersey and Montana, for example—that inequalities are unconstitutional. In Tennessee, 77 school districts asked a state court to take the same approach, and won. A similar suit has been launched by 108 of Michigan's 500 school districts.

The reform movement is already producing some results. In 1989 Kentucky's supreme court ruled that the state's school-finance system was unconstitutional; the richest schools were allocated as much as $4,200 a year for each pupil, while poorer ones received only $1,700 per student. Under a plan that is in its second year, virtually every school district now has at least $3,200 to spend per student; over the years, the gap between rich and poor districts will be further narrowed. Children from low-income families now have new preschool programs, and there is a wide range of Saturday and after-school projects for students with special needs.

But in other parts of the country the fight over redistributing privilege remains bitter. Texas' state supreme court ruled in 1989 that gross educational inequality could no longer be condoned. Since then Texas lawmakers have come up with two plans that the judiciary found unsatisfactory. Governor Ann Richards signed a compromise law last year that shifted millions of dollars in property-tax revenue to poorer districts, but the bill's constitutionality is still under challenge in the courts.

"Surely there is enough for everyone within this country. It is a tragedy that these good things are not more widely shared. All our children ought to be allowed a stake in the enormous richness of America."

—Jonathan Kozol

In New Jersey, Democratic Governor James Florio did some fast backpedaling after prompting the state legislature to enact a Robin Hood plan last year that would have used $1.1 billion in state taxes to raise the level of funding in poor school districts. When affluent voters expressed outrage, Florio agreed to shift $360 million of the school aid back to property-tax relief. His political standing was badly damaged; at board of education meetings in Florham Park, N.J., angry parents showed up seeking to turn their public school district into a private one.

IT IS EASY ENOUGH TO CONDEMN THOSE self-protective actions as selfishness, but as author Kozol points out, in most cases better-off Americans simply have a narrower view of what they are doing. "They do not want poor children to be harmed," he writes, "they simply want the best for their own children." Those sentiments are echoed by New Jersey school-district superintendent Timothy Brennan, whose Holmdel district spends $7,450 per pupil, vs. $3,086 in the state's poorest jurisdiction. "The point of reform was to make all schools quality schools. But I fear that everything will settle into mediocrity." The belief even extends to children. Kozol spoke to a student in a wealthy New York City suburb whose family had moved from the problem-plagued Bronx. "There's no point in coming to a place like this, where schools are good," she said, "and then your taxes go back to the place where you began."

Yet anyone who has seen the shameful disparities between public schools in rich and poor areas, or who has read Kozol's vivid account, will find it difficult to deny that the differences in funding make a mockery of the nation's ideal. Fifth-grade teacher Madelyn Cimaglia has no doubt of the wonders that could be worked in San Antonio's Edgewood school district if more funds were available. Like thousands of her peers, Cimaglia supplements meager classroom supplies with her own money, buying her students books such as *Alice in Wonderland* and *Charlotte's Web.* "Our kids would fly if we had resources similar to the rich districts," she says. —*Reported by Deborah Fowler/Houston and Lisa H. Towle/New York*

CARL SCHURZ HIGH SCHOOL, CHICAGO
ANNUAL EXPENDITURE PER STUDENT: $5,276
NUMBER OF STUDENTS: 3,100; TEACHERS: 184

AFTER YOU READ

Comprehension Questions

1. What kinds of facilities do many schools in wealthy areas have?
2. What is the condition of many schools in poor areas?
3. According to Jonathan Kozol, what is the cause of these differences in schools?
4. What three sources of funding do U.S. school districts have?
5. What do educational reformers want to change?

Discussion and Analysis Questions

1. Were you surprised to learn about the inequalities of education in the United States? Why or why not?
2. Do you think the reform movement will be successful? Explain your answer.
3. The writer uses many statistics in the article. Find examples of these. Do you think the numbers are effective? Why or why not?

Group Activity

In groups of four or five, discuss what facilities and courses you think the ideal elementary or secondary school should have. Do you know of any such schools? If so, where are they located? Describe your ideal school to the class.

Individual Work

Pretend that you are a student in one of the poor schools discussed in the article. Write a one-page letter to the editor of the local newspaper describing your school and asking for help from the public. Be prepared to read your letter to the class.

5 BIG CHILL ON CAMPUS

BEFORE YOU READ

Preview

Financial problems are forcing many U.S. colleges and universities to raise fees and cut expenses.

Getting Started

1. What kinds of institutions of higher education are there in your home country? What is their source of funding? Must students pay fees for higher education? Does every university offer the same courses of study?
2. Describe the reputation of American higher education. On what do you think this reputation is based?

Culture

catalog ['kædə,lɔg]   a publication that gives information about a college or university, including descriptions of its courses and degree programs

infrastructure ['ɪnfrə,strəktʃɚ]   the support system for an organization

regent ['ridʒɛnt]   an appointed or elected member of the governing board for a system of higher education

sit-in ['sɪt ɪn]   a nonviolent demonstration in which people enter a place and refuse to leave until their demands are met. Sit-ins were very common during the civil-rights movement of the 1960s.

tuition [,tu'ɪʃən]   the fee students pay to a college or university in order to take courses

Vocabulary

byword ['baɪwɚd]   a word or phrase that is often used

cutback ['kətbæk]   a reduction

(to) epitomize [i'pɪdə,maɪz]   to represent ideally

hottest ['hadəst]   most popular

leaner ['linɚ]   thinner; smaller

pinch [pɪntʃ]   a shortage of needed things, like money

(to) prune [prun]   to cut away unnecessary parts

(to) shave [ʃev]   to reduce or lessen something

squeeze [skwiz]   a tight situation; a situation in which pressure is felt

stripe [straɪp]   kind; variety

Culture and Vocabulary Activities

1. Which items on the Culture list refer to college and university life? As you read the article, make a list of all the words you find that pertain to higher education. If there are any you don't understand, discuss them in class.
2. Which words on the Vocabulary list are synonyms for *decrease*? As you read the article, make a list of other words that mean *decrease*.
3. As you read the article, make a list of words that mean almost the same as *increase*.

Big Chill on Campus

After decades of growth, U.S. colleges are facing a financial squeeze that threatens the quality and breadth of higher education

By RICHARD N. OSTLING

FOR A HALF-CENTURY, EXPANSION HAS been the byword of American higher education. More course offerings, bigger and better-paid faculties, new graduate schools and elaborately equipped laboratories, more diverse student bodies. The emphasis on bigger and better helped make American universities the envy of the world and their degrees one of the nation's hottest exports.

But suddenly, with a shifting of economic winds, contraction is the order of the day. As state, federal and private sources of funds dry up and bills from the fast-spending '80s come due, even the most elite colleges find themselves facing a financial crunch that promises to reshape the contours of higher education. "Now they have to pay for their prosperity," says Robert Rosenzweig, president of the Association of American Universities in Washington. "It is the morning after."

Colleges of all stripes—public and private, princely and proletarian—are retrenching in an effort to stay afloat. Meanwhile, expenses are rising. A declining pool of 18-year-olds has forced schools into a pricey competition for students. The cost of high-tech equipment and high-profile professors continues to grow, along with such expenses as medical insurance. The cutbacks are causing alarm among faculty members and a furor among students, who are worried that schools will be unable to deliver on the educational promises made in their glossy catalogs.

At Yale University, administrators see the current $8.8 million operating deficit ballooning to a staggering $50 million within a few years, and contemplate deep cuts in faculty and programs. Having already trimmed nearly 10% in administrative costs and 5% in academic expenses last year, along with such marginal items as the water-polo team, the New Haven institution is proposing to eliminate two departments—linguistics and operations research. It hopes to consolidate three engineering departments into one, with a 23% loss of faculty. And it anticipates a 10.7% overall reduction in its professorial ranks.

After 90 years of service, Commons is closed for dinner

YALE UNIVERSITY

GONE
- 130 support staff
- Varsity wrestling and water polo
- Dinner in Commons

GOING?
- 10.7% of arts-and-sciences faculty
- Departments of linguistics and applied physics
- Three specialized engineering departments

Similar cuts are looming at Stanford, which is planning to slash $43 million over the next two years. And Columbia University, which faces a $50 million deficit, will probably follow suit, although the heads of 26 arts-and-sciences departments have threatened to quit if the cutbacks are too harsh. Adding to the woes of such élite and venerable universities are harrowing upkeep costs for aging buildings: at Yale the tab for deferred maintenance is said to be $1 billion.

While the pinch at private schools has been tightening for some time, troubles cascaded rather suddenly upon the public campuses. State governments, having lavished funds on their colleges in the '80s, are grappling with large budget deficits, declining tax revenues and increased outlays as a result of the recession.

California epitomizes the problems. The celebrated Master Plan of 1960 calls for the top high school graduates in the state to have access to the world-class University of California system, which has nine campuses. Somewhat less accomplished students—those in the top third of their classes—can enter 20 California State University campuses, while everyone else is eligible for the 107 community colleges. Then came last year's crushing state deficit and a $369 million cut in higher-education spending. Barry Munitz, chancellor of the Cal State system, says his domain "is so dangerously underfunded" that the

Can marriage to another college save the sinking school?

Master Plan "becomes more of a myth every day."

To make ends meet, the University of California, Berkeley, has cut 163 full- and part-time faculty and increased fees 40% this year. Governor Pete Wilson wants a new 22% hike for next year. (Even then, residents would pay only $3,036, a big bargain compared with the tab at private campuses of similar excellence.) Hundreds of infuriated students at the university campus in Davis conducted a 1960s-style sit-in for four days after U.C. regents approved the latest increase.

California is hardly alone in ordering steep tuition hikes. Charges for many State University of New York students will double in two years if a budget unveiled last week is approved. This year, fees jumped 36% at Oregon State University. The University of Maine administered a rare midyear tuition hike of 15.6%. Mississippi's public-university students may face a 25% jump next year.

Tuition increases are a seemingly simple way for public colleges to meet deficits, but if taken too far they undermine the principle of state-supported education. A steep price means that "education is no longer seen as a public good, but as a private benefit," enriching the individual as opposed to society, says University of Oregon provost Norman Wessells. Joseph Duffey, president of American University in Washington, shares that concern: "People think they don't have obligations to any children but their own."

While private campuses do not face such philosophical scruples about raising fees, they seem to have reached a practical limit. After rapid increases throughout the 1980s, market resistance is forcing tuitions to level off. Thus schools are compelled to reduce expenses. Just how intelligently this is done will determine the future strength of each college. "We're all going to have to do more with less," says James Pickering, academic-affairs vice president at the University of Houston.

Unfortunately, it is already clear that many schools are doing considerably less with less. The California State system, which is distinct from the U.C. system, has laid off 3,000 full- and part-time teachers and canceled 5,000 course sections. This meant that last fall 1,162 hapless students at the San Diego State campus were initially unable to find a spot in a single course that they needed to meet their graduation requirements. At Cal State Long Beach, president Curtis McCray described the damage to a local reporter: "In chemistry, we have no chemicals. In art, there is no paint. In other parts, it's simply impossible to get paper. Hallways go uncleaned. Light bulbs go unchanged. We can't offer classes because we've laid off faculty."

The consequences of some cutbacks are less obvious, more insidious. The University of Maryland and the University of Massachusetts have cut library expenses and subscriptions to academic journals and postponed maintenance on buildings. They have trimmed back on teaching assistants, shaved the overall ratio of professors to students. "You can't see the damage now," says Sherry Penney, chancellor of U. Mass's Boston campus, "but in five years there will be no journals in the library, the best people will have left, the infrastructure will be falling apart."

Still, many educators believe that the contraction of the 1990s need not spell doom for U.S. universities. If major institutions concentrate on what they do best and stop trying to be all things to all students, they may actually emerge stronger than ever. "What we are witnessing is the death of the 19th century research

university," says David Scott Kastan, chairman of Columbia's department of English and comparative literature. Such institutions are enormously inefficient, but there are good ways and bad ways to prune them. "There's the democracy-of-pain option," he explains, "whereby you cut across the board, which runs a terrible risk of mediocritizing and demoralizing the university. Or you can make more selective cuts, which require real leadership."

At Northwestern University, decisions to close the nursing and dental-hygiene programs probably represent intelligent pruning, as does Yale's decision to consolidate applied physics with physics. Kastan and others point out that universities within a given city or region could save money by sharing resources. "It's odd that every university needs to have its own molecular-biology course and pre-Tudor theater course," Kastan says.

Among the financially weakest colleges, however, intelligent cutting will not suffice. "Some colleges will either have to consolidate or shut down," says Sara Melendez, who until recently served as vice provost and dean of arts and humanities at Connecticut's University of Bridgeport. The school, hard hit by the deterioration of its hometown, has been struggling to stave off its own demise. Late last year it began negotiations for an emergency loan of $2 million to $3 million in order to keep operating. Administrators now believe that the school can survive only by merging with nearby Sacred Heart University, though the law school prefers another partner.

Such decisions promise to make the coming decade the most difficult ever faced by America's institutions of higher learning. By the year 2000, many educators predict, the country will have leaner universities and a smaller system of higher education. But that may be appropriate. In the past 20 years, too many colleges overbuilt, too many aspired to do too much, and as a result, too many are competing frantically—and wastefully—for the same students. "We need more community colleges and fewer research universities," observes Duffey of American University, "and there should be more liberal-arts schools focusing on undergraduate education." A smaller system might turn out to be a better system, particularly if colleges concentrate on developing their unique strengths. But to do so will require all the brainpower and ingenuity that American educators can muster.   —*Reported by Ann Blackman/Washington and Jeanne Reid/Boston, with other bureaus*

AFTER YOU READ

Comprehension Questions

1. What characterized the expansion period of higher education in the United States?
2. What has caused the need for contraction of services at American colleges and universities?
3. What kinds of reductions have taken place at various universities?

Discussion and Analysis Questions

1. The writer describes the "consequences of some cutbacks" as "insidious." What examples does he give? Do you agree with his evaluation?
2. What is the "democracy-of-pain option"? What is its alternative?
3. Do you think the writer is optimistic or pessimistic about the changes in American higher education? Identify sections of the article to support your opinion.

Group Activity

In groups of four to six, discuss the advantages and disadvantages of the "democracy-of-pain option" and of the "intelligent pruning option." Decide which choice is better for a university that must make financial reductions. Present your conclusions to the class.

Individual Work

Interview a faculty member or an administrator at your institution to learn what cuts (if any) have occurred in the last five years. Take notes on the conversation and be prepared to give a five-minute oral summary of your findings to the class.

6 THE PURSUIT OF EXCELLENCE

BEFORE YOU READ

Preview

Foreign students often come to American colleges and universities to find what they can't find at home.

Getting Started

1. Look at the graph titled "Students from Abroad." How many international students attended U.S. institutions of higher education in 1990? How many are expected to attend in the year 2000?
2. Look at the other graph. What eight countries do approximately half of the international students in the United States come from?

Culture

constituency [kən'stɪtʃuən,si]   a portion of the population being served or represented

corporate donor ['kɔrprət 'donɚ]   a company that gives money to a college or university

curfew ['kɚfju]   the time at which residents of a dormitory must be inside. During the 1960s, curfews for female college students were common.

dorm-visitation rules [,dorm vɪzɪ'teʃən ,rulz]   rules indicating the times at which students may have visitors of the opposite sex in their dormitory rooms. Visitation rules used to be very strict; today they are quite liberal.

G.I. bill ['dʒi aɪ 'bɪl]   a U.S. legislative act passed after World War II that gave veterans financial assistance to attend college. A G.I. is a member or former member of the U.S. armed services. The initials commonly stand for "government issue."

in loco parentis [ɪn 'loko pə'rɛntɪs]   in the place of one's parents

minority [maɪ'norɪti]   a person belonging to a group whose members are few in number and/or have relatively little political power

Vocabulary

cachet [kæ'ʃe]   prestige; social value

cutback ['kətbæk]   a reduction

(to) earmark ['ɪrmɑrk]   to designate; to indicate for a special purpose

hallmark ['hɔlmɑrk]   a distinguishing characteristic

(to) run out ['rən 'aʊt]   to use up the last of something and have no more

shut out ['ʃət 'aʊt]   excluded; denied entrance

(to) soak up ['sok 'əp]   to absorb something; to take in something

(to) take seed ['tek 'sid]   to begin to grow; to start to develop

Culture and Vocabulary Activities

1. Which words and phrases in the Culture and Vocabulary lists have been borrowed directly from other languages? Which languages did they come from?
2. Find the two-word verbs in the Vocabulary list. What seems to be the rule for pronouncing two-word verbs?

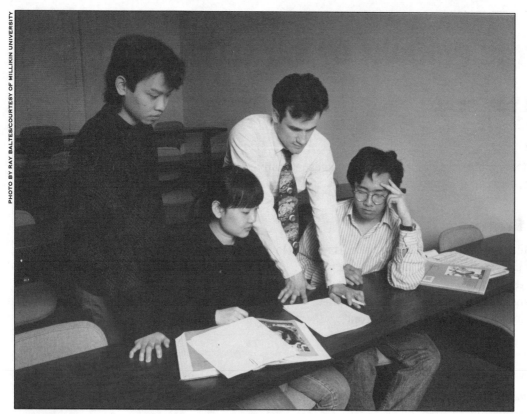

MILLIKIN UNIVERSITY:
Foreign students benefit from the personal attention of their professors at this small midwestern university

EDUCATION

The Pursuit of Excellence

For all their abiding troubles, U.S. universities and colleges are a powerful magnet for foreign students in search of freedom and diversity

By JILL SMOLOWE

SOMETIME AROUND THE SEVENTH GRADE, many American students are introduced to the tale of 10 blind men inspecting an elephant. When each blind man reaches different conclusions about the creature, the students are invited to consider whether truth is absolute or lies in the eye of the beholder. College professors and administrators might want to remember that fable when they take the measure of American higher education. Many of them, who tend to see only what they stand to lose, perceive the beast as wounded, suffering from the shocks of rising costs, dwindling resources and life-draining cutbacks. But foreigners, who compare America's universities with their own, often reach very different conclusions about the nature of the beast.

If sheer numbers provide any proof, America's universities and colleges are the envy of the world. For all their abiding troubles, this country's 3,500 institutions were flooded with 407,530 students from 193 different countries last year. Asia led the way with 39,000 students from China and 36,610 from Japan, followed by India and Canada. Many of the foreigners, who entered graduate and undergraduate programs in roughly equal numbers, felt they had to go abroad to escape narrow and restrictive systems at home. They came in search of academic excellence certainly, but they also came looking for freedom, diversity and the cachet that an American degree continues to provide.

Some students come simply because they are shut out of the system at home. Most European and Asian universities provide an élite service to a small and privileged clientele. While fully 60% of all

U.S. high school graduates attend college at some point in their life, just 30% of the comparable German population, 28% of the French, 20% of the British and 37% of the Japanese proceed beyond high school. German students who survive the *Abitur* or Britons who pass their A levels may still not qualify for a top university at home, but find American universities far more welcoming. Some U.S. schools acknowledge the rigor of European secondary training and will give up to a year's credit to foreigners who have passed their high school exams.

"The egalitarian conception that everyone has a right to an education appropriate to his potential is a highly democratic and compassionate standard," says Marvin Bressler, professor of sociology and education specialist at Princeton University. True, not all U.S. collegians can match the performance of their foreign counterparts, but American institutions do offer students from rich and poor families alike the chance to realize their full potential. "America educates so many more people at university that one can't expect all those who go to be either as well informed or intelligent as the much narrower band who go to English universities," says Briton Christopher Ricks, professor of English at Boston University. Having instructed at Cambridge, Ricks knows that teaching T.S. Eliot to British undergraduates is an easier task. Yet he finds teaching at B.U. very rewarding. "I'm not against élitism," he says. "But I happen to like having people who are more eager to learn."

The democratic impulse to reach out to so many first took seed after World War II, when the G.I. bill made funding for higher education available to all returning soldiers. As universities expanded to handle the sudden influx, they developed the flexibility that has become one of the hallmarks of American higher learning. "In the U.S. there is a system of infinite chances," says Diane Ravitch, Assistant Secretary of Education. "At 35, you can decide to go back to college, upgrade your education, change your profession."

While Americans take such flexibility for granted, foreigners do not. To French students, who are commonly expected at age 16 to select both a university and a specific course of study, the American practice of jumping not only from department to department but also from school to school seems a luxury. Japanese students find it all but impossible to transfer credits from one school to another. Thus students who initially enter a junior college and subsequently decide to earn a bachelor's degree must head overseas.

Many are attracted not only to the academic programs at a particular U.S. college but also to the larger community, which affords the chance to soak up the surrounding culture. Few foreign universities put much emphasis on the cozy communal life that characterizes American campuses: from clubs and sports teams to student publications and theatrical societies. "The campus and the American university have become identical in people's minds," says Brown University President Vartan Gregorian. "In America it is assumed that a student's daily life is as important as his learning experience."

WHILE CURFEWS AND DORM-VISITATION rules have long been relaxed, university administrators and staff members still perform an in loco parentis role. They are expected to provide counseling and supervision on everything from career and family planning to the dietary habits of vegetarians and anorexics. Indeed, such painstaking attention is paid to the personal needs of students that Gregorian likens running a U.S. college to presiding over a Greek city-state. "You have your security force, your dormitories, your food services, a judiciary to impose discipline, whether somebody harassed somebody, and so forth," he says. "I can't imagine the president of the Sorbonne being bothered with these things."

Foreign students also come in search of choices. America's menu of options—research universities, state institutions, private liberal-arts schools, community colleges, religious institutions, military academies—is unrivaled. "In Europe," says history professor Jonathan Steinberg, who has taught at both Harvard and Cambridge, "there is one system, and that is it." While students overseas usually must demonstrate expertise in a single field, whether law or philosophy or chemistry, most American universities insist

that students sample natural and social sciences, languages and literature before choosing a field of concentration.

Such opposing philosophies grow out of different traditions and power structures. In Europe and Japan universities are answerable only to a Ministry of Education, which sets academic standards and distributes money. While centralization ensures that all students are equipped with roughly the same resources and perform at roughly the same level, it also discourages experimentation. "When they make mistakes, they make big ones," says

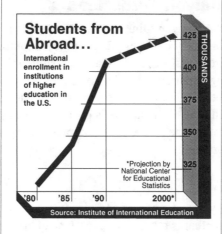

Students from Abroad...
International enrollment in institutions of higher education in the U.S.

*Projection by National Center for Educational Statistics

'80 '85 '90 2000*

THOUSANDS: 425 400 375 350 325

Source: Institute of International Education

Robert Rosenzweig, president of the Association of American Universities. "They set a system in wrong directions, and it's like steering a supertanker."

U.S. colleges, on the other hand, are so responsive to cultural currents that they are often on the cutting edge of social change. Such sensitivity—some might argue hypersensitivity—to the culture around them reflects the broad array of constituencies to which college administrators must answer. The board of trustees, composed of community and national leaders, serves as a referee between the institutional culture and the surrounding community; alumni and corporate donors, who often earmark monies for specific expenditures; student bodies that demand a

voice in university life; legislators who apportion government funds; and an often feisty faculty.

Smaller colleges are particularly attractive to foreign students because they are likely to offer direct contact with professors. "We have one of the few systems in the world where students are actually expected to go to class," says Rosenzweig. With the exception of Britain, where much of the teaching takes place in one-on-one tutorials, European students rarely come into direct contact with professors until they reach graduate-level studies. Even lectures are optional in Europe, since students are graded solely on examinations, with no eye to class attendance or participation. In Japan students are expected to ingest their professors' teachings so passively that it is possible for a student to graduate without ever opening his mouth.

In some respects, the independent spirit of the American university that foreigners admire comes down to dollars and cents. All U.S. colleges, private and public alike, must fight vigorously to stay alive. They compete not only for students but also for faculty and research grants. Such competition, though draining and distracting, can stimulate creativity and force administrators to remain attentive to student needs. "U.S. students pay for their education," says Ulrich Littmann, head of the German Fulbright Commission, "and demand a commensurate value for what they—or their parents—pay."

Most universities abroad have state funding, but that luxury has a steep price: universities have less opportunity to develop distinctive personalities and define their own missions. "There isn't a lot of competition or innovation in Japanese higher education because there's too much government control," says Nana Regur, an international-education specialist.

If the financial crisis besetting U.S. campuses is mishandled, Americans may discover they don't know what they've got until it's gone. "By the year 2000, American higher education will no longer be dominant in the world," warns Joseph Duffey, president of American University in Washington. "Our general belief in education and our ability to finance it are running out." Unless real corrections are made—and fast—the U.S. will relinquish its standing as the most desirable place in the world to get a higher education. —*With reporting by Ann Blackman/Washington, Rhea Schoenthal/Bonn and Sidney Urquhart/New York*

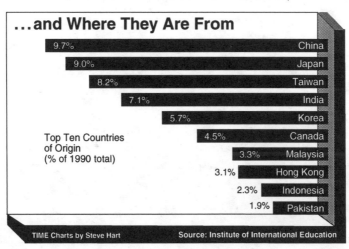

...and Where They Are From

Top Ten Countries of Origin (% of 1990 total)

Country	%
China	9.7%
Japan	9.0%
Taiwan	8.2%
India	7.1%
Korea	5.7%
Canada	4.5%
Malaysia	3.3%
Hong Kong	3.1%
Indonesia	2.3%
Pakistan	1.9%

TIME Charts by Steve Hart   Source: Institute of International Education

AFTER YOU READ

Comprehension Questions

1. How many institutions of higher education are in the United States?
2. From how many different countries do international students come?
3. Why do international students come to the United States?
4. What kind of flexibility do U.S. colleges and universities offer?
5. Why are smaller colleges especially attractive to international students?

Discussion and Analysis Questions

1. Based on your experience, do you think the contrasts made in the article between U.S. universities and those in other countries are accurate? Explain your answer.
2. According to Vartan Gregorian, "In America it is assumed that a student's daily life is as important as his learning experience." What examples are given in the article to support this statement? Do you think the statement is explained enough?
3. Do you think the overall tone of the article is positive or negative? Give examples to support your answer. Is the tone of the last paragraph optimistic or pessimistic? Does it fit with the rest of the article?

Group Activities

1. In groups of six, identify the advantages and disadvantages of a university system that is more egalitarian and one that is more selective. Present your conclusions to the class.
2. In groups of six, discuss whether you think universities should be responsible only for academics, or whether they should be concerned with other parts of student life such as housing, meals, and extracurricular activities. Be prepared to report to the class.

Individual Work

In a one-page paper, describe the advantages and disadvantages of studying in another country.

Nature & the Environment

1 INVASION OF THE SUPERBUG

BEFORE YOU READ

Preview

An insect from another part of the world is destroying fruits and vegetables in California.

Getting Started

1. What kinds of fruits and vegetables are grown in your home country? Are they grown in specific areas?
2. What can cause fruit and vegetable crops to fail?

Culture

bugbuster ['bəg,bəstɚ]   a person who fights insects. The name is based on the popular movie *Ghostbusters*, in which a team of men fought ghosts.

continental U.S. ['kɑntɪ,nɛntəl 'ju,ɛs]   the United States excluding the states of Alaska and Hawaii

smorgasbord ['smorgəs,bord]   a buffet meal offering a wide variety of hot and cold foods. Diners serve themselves at a smorgasbord.

wholesale price ['holsel 'praɪs]   the price a distributor pays to the producer of a product. Consumers then pay the distributor a *retail price,* which is higher.

Vocabulary

crop [krɑp]   the amount of a plant or other product grown in a season

entomologist [,ɛntə'mɑlədʒəst]   a specialist in entomology, the study of insects

(to) feel at home ['fil æt 'hom]   to be comfortable

habitat ['hæbɪ,tæt]   the place where a kind of plant or animal naturally lives

hybrid ['haɪbrɪd]   a mixture of different varieties of plants or animals

innocuous [ɪn'ɑkjuəs]   harmless; causing no injury

insecticide [ɪn'sɛktɪ,saɪd]   a chemical that kills insects

parasite ['pɛrə,saɪt]   an organism that lives in or on another organism

pesticide ['pɛstə,saɪd]   insecticide; a chemical used to destroy pests. Some pesticides are harmful to the environment.

predator ['prɛdətɚ]   an animal that kills another animal for food

quarantine ['kwɔrən,tin]   the isolation of infected plants, animals, or people

Culture and Vocabulary Activities

1. Look at the Culture list. Which word is the newest? Which word is borrowed from another language? What language is it from?
2. Look at the Vocabulary list. What do you think the following suffixes (word endings) mean: *-ist, -ite, -ide, -or?*

The whitefly sucks the juices from a plant, causing it to wither and die. Melons were the first victims, but the insect attacks virtually every fruit and vegetable—except asparagus.

Invasion of the Superbug

A voracious insect is chewing its way through California crops, and consumers across the U.S. may pay the price

By MICHAEL D. LEMONICK

BY LATE NOVEMBER, FIELDS IN THE IMperial valley, which straddles the California-Mexico border, should be bursting with ripe melons ready for shipment to markets around the U.S. Instead, 95% of this fall's crop has been lost and much of the rest lies rotting on the vine. Harvests of lettuce, broccoli, cauliflower, squash, citrus fruits, table grapes, sugar beets, carrots and cabbages are threatened as well. Total crop losses in Imperial County and nearby Riverside County have already reached $90 million. Says melon grower Ben Abatti, who has been farming in the area since 1956: "It is total disaster."

The agent of disaster is a 3-mm (onetenth-in.) insect known to scientists as the poinsettia strain of the sweet-potato whitefly but to farmers as the Superbug. Millions of these voracious insects have spread over the Imperial Valley, massing on the undersides of leaves and sucking plants dry, weakening or killing them in the process. Farmers first noticed the flies getting worse in July, and by September swarms of them looked like white clouds. They covered windshields and got stuck between people's teeth. Farm workers had trouble inhaling and eventually had to wear masks. Not since the Mediterranean fruitfly scares of the early and late 1980s has California's $18 billion agriculture industry, which during winter supplies close to 90% of the fresh produce in the continental U.S., been so alarmed by a pest.

The first hint of a visit by fruit flies is invariably met with quarantines and airborne-insecticide spraying campaigns. The new Superbug has no effective native predators in California, and pesticides are largely useless against it. If it continues unchecked, Imperial Valley could be put out of business for months. That could cause an estimated $200 million in farm losses by spring and higher prices at the produce counter. The wholesale price of melon has tripled, and by one reckoning, the average cost of a head of lettuce in a supermarket could go from $1.19 to about $1.50. In some areas, these foods may be in short supply.

California farmers have been fighting other types of sweet-potato whiteflies for years. But the poinsettia strain, so named because it first appeared in the U.S. on poinsettia plants in Florida greenhouses, reproduces twice as fast as its relatives and consumes five times as much food from its victims. It comes originally from somewhere halfway around the world, possibly Iraq or Pakistan, and apparently reached America in 1986, probably hidden away in a cargo shipment.

Florida is a little too cool and rainy, on average, for the Superbug's taste, and the infestation there was never as serious. But when the fly arrived in Southern California, probably in a fruit basket or vegetable shipment, it felt right at home in the dry weather and summer temperatures that can reach 46°C (115°F). Because the insect is happy eating some 500 varieties of plants (one of the only vegetables it doesn't seem to like is asparagus), it found the fertile Imperial Valley to be a veritable smorgasbord.

Since all pesticides approved for use in California have been ineffective against the bug, the best advice agriculture officials can give is for farmers to plow under devastated fields, denying the pests their food sources. In addition, roadways and ditches around the valley are being cleared of weeds that help sustain the whitefly. Farmers are considering a "host-free" period in which they will do no planting at all. Says John Pierre Menvielle, who farms 900 hectares (2,200 acres) in Calexico: "If that is what it takes, we will do it."

ONE POSSIBLE LONG-TERM SOLUTION, says Nick Toscano, an entomologist at the University of California at Riverside, is a tiny stingless wasp that lives in the California desert. It lays eggs on the immature whitefly, and when they hatch, the baby wasps eat the fly. Other researchers are cross-breeding the poinsettia whitefly with more innocuous varieties in hopes of developing a mild-mannered hybrid that might displace the Superbug. In the next six or nine months, a team of scientists will leave for the Middle East in search of a parasite from the fly's native habitat that could combat it. A promising natural pesticide is neem-seed extract from the Indian *Azadirachta indica* tree. The bugbusters may have to resort to synthetic insecticides that are not approved in California but may have to be—in a hurry.

Unfortunately, that last option could end up causing more trouble in the long run. The toughness of the poinsettia whitefly has evolved over generations. "It has been exposed to pesticides for a long period of time and developed resistance," explains Toscano. Using new pesticides could halt the bug's advance for now—but given its ability to adapt, the result could be some sort of Ultimate Bug that would make Superbug look tame. —*Reported by Jeanne McDowell/Los Angeles*

AFTER YOU READ

Comprehension Questions

1. Why is California's agriculture industry so important?
2. How does the whitefly kill plants?
3. Why is the poinsettia strain worse than other varieties of whiteflies?
4. What advice are agriculture officials giving to California farmers?
5. What four other solutions to the problem are possible?

Discussion and Analysis Questions

1. Discuss the possible solutions to the whitefly problem. What are the advantages and disadvantages of each?
2. This article uses many technical words like *entomologist* and *quarantine*. Do these words help you to understand the article, or do they make the article more difficult?

Group Activity

New compound words in English can be made using the suffix (word ending) *-buster* (someone or something that fights, breaks, or destroys). For example, one brand of hand-held vacuum cleaner is called a Dustbuster. In groups of three, invent new words using *-buster* and write their definitions. Present your inventions to the class.

Individual Work

Identify words in the article with negative connotations (additional meanings). *Pest* is one example. Share your list with the class.

2 BREEZING INTO THE FUTURE

BEFORE YOU READ

Preview

Windmills can help meet the energy needs of the United States.

Getting Started

1. Look at the drawing of the windmill and read the descriptions. What do these descriptions suggest were the problems of previous windmills?
2. Look at the small graph entitled "Power Costs." What happened to the costs of gas and wind power between 1982 and 1990?

Culture

alternative energy [ɔl'tɚnətɪv 'ɛnɚdʒi]   energy produced by a source other than fossil fuels. Water is one example of an alternative energy source.

fossil fuel ['fɑsəl 'fju(ə)l]   a source of energy that comes from ancient plant or animal remains in the earth. Coal is one example of a fossil fuel.

nickel ['nɪkəl]   a U.S. coin worth five cents

pilot project ['paɪlət 'prɑ,dʒɛkt]   a trial activity; an experiment to see if a plan will work

renewable energy [ri'nuəbəl 'ɛnɚdʒi]   energy produced by a source that never runs out. Solar energy is one example of a renewable energy source.

Vocabulary

(to) come full circle ['kəm ,fʊl 'sɚkəl]   to arrive at the starting point again; to return to where one began

dicey ['daɪsi]   touchy; chancy; potentially controversial

free as the breeze ['fri æz ðə 'briz]   having no cost

incentive [ɪn'sɛntɪv]   a motive; a reason to do something. Incentives are often financial.

lost cause ['lɔst 'kɔz]   a project or plan with no hope of success

on the drawing board [ɔn ðə 'drɔɪŋ 'bord]   being planned; in the process of development

scam [skæm]   a swindle; a deceptive act or plan

(to) shave off ['ʃev 'ɔf]   to reduce or lessen something

trial and error ['traɪ(ə)l ænd 'ɛrɚ]   trying repeatedly for success; experimentation

wildcatter ['waɪld,kædɚ]   someone who looks for energy sources in untried areas. The word usually refers to people who drill for oil or gas.

Culture and Vocabulary Activities

1. English uses many phrases like "free as the breeze" to describe people or things. Look at the following phrases and discuss their meanings:

   strong as an ox   wise as an owl   quiet as a mouse
   gentle as a lamb   happy as a lark   wily as a fox

   Does your native language have similar phrases? If so, discuss them with the class.
2. *Nickel* is the name of one piece of American money. Be sure you know the meanings of the following money names: *penny, dime, quarter, half-dollar,* and *buck.*

Breezing into the Future

How can America curb its dangerous dependence on scarce, nasty fossil fuels? The answer, my friend, is blowing in the wind.

Oil wells of the 1990s? Advanced wind turbines such as these in central California are capable of meeting 10% of the nation's energy needs.

By DICK THOMPSON WASHINGTON

A DECADE AGO, WINDMILLS PROMISED to be a clean, reliable source of power that could help wean America from its dependence on dirty fuels and foreign oil. The idea of harnessing an energy supply that was free as the breeze generated enough megawatts of excitement to light up an entire new industry. Spurred by generous government tax incentives, investors poured more than $2.5 billion into U.S. wind projects during the early 1980s.

But enthusiasm was not enough to propel the dream into reality. "Wind developed a reputation for not working, and it had the stigma of a tax scam," says Robert Thresher, the wind-program manager at the National Renewable Energy Laboratory in Golden, Colo. Eventually the problems caused power companies to back away. And by 1985, when the tax credits expired, the remaining wind towers began looking more and more like monuments to a lost cause.

Now, however, there's new energy in the wind. Engineers have used advanced technology to make wind turbines that are far more efficient and cost effective than those of yesteryear. Says J. Michael Davis, chief of renewable-energy programs at the U.S. Department of Energy: "These machines are real and reliable." Today's models are capable of meeting 10% of America's energy demand, and within 30 years, newer versions could provide for a quarter of the nation's power needs. Such figures have re-energized the manufacturers of wind-power equipment and attracted the interest of foreign competitors. Utilities are conducting wind surveys and starting pilot projects. And a new breed of wildcatter is scurrying to buy up wind rights—licenses to erect what may be the oil wells of tomorrow.

For years, the wind industry's goal has been to produce power at rates similar to oil's: roughly a nickel for a kilowatt. Machines now operating in California can produce energy at 7¢ per kW. In areas of consistent high winds, the next generation, currently being deployed, will bring

that cost down to 5¢ by 1995, and more advanced designs are likely to shave off another penny by the year 2000. While many locales do not have enough wind to use the technology, enhancements already in the works will expand by a factor of 20 the area of land that can generate wind power profitably, according to experts at the National Renewable Energy Lab.

Wind's success says something about a dicey political issue: Should government tamper with free enterprise to nurture a new technology? The answer for renewable energy sources is definitely yes. Had manufacturers and utilities not received state and federal assistance early on, the future of wind power would now be controlled by either Japan or Europe; both have consistently funded wind research. Today American technology dominates the field.

In a sense, wind power has come full circle. In the early 1900s, most of the electricity on U.S. farms was provided by windmills. Those were replaced during the 1930s when the Rural Electrification Administration wired the countryside. But

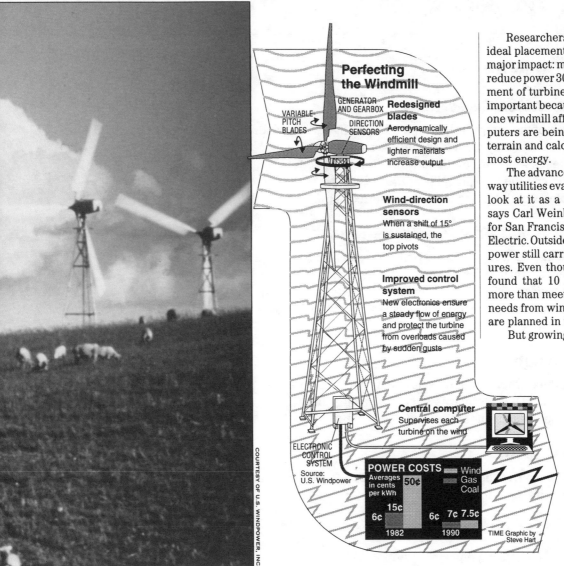

COURTESY OF U.S. WINDPOWER, INC.

Perfecting the Windmill

VARIABLE PITCH BLADES

GENERATOR AND GEARBOX

DIRECTION SENSORS

Redesigned blades
Aerodynamically efficient design and lighter materials increase output

Wind-direction sensors
When a shift of 15° is sustained, the top pivots

Improved control system
New electronics ensure a steady flow of energy and protect the turbine from overloads caused by sudden gusts

Central computer
Supervises each turbine on the wind

ELECTRONIC CONTROL SYSTEM

Source: U.S. Windpower

POWER COSTS Averages in cents per kWh

Wind / Gas / Coal

6¢ 15¢ 50¢ — 1982

6¢ 7¢ 7.5¢ — 1990

TIME Graphic by Steve Hart

Researchers also found that less than ideal placement of a windmill can have a major impact: missing 10% of the wind can reduce power 30%. Moreover, the arrangement of turbines within a wind "farm" is important because the wake produced by one windmill affects those around it. Computers are being used to simulate varied terrain and calculate how to produce the most energy.

The advances are slowly changing the way utilities evaluate the technology. "We look at it as a real competitive option," says Carl Weinberg, director of research for San Francisco–based Pacific Gas and Electric. Outside California, however, wind power still carries the burden of past failures. Even though a government survey found that 10 Midwestern states could more than meet all their electrical power needs from wind, no major wind projects are planned in the region.

But growing public concern over pollution from burning fossil fuels will increase the pressure for renewable energy. Several states are starting to require utilities to factor the cost of environmental damage into the cost of power production. In California, where the process of calculating environmental cost is just beginning, wind power may be assigned a price 15% lower than that for energy from traditional sources.

Seven different proposals are before Congress to provide incentives for new wind-turbine purchases. Surprisingly, the energy industry itself is divided on the value of such incentives. Turbine manufacturers believe that wind should prove itself competitive without further special assistance. But utilities would like a tax credit to make investment more attractive.

Additional technological advances now on the drawing board are likely to make wind power even more appealing. Engineers plan to boost the towers in some areas higher than they are at present so that the machines can escape ground turbulence and tap more consistent winds. Lighter materials could reduce the cost of building the towers. And researchers are looking into ways to store excess energy produced during windy periods so that it could be banked for use on calmer days or during peak energy demand.

If wind power does not fulfill its promise as a major energy source by the end of the century, it will not be a failure of technology. It will be a failure of vision on the part of society to make the necessary commitment. ∎

---

the oil embargoes and environmental concerns of the '70s prodded politicians to encourage the investigation of alternative energy sources. States began requiring their utilities to spend between 1% and 2% of profits on research, and the federal government added its generous tax credits for investments in renewables.

Unfortunately, the credits were for investment, not performance. Consequently, many wind-power machines seemed to be designed on an accountant's calculator to capture more deductions than breezes. Some towers were planted in fields of feeble winds. Others broke down with frustrating regularity. But a few companies persisted, and California in particular became the nursery for advanced technology. The state's hot central valleys are linked to the cool ocean by a series of gorges and valleys along the coast that act like wind tunnels. It was in these natural labs that engineers began testing new designs.

The failures of the 1980s showed the researchers that they knew almost nothing about building machines that could withstand and harness the turbulence of

wind. Early models used blades of a type originally designed for helicopters. Since wind pressure could vary considerably from one end of the blade to the other, the rotor would wobble wildly and eventually break off. Sudden gusts of wind could overpower the machine and burn out its energy-converting turbine. Some engineers tried solving the problems by building heavier machines, but that simply made them more expensive.

After much trial and error, researchers modified the contours of the blades; some, for instance, are thicker in the middle in order to provide more stability. Engineers put electronic sensors atop the towers that could constantly monitor wind direction and turn the machine to correct for changes. The sensors do not respond to every fluctuation, but when a computer calculates a sustained 15° shift, it signals for a turn into the wind. The leading American manufacturer, U.S. Windpower of Livermore, Calif., has built machines with electronic components that act as a giant surge protector, keeping sudden bursts of energy produced by gusts from overpowering the turbine.

AFTER YOU READ

Comprehension Questions

1. How much of the energy needed in the United States can windmills provide today? How much could they provide in thirty years?
2. Why were the windmills of the early 1900s replaced?
3. What problems did the windmills of the 1980s have?
4. What features do 1990s models have to correct these problems?

Discussion and Analysis Questions

1. Do you think that governments should give companies financial incentives for developing alternative energy sources? Why or why not?
2. What problems do windmills have that still need to be solved?
3. Do the drawing of the windmill and its descriptions help you to understand how windmills work? Is the drawing essential to the article?

Group Activity

In groups of three or four, identify sources of energy that are used today or that could be developed. Discuss the advantages and disadvantages of each one. Be prepared to summarize your discussion for the class.

Individual Work

Do you think countries should use nuclear power as a source of energy? Explain your position in a half-page paper.

3 NATURE'S TIME CAPSULES

BEFORE YOU READ

Preview

Ancient pack-rat nests hold valuable information about the earth's past.

Getting Started

Read the subtitle information and look at the pictures and caption. Are you interested in reading this article? Why or why not?

Culture

DNA ['di 'ɛn 'e]   deoxyribonucleic acid, the material found in all living cells that controls genetics

Forty-Niner [ˌfordi 'nɑɪnɚ]   a person who participated in the California Gold Rush of 1849

Gold Rush ['gold rəʃ]   the discovery of gold in California and the resulting rush of people to mine it

time capsule ['tɑɪm ˌkæpsəl]   a container filled with objects that represent a particular time and culture. Time capsules are often buried for future generations to find.

Vocabulary

(to) find one's way ['fɑɪnd wənz 'we]   to discover the route to a place; to end up in a place

(to) make the grade ['mek ðə 'gred]   to be satisfactory; to be what is expected

pack rat ['pæk ræt]   an animal of the rodent family; a person who collects and hoards things

(to) pay off ['pe 'ɔf]   to bring good results; to result in something positive

(to) pin down ['pɪn 'dɑʊn]   to identify; to locate

snack [snæk]   a light meal; food eaten between meals

snapshot ['snæpʃɑt]   a photograph

tome [tom]   a very long and scholarly written work

Culture and Vocabulary Activities

1. Look at the caption to the photographs. What is another word for *nest*? What category of animal is the pack rat?
2. If *paleonidology* means "the study of old nests" (see paragraph five), what do *paleobotany, paleoecology,* and *paleozoology* mean?

Nature's Time Capsules

Nests built long ago by the humble pack rat provide tantalizing peeks into the earth's past

By LEON JAROFF

Part way up we came to a high cliff and in its face were niches . . . and in some of them we found balls of a glistening substance looking like pieces of variegated candy . . . it was evidently food of some sort, and we found it sweet but sickish, and those who were hungry, making a good meal of it, were a little troubled with nausea afterwards.

— from the diary of a lost prospector in the Gold Rush of 1849

NAUSEA? LITTLE WONDER. THE GLIStening balls mistaken for a snack that day in Nevada were later identified as pack-rat middens—globs of crystallized packrat urine containing sticks, plant fragments, bones and animal dung. Still, while the middens failed to make the grade as cuisine, they have begun to excel in another role—as a kind of natural time capsule.

From the well-preserved contents of middens, scientists using radiocarbon dating can peer thousands of years into the past to discern when climates changed, why civilizations withered and how plants and animals migrated.

Pack-rat middens are found in arid regions of North and Central America and take shape when the acquisitive rodent, like its human namesake, collects and carries home virtually all the trash it can find. It piles the debris in its den, where it becomes saturated with urine. As the urine evaporates in the dry climate, it crystallizes, gradually enveloping the collection and forming a large, hard clump. Protected from the elements, the pack rat's trophies, like insects entombed in amber, are preserved for millenniums.

"A pack-rat midden is a snapshot of the flora and fauna existing within about 50 m [164 ft.] of the midden at the time it was accumulating," explains Peter Wigand, a paleoecologist at the University of Nevada's Desert Research Institute. Scientists can pin down the approximate time the snapshot was taken by radiocarbon dating of a preserved twig or fecal pellet; the technique can date specimens that are more than 40,000 years old. And by studying middens of different vintages in the same area, researchers can in effect create a movie from a sequence of snapshots, showing changes in local ecosystems.

The analysis of middens is emerging as a distinct scientific specialty. Its handful

In the Mojave Desert botanist Alan Riggs examines a 48,000-year-old pack-rat midden. At right, the bushy-tailed rodent.

of practitioners have already published a 472-page tome on the subject (*Packrat Middens;* University of Arizona) and have considered naming the specialty paleonidology, which roughly translated means "study of old nests."

By whatever name, the investigation of middens is paying off with a host of new insights about the past. Using midden evidence of tree growth and distribution in the Mojave Desert, botanist W. Geoffrey Spaulding of the University of Washington determined that average desert temperatures during the height of the last Ice Age, about 18,000 years ago, were 6°C (11°F) colder than they are today.

In a midden study covering 11,000 years of vegetation change in New Mexico's Chaco Canyon, Julio Betancourt of the U.S. Geological Survey and Thomas Van Devender of the Arizona–Sonora Desert Museum found evidence that could explain why a once thriving Anasazi Indian community was abandoned 800 years ago. Simply stated, the Indians eventually used all the surrounding pine trees for their dwellings and firewood, depleting the woodland and eroding the farmland vital to the tribe's survival.

Middens made by hyraxes—rodents found in Africa and the Middle East—have provided similar evidence that human clearing of surrounding forests and shrubbery led to the sudden collapse in A.D. 900 of the ancient metropolis of Petra, in what is now Jordan.

Middens can reveal changes in the heavens as well as on earth. That was demonstrated by hydrologist Fred Phillips of the New Mexico Institute of Mining and Technology, who checked an ancient pack-rat midden for evidence of cosmic-ray bombardment of the earth. He knew that highly energetic cosmic-ray particles create the radioisotope chlorine 36 when they strike argon atoms in the atmosphere, and that the isotope finds its way into plants and the urine of mammals, including the pack rat.

With the aid of radiochemist Pankaj Sharma of the University of Rochester, he compared the amount of the isotope in the midden urine with contemporary values, and concluded that cosmic-ray bombardment was 41% more intense 21,000 years ago than it is now. This suggests that the earth's magnetic field, which acts as a partial barrier to cosmic rays, was then considerably weaker. One implication: terrestrial life had been—and could someday again be—exposed to higher doses of dangerous radiation from space.

Researchers are gleaning other secrets from plant leaves preserved in the middens. At the end of the last Ice Age, for example, plant structures called stomata, which are used to process carbon dioxide, were far denser than they are today. This suggests that the ancient atmosphere contained much less carbon dioxide. Middens have even more to reveal. The well-preserved plant and animal DNA in midden specimens promises to be a bonanza for genetic researchers.

History does not record if the band of nauseated Forty-Niners eventually reached California or how they fared in their quest. Yet on that day long ago in Nevada, they had already struck gold. ∎

AFTER YOU READ

Comprehension Questions

1. Where are pack-rat middens found? What are they made of?
2. What have scientists learned from middens about ancient civilizations?
3. What have scientists learned from the nests about the earth's climate and atmosphere?
4. What other information can be learned from pack-rat middens?

Discussion and Analysis Questions

1. Do you think pack-rat middens are a worthwhile subject of study? Support your answer.
2. Paragraph three describes how middens are formed. Is this paragraph necessary to the article? The ninth and tenth paragraphs give scientific descriptions. Do you think these are too technical for most readers?

Group Activity

In groups of six, think of other unusual areas of study that you have heard about or that might be valuable to pursue. Present your ideas to the class.

Individual Work

Did you enjoy reading this article? Write a half-page discussion of what you did or did not like about it.

4 LIVING HAPPILY NEAR A NUCLEAR TRASH HEAP

BEFORE YOU READ

Preview

Residents of Oak Ridge, Tennessee, don't appear to be worried about the local nuclear facilities.

Getting Started

1. Find Tennessee on the map of the United States at the back of this book. What might have been the reasons for locating a secret project there?
2. Would you like to work at a nuclear research facility? Would you like to live near one? Explain your answers.

Culture

Bhopal [bo'pɑl]   a city in India. In 1984, a chemical accident at a U.S.-owned company in Bhopal caused about 1,700 deaths and 200,000 injuries.

Bomb [bɑm]   the atomic bomb

Centers for Disease Control (CDC) ['sɛntɚz for dɪ'ziz kən,trol]   federally supported medical research facilities located in Atlanta, Georgia

cold war ['kold 'wor]   the tension between the United States and the former Soviet Union that lasted from the end of World War II until 1990

Geiger counter ['gɑɪgɚ ,kɑʊntɚ]   an instrument that detects the presence of radioactivity. It was named for the physicist Hans Geiger.

Manhattan Project [mæn'hætən 'prɑdʒɛkt]   the code name for the secret American research to develop the atomic bomb during World War II

U.S. Department of Energy ['ju ɛs dɪ'pɑrtmənt əv 'ɛnɚdʒi]   a federal agency in charge of energy development and usage

Vocabulary

activist ['æktə,vəst]   a person who actively supports a cause or ideal

by-product ['bɑɪ ,prɑdəkt]   a result; something produced

(to) hunker down ['həŋkɚ 'dɑʊn]   to settle down to do something

(to) keep from ['kip 'frəm]   to prevent

on the spot ['ɔn ðə 'spɑt]   immediately; at exactly the same place and time

plant [plænt]   a factory; a manufacturing facility

(to) skew [skju]   to alter; to change

(to) ward off ['word 'ɔf]   to keep away; to prevent from happening

Culture and Vocabulary Activities

1. The Geiger counter was named after its developer, Hans Geiger. Can you think of any other things that are named after their inventors? (Hint: See the Culture list for "Do the Poor Deserve Bad Schools?")
2. Create sentences using *to keep from, on the spot,* and *to ward off.*

Living Happily Near a Nuclear Trash Heap

Enough nuclear material and other hazardous wastes have piled up to keep this incinerator operating every day for nearly six years

The frogs and trees are radioactive, you can't catch the fish or wade in the streams, and a doctor warns of cancer risks, but that doesn't ruffle the people of Oak Ridge

By DICK THOMPSON OAK RIDGE

DR. WILLIAM REID WAS NEW TO OAK Ridge, Tenn., and disturbed by what he was seeing. Soon after he joined the staff of Methodist Medical Center in early 1991, he was treating four patients with kidney cancers, an unusually large number for one small area, and a cluster of other people who appeared to have weakened ability to ward off infections. Reid suspected that something in the local environment was attacking the residents' immune systems.

It didn't take much imagination for Reid to figure out possible sources of contamination. For 49 years, federal installa-

tions at Oak Ridge have manufactured the innards of nuclear bombs. In the process, the plants have produced—and carelessly disposed of—mountains of radioactive material and hazardous wastes. Even the U.S. government admits the Oak Ridge labs have littered the surrounding countryside with everything from asbestos and mercury to enriched uranium. The story is much the same at all the country's now notorious nuclear weapons plants, scattered from Hanford, Wash., to Los Alamos, N. Mex., to the Savannah River plant. The Department of Energy has launched a major clean-up effort, but it might be too late to prevent a host of medical problems in people who have lived in the shadow of the toxic plants for decades.

Could a health disaster be hitting Oak Ridge? Reid was determined to find out. Last August he called Martin Marietta Corp., which took over management of the government's nuclear complex from Union Carbide in 1984. The doctor wanted to report his concerns and ask what chemicals he should test for in his patients. If Reid thought that Martin Marietta and his employers at Methodist Medical Center would appreciate his initiative, he was wrong. Three weeks later, the hospital began a disciplinary process aimed at forcing him off the staff. The doctor suspects that the hospital and Martin Marietta were trying to thwart his investigation. Says Reid: "They are worried they're going to have a Bhopal on their hands." The hospital denies there is any connection between the disciplinary action and Reid's allegations about health problems.

When Reid's dispute with the hospital hit the Oak Ridge newspapers this year, the public response was strangely muted. Residents long ago learned to live with radioactivity and risk. This, after all, is one of the birthplaces of the Bomb, a town whose very existence was a by-product of nuclear reactions. The federal complex is still the largest employer of the population of 30,000. Even the mayor is a physicist, and newspapers report levels of background radiation each week. But decades of studies have failed to find any gross health problems. Says Oak Ridge physicist Chester Richmond: "People here just don't accept the arguments that this material is going to give you cancer."

Still, Oak Ridge is no ordinary place. Earlier this year a visitor to one of the nuclear facilities accidentally turned off the main road. When he tried to leave, alarms rang, and the government bought his radioactive rental car on the spot. In the reservation surrounding the plants, creatures ranging from deer to frogs and water fleas have all excited Geiger counters. Contaminated trees, which take up nuclear liquids through their roots, have been chopped down and buried lest the autumn winds spread radioactive leaves. And the streams have carried toxic chemicals and nuclear products—including strontium, tritium and plutonium—for distances of 64 km (40 miles). Posted along the town's creek are NO FISHING signs and Department of Energy warnings: NO WATER CONTACT.

No one worried much about environmental contamination when Oak Ridge quietly sprang up as part of the Manhattan Project during World War II. By 1944, two years after construction started, Oak Ridge had become Tennessee's fifth largest city, and it was all behind a guarded fence. At peak production, the "secret city" used 20% more power than New York City.

After the products of the Manhattan Project exploded over Japan and ended the war, the mania for secrecy diminished. The fences surrounding the city came down, and Oak Ridge started appearing on maps. But its work was far from done. Once the arms race with the Soviets began, Oak Ridgers hunkered down to help produce an arsenal of American hydrogen bombs. A recently declassified report done for the Department of Energy found that the weapons factories "operated in an atmosphere of high urgency" that resulted in astounding environmental and health assaults.

Between 1951 and '84, the Oak Ridge plants pumped 10.2 million L (2.7 million gal.) of concentrated acids and nuclear wastes into open-air ponds, called the "witches' cauldron," from which the chemicals would evaporate or leach into a nearby stream. Barrels of strange brews and experimental gases, some so volatile that they would explode on contact with oxygen, were sealed and dropped into a quarry pool. A neatly stacked collection of 76,600 barrels and oil drums, filled with nuclear sludge and now rusting, is larger than the main building at Oak Ridge. Millions of cubic meters of toxic material, including PCBS and cobalt 60, were dumped in trenches and covered with soil. In 1983 the Department of Energy acknowledged that 1.1 million kg (2.4 million lbs.) of mercury had been lost. It went up the smokestacks, drained into the soil and flowed into the stream that runs through town. After that revelation, mercury was found at the city's two high schools and in the blood of workers at one of the atomic-research sites. An unknown amount of enriched uranium went out smokestacks.

Given this legacy, one might expect Oak Ridgers to be dying prematurely in droves. But nothing like that has occurred. Between 1988 and '90, cancer deaths in the county that contains Oak Ridge were 142 per 100,000 people—less than the 145 per 100,000 recorded for the entire state. Research shows that Oak Ridge employees are 20% less likely to die of cancer than Americans as a whole, perhaps because the nuclear workers all have health insurance and good medical care.

Local environmental activists, who tend to live outside the city of Oak Ridge, suspect the results of reassuring studies have been skewed. They focus on workers and not on other members of the community. The studies look largely, though not exclusively, at cancer deaths, rather than cases of cancer that haven't yet proved lethal. And the best indication of radiation hazards might not be cancer but some other disability, such as neurological damage, immune dysfunction or birth defects. The worst flaw seems to be that no study has been carried out on women.

The culture of secrecy and concern about job security may have kept information from health investigators. Says Robert Keil, president of the Oak Ridge Atomic Trades and Labor Council: "One thing that kept people from coming forward is that they were afraid they might jeopardize their security clearance by talking about something that was classified."

The end of the cold war provides an opportunity to get at the truth. At Oak Ridge, as at other weapons labs, the threat of a nuclear conflict has been replaced by the threat of massive layoffs. The big job in town now seems to be cleaning up the nuclear trash heap. More than $1.5 billion has already been spent on detoxifying Oak Ridge, and the end isn't in sight. The government is beginning an exhaustive medical survey of the people who live around Oak Ridge, including the women. The Centers for Disease Control has been asked to look into Reid's allegations.

But confident of the outcome, the people of Oak Ridge still sleep soundly. They have lived with danger for decades and see no reason to start panicking now. ∎

AFTER YOU READ

Comprehension Questions

1. Why was Dr. Reid suspicious when he saw patients at Oak Ridge? What did he think caused their problems? What happened to Dr. Reid when he tried to investigate?
2. Why was Oak Ridge built? What has happened to its environment?
3. Some people criticize the existing medical studies on Oak Ridge residents. What are some possible problems with the studies?

Discussion and Analysis Questions

1. Why do you think some people don't want medical research done at Oak Ridge?
2. What is your opinion of the medical studies that have been done? Do you think more studies are needed?
3. The writer states that the people of Oak Ridge aren't worried about the nuclear facilities. Does the writer think they should be worried? Find parts of the article to support your answer.

Group Activity

In groups of five or six, develop a brief plan for medical research in Oak Ridge. What diseases or conditions would you look for? What groups of people and what ages would you examine? Present your plan to the class.

Individual Work

Do you think nuclear research should be conducted? State your answer and supporting reasons in a half-page paper.

5 IN SEARCH OF THE GREAT WHITE BEAR

BEFORE YOU READ

Preview

Researching polar bears is dangerous but important work.

Getting Started

1. What do you know about polar bears? Share your information with the class.
2. Read the first paragraph of the article. What emotion do you think the writer wants you to feel?

Culture

Native American [ˈnedɪv əˈmɛrəˌkən]   a descendant of the original inhabitants of the area now known as the United States. Native Americans include such groups as the Eskimo, Cherokee, Navajo, and Seminole.

U.S. Fish and Wildlife Service [ˈju ɛs ˈfɪʃ ænd ˈwaɪldlaɪf ˌsɚvəs]   a federal agency in charge of the maintenance and preservation of nondomestic animals

Vietnam [ˌviɛtˈnɑm]   the war fought in Vietnam in the 1960s and 1970s. More than fifty-five thousand Americans died in this war.

wind-chill factor [ˈwɪnd tʃɪl ˈfæktɚ]   the temperature that the air feels to bare skin. The number is based on the actual air temperature and the speed of the wind.

Vocabulary

all in a day's work [ˈɔl ɪn ə ˌdez ˈwɚk]   part of what is expected; typical or normal

as good as it gets [æz ˈgʊd æz ɪt ˈgɛts]   the best possible

bunkhouse [ˈbəŋkhaʊs]   a building with beds for many people. The beds are called bunks.

charismatic [ˌkɛrɪzˈmædɪk]   having qualities that are attractive to others

done deal [ˈdən ˈdil]   something that is settled or finished

ground-breaking [ˈgraʊnd ˌbrekɪŋ]   revolutionary; new and inventive

incarnate [ɪnˈkɑrnət]   personified; having all the qualities of someone or something

predator [ˈprɛdətɚ]   an animal that kills another animal for food

(to) put in [ˈpʊt ˈɪn]   to land an aircraft

spartan [ˈspɑrtən]   without attention to comfort; simple and severe. The word refers to Sparta in ancient Greece.

Culture and Vocabulary Activities

1. Look at the Vocabulary list. Which entries do you think are casual (not formal) English?
2. Read the first two paragraphs of the article. Which two words are synonyms for the *posterior* of an animal? Look at paragraph seven. Which two words are synonyms for *isolated*?

In Search of the Great White Bear

A handful of hearty U.S. government researchers brave dangerous Alaskan ice and cold to track and protect elusive arctic polar bears

By **TED GUP** ST. LAWRENCE

ABOVE A GLISTENING ICE PACK IN the Bering Sea, a helicopter stalks a polar bear, following paw prints in the snow. The bear suddenly appears as a hint of movement, white against white, padding its way across the ice. The helicopter descends, hovering over the frightened creature, and a shotgun slides out the window, firing a tranquilizer dart into the massive fur-covered rump. Minutes pass. The bear shows no effects. The helicopter drops for a second shot. This time the bear stands its ground, and the pilot, fearing the animal is about to lunge for the aircraft, abruptly noses the chopper skyward. He remembers how a 9-ft. bear once swiped at a helicopter's skids, shredding the pontoons.

But this bear finally staggers, then stretches out on the ice like a giant sheep dog. The helicopter sets down, and biologist Gerald Garner advances, kicking the bear in the behind to make sure it is immobilized. A swivel of its head and a flashing of teeth warn Garner that there is plenty of defiance left in this 272-kg (600-lb.) carnivore. With a syringe, he injects more drug. At last the head droops, and Garner can proceed. Around the Bear's neck he fastens a vinyl collar containing a computer that will send data to a satellite, allowing scientists to keep track of the animal for a year. By the time Bear No. 6,886 raises its head, the helicopter is safely aloft.

Those tense moments were all in a day's work for Garner, one of a handful of hearty scientists, pilots and technicians taking part in a ground-breaking and hazardous $700,000 annual U.S. Fish and Wildlife Service study of arctic polar bear populations. In an effort to follow the fate of more than 600 bears since the program's inception, the researchers have braved wind-chill factors of −59°C (−75°F), spartan living conditions, the constant threat of mechanical failures and the peril of being stranded on an ice pack. Last October two government biologists and a pilot vanished while tracking polar bears from the air. Officials believe their helicopter plunged under the ice, muffling their emergency signal. Other researchers have been rescued after a wakeful night on an ice floe.

"This is a very unforgiving environment," says mechanic Lester Hampton. "The biggest danger is getting caught in bad weather and running low on fuel. The second biggest danger is having a mechanical failure and having to put in out there. The third biggest danger is that after you do, the bears are going to come in and try to eat you up—and that's if you don't freeze to death. If you go in that water, it's a done deal—you're dead."

Two decades ago, big-game hunters, not researchers, pursued polar bears from the air and on the ground. A thousand carcasses a year littered the Arctic. The number of ice bears dwindled, and there was worldwide concern that the animal might be hunted to extinction. Today the bears' recovery is one of the success stories of conservation. Worldwide, polar bears now number at least 20,000, all of which are protected by a 1976 international agreement. Alaska has 3,000 to 5,000 polar bears, and only the state's Native Americans can hunt them—and strictly for subsistence purposes.

The Fish and Wildlife Service project is part of a continuing effort to advance biologists' understanding of the polar bear and assess potential new threats against the creature. Researchers, for example, are most concerned about the impact of increasing oil and gas exploration in the Arctic. Another concern comes from the Soviet Union, which has proposed to lift its 35-year-old ban on polar bear hunting. Many of western Alaska's bears migrate as much as 1,609 km (1,000 miles) to set up winter dens in the Soviet Union. U.S. and Soviet biologists are working together to find out how many bears migrate in this fashion to ensure that one country does not undermine the conservation efforts of the other.

In search of the bears, the Fish and Wildlife Service has dispatched scientists to some of the most remote regions of the U.S. One expedition earlier this year was based on St. Lawrence Island's desolate expanse of tundra and mountains rising out of the Bering Sea. In Savoonga, an Eskimo village on the edge of the frozen sea, researchers lived in a bunkhouse with no running water and snow drifts above the windowsills. "We're stretching every-

Studying the ultimate predator: after a bear is felled by a tranquilizing dart, one scientist stands watch for cubs as another ensures that the big bear has been immobilized

thing to the limit in terms of safety to accomplish these research objectives," says Larry Pank of the Alaska Wildlife Research Center. "We have a real interest in ensuring we have a polar bear population at the same or similar levels 50 or 100 years from now."

MANY OF THE PILOTS AND MECHANics have Vietnam combat experience. "Most of these guys have been shot out of the air a time or two. That's valuable experience if you have a mechanical problem," says biologist Garner. Pilot Paul Walters flew low-level reconnaissance in Vietnam. Before taking off to track polar bears, he tells any neophyte on board that if the chopper crashes, survivors should kick out the glass, retrieve the orange survival bag and activate the emergency transmitter.

"Risk goes with the territory," says biologist Tom McCabe, who lost a third of his arm to shrapnel in Vietnam. If another bear charges while he is examining a bear, he will try to scare it off with Teflon bullets. If that fails, he has a shotgun and a .44 Magnum pistol in a shoulder holster. "The polar bear is the ultimate predator," he says. "He doesn't seem to fear anything." Alaska polar bear expert Jack Lentfer remembers how a bear that was thought to have been tranquilized suddenly reared up and chased him. When the bear was almost upon him, a colleague shot the animal. "It would have chewed me up," says Lentfer.

"You develop a fatalistic attitude. If something happens, it happens," says Garner. He has handled 250 polar bears— and 450 grizzly bears. At times he resembles a bear. He stands 6 ft. 2 in., weighs 225-plus lbs., chomps cigars through a wild beard and is girded in layer upon layer of insulated clothing, topped off with a beaver hat. He has little time for worry. Mornings he contacts Anchorage for the latest satellite fixes on his bears. During the day, he tracks and collars the animals. Each is subjected to an exhaustive exam. A tooth is removed to determine age. Vials of blood are drawn for immunological and genetic study. A hole is punched in the ear for an identification tag. A number is tattooed on the bear's upper lip. A snippet of fur is cut. At night Garner spins bear blood in a centrifuge, readies his darts and cleans the barrels of his shotguns.

Any hardship is offset by the chance to work with mammals as charismatic as they are inaccessible. "This is as good as it gets," says Garner. "I'm surprised people would pay me to do this." Ian Stirling of the Canadian Wildlife Service sums up the admiration felt by most of the bears' scientific followers: "The polar bear is the Arctic incarnate. When you watch one sauntering across the ice and it's 30 below, he looks as comfortable as someone in a pair of shorts on the beach in Hawaii." ∎

AFTER YOU READ

Comprehension Questions

1. What do scientists do to polar bears after the bears are tranquilized?
2. What do researchers hope to learn by studying polar bears?
3. What was happening to the polar bear population prior to 1976? What currently threatens the bears?
4. What dangers face the scientists as they do their work?

Discussion and Analysis Questions

1. Why are some scientists willing to risk their lives to do this research?
2. Would you like to participate in such research? Why or why not?
3. Look at the quotations used in the last four paragraphs. What do these quotes tell you about the researchers?

Group Activity

In groups of four or five, identify animal species that have become extinct or that are endangered. How many can you think of? Compare your answers with those of other groups. How many did you name in total?

Individual Work

Do you think countries should cooperate to protect certain animal species? State your position in a half-page paper.

6 THE BEEF AGAINST . . . BEEF

BEFORE YOU READ

Preview

Activists claim that cattle are a major source of world problems.

Getting Started

1. Look at the graphic entitled "Costly Cattle." Which food uses the most water in its development? What is the greatest source of methane? Which animal needs the most feed?
2. Do people of your culture eat beef? If so, how often? If not, why not?

Culture

ecotourism [ˌikoˈtʊrɪzm]   visitation of unique and interesting natural sites without damaging or otherwise affecting the environment. The Amazon river is a popular destination for ecotourists.

Stephen King [ˈstivən ˈkɪŋ]   an American writer of best-selling horror stories

New Age [ˈnu ˈedʒ]   relating to the newest—and often unusual—cultural developments. New Age music, for example, relies on computer-generated sounds.

think tank [ˈθɪŋk tæŋk]   an organization of individuals whose purpose is to study and propose solutions to critical societal issues

U.S. Department of Agriculture [ˈju ɛs dɪˈpɑrtmənt əv ˈægrəkəltʃər]   a federal agency concerned with the growing of plants and animals for food

U.S. Forest Service [ˈju ɛs ˈfɔrəst ˈsɚvəs]   a federal agency in charge of maintaining and preserving the country's public lands

Vocabulary

by-product [ˈbaɪ ˌprɑdəkt]   a result; something produced

(to) cut down [ˈkət ˈdaʊn]   to reduce

(to have a) beef against [ˌhæv ə ˈbif əˈgɛnst]   to have a complaint about someone or something

(to) lock horns [ˈlɑk ˈhornz]   to disagree; to argue

locust [ˈlokəst]   a type of flying insect. Swarms of locusts can destroy fields of crops.

rhetoric [ˈrɛdɚɪk]   speech or writing used to persuade. The word sometimes has negative connotations.

(to) send shudders [ˈsɛnd ˈʃədɚz]   to cause to worry

(to) shoulder [ˈʃoldɚ]   to take responsibility for

(to) swear off [ˈswɛr ˈɔf]   to promise not to do something that one normally does

Culture and Vocabulary Activities

1. Read the first paragraph of the article. Based on the information given, what is the meaning of *desertification*?
2. Read the third paragraph of the article. Based on the information given, what do you think a *coalition* is?

THE BEEF AGAINST . . .

Do cows cause global warming and human hunger? The fault, dear Jeremy, lies not in our cattle but in ourselves . . .

By J. MADELEINE NASH

VERMIN. THE WORD REminds most people of cockroaches scuttling across kitchen floors and rats skulking in dark basement corners. But to Jeremy Rifkin, the environmental movement's most prominent polemicist, vermin are big, brown-eyed ungulates that graze the rolling countryside, chew their cud and moo. In his controversial new book, *Beyond Beef: The Rise and Fall of the Cattle Culture,* Rifkin manages to blame the world's burgeoning population of bovines for a staggering spectrum of ecological ills. In the U.S., he charges, runoff from mammoth feedlots is despoiling streams and underground aquifers. In sub-Saharan Africa, cattle are contributing to desertification by denuding arid lands of fragile vegetation. In Central and South America, ranchers are felling tropical rain forests and turning them into pastures for their voracious herds. "The average cow," claims Rifkin, "eats its way through 900 lbs. of vegetation every month. It is literally a hoofed locust."

According to Rifkin, civilization began a long slide downhill when 18th century British gentry acquired a taste for fatmarbled beef and proceeded to spread that proclivity, like a plague, throughout the Western world. Rifkin's real argument, of course, is not with the 1.3 billion bovines that roam the planet but with modern methods of mass-producing beef that

include plumping animals with hormones and stuffing them with "enough grain to feed hundreds of millions of people." Although he did not personally visit a ranch or a meat-packing plant, his stomach-churning descriptions of how cattle are treated from birth to slaughter brim with righteous indignation. (A reformed carnivore, Rifkin says he swore off beef 15 years ago after taking three bites of a revolting blue-gray hamburger, then throwing the rest away.)

Such inflammatory rhetoric sends shudders through the U.S. beef industry, which is already reeling from a nearly one-third drop in per capita consumption since 1976—the result of popular concern about fat in the diet. Now Rifkin hungers for a more decisive blow. This week he is leading a coalition of environmental, food-policy and animal-rights groups in launching a well-financed advertising campaign aimed at slashing worldwide beef consumption by 50% over the coming decade. Members of the coalition range from the Rainforest Action Network, which blames cattle for "killing the Amazon," to the

Fund for Animals, which criticizes the use of poisons and traps to control coyotes that prey on calves. The International Rivers Network blames cattle for wasting scarce water resources, while Food First denounces the feedlot system for wasting grain that could otherwise be used for human consumption.

Not since he took on the biotechnology industry over the safety of genetic engineering has Rifkin been embroiled in a higher-profile controversy, or one with the potential for greater economic consequences. With so much at stake, it is hardly surprising that environmentalists and meat-industry advocates have locked horns over Rifkin's charges. Among the most notable areas of dispute:

Cattle ranching is destroying tropical forests. Without question, ranching is a factor in tropical deforestation, and a major one at that. But University of Pennsylvania biologist Daniel Janzen, for one, believes that this unfortunate epoch in the history of Latin America is rapidly drawing to a close. In Costa Rica, he says, "most of the pastureland that was easily cleared of forest has already been cleared." At the same time, the remaining forest has begun to rise in value. "Two decades ago," explains Janzen, "the choice was simple. Either the forest stood there, or someone tore it down to plant a crop." Now leaders of countries like Costa Rica are beginning to view forests as valuable assets that can help control erosion, protect watersheds and generate income from New Age industries like biotechnology and ecotourism.

Cows are contributing to global warming. To a measurable extent, they are. The symbiotic bacteria that dwell in every cow's gut enable grazers to break down the cellulose in grass. As a by-product, these bacteria produce considerable amounts of methane, which, like carbon dioxide, is a heat-trapping greenhouse gas. The methane periodically gusts forth from grazing herds in the form of rumbling postprandial belches. But if cattle contribute to the global methane load, they are hardly alone. Swamps, termite mounds and rice paddies are all hosts to similar sorts of bacterial methane factories.

Overgrazing by cattle has destroyed grasslands. The "cowburnt" ranges of the American West testify to the damage wrought by decades of uncontrolled grazing, which transformed once verdant land into desert. Of more than 50 million acres of U.S. Forest Service land that is open to grazing, half remains in poor condition. Lands under control of the Bureau of Land Management are in equally bad shape. Driving the cattle off, however, as some radical environmentalists would like, is not necessarily the solution. Properly managed grazing, range ecologists agree, serves to enrich rather than impoverish grasslands. In exchange for forage, hoofed beasts deposit tons of that old-fashioned organic fertilizer known as manure.

Grain fed to cattle could feed the hungry. "Hunger isn't about actual scarcity," declares Stephanie Rosenfeld, a researcher for San Francisco–based Food First. "It's about the maldistribution of resources. People are hungry for different reasons at different times, but quite often the reasons have to do with beef." The link is often very subtle: in countries like Egypt and Mexico, for instance, farmland that formerly grew staples for human consumption is being switched to grow grain for beef that only the wealthy can afford. Indirectly, then, a growing cattle population threatens humans on the low end of the economic scale with hunger. D. Gale Johnson, an agricultural economist at the University of Chicago, questions this assumption. He notes that in China, beef consumption has risen in tandem with overall improvements in diet.

Rifkin's critics—and there are many—regularly accuse him of taking a nugget of truth and enlarging it beyond reason in ways calculated to raise public fears. "*Beyond Beef* is about the worst book I've ever read," exclaims Dennis Avery, director of Global Food Issues for the Hudson Institute, a think tank in Indianapolis. "It establishes Rifkin as the Stephen King of food horror stories." Among other things, Rifkin raises the specter of beef contaminated with viruses, including a bovine immunodeficiency virus that he provocatively labels "cow AIDS," though there is no evidence that the virus can infect humans. Rifkin also charges that inspection of carcasses is shoddy, which the U.S. Department of Agriculture flatly denies. However, even the American Meat Institute allows that the inspection system, which still relies on visually examining and touching meat, hasn't changed much since 1906 and needs more up-to-date techniques to detect invisible contaminants like microbes. Ironically, the primary tools for improvement could well come from biotechnology, an industry that Rifkin loves to bash.

Rifkin is using beef as a metaphor for all that has gone rotten in the modern world, wrongs that he attributes to a meta-physical loss of humans' sacred relationship to nature. And cattle, because of their prominent role in ancient mythology and their haunting presence in prehistoric pictographs, lend themselves well to this moralistic exercise.

But how much blame for environmental degradation should the cattle industry rightly shoulder? In the Netherlands, for instance, manure from pigs poses a major ecological threat, defiling water supplies with excessive nitrates and acidifying local soils. Sheep have permanently scarred the landscape in Spain and Portugal, while in India—a country that Rifkin praises for its kindness to cows—bovines are ravenous wraiths whose constant quest for food drives them to ravage standing forests. Holy or not, most of India's 200 million cows go hungry much of the time.

Cutting down on beef consumption in protein-sated countries like the U.S. is a prudent prescription that would go a long way toward enhancing general health. Red meat is the primary source of saturated fat in the American diet, and too much dietary fat has been linked to the development of both heart disease and certain types of cancer. But trimming beef in the American diet, emphasizes Felicia Busch of the American Dietetic Association, "will not solve world hunger, and it isn't going to save our planet." The environmental cost of beef is just one aspect of the multiplying burdens of producing food for an exploding human population. The real threat to the carrying capacity of planet Earth, dear Jeremy, comes not from our cattle but from ourselves. —*With reporting by Janice M. Horowitz/New York and David S. Jackson/San Francisco*

COSTLY CATTLE

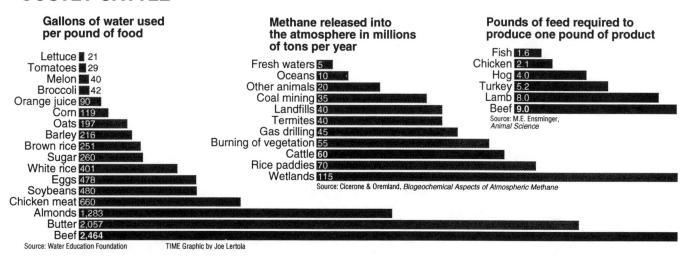

Gallons of water used per pound of food

Lettuce	21
Tomatoes	29
Melon	40
Broccoli	42
Orange juice	90
Corn	119
Oats	197
Barley	216
Brown rice	251
Sugar	260
White rice	401
Eggs	478
Soybeans	480
Chicken meat	660
Almonds	1,283
Butter	2,057
Beef	2,464

Source: Water Education Foundation   TIME Graphic by Joe Lertola

Methane released into the atmosphere in millions of tons per year

Fresh waters	5
Oceans	10
Other animals	20
Coal mining	35
Landfills	40
Termites	40
Gas drilling	45
Burning of vegetation	55
Cattle	60
Rice paddies	70
Wetlands	115

Source: Cicerone & Oremland, *Biogeochemical Aspects of Atmospheric Methane*

Pounds of feed required to produce one pound of product

Fish	1.6
Chicken	2.1
Hog	4.0
Turkey	5.2
Lamb	8.0
Beef	9.0

Source: M.E. Ensminger, *Animal Science*

AFTER YOU READ

Comprehension Questions

1. When did beef eating supposedly become popular?
2. According to Jeremy Rifkin and others, what problems are caused by cattle? Discuss each one briefly.
3. Why has the amount of beef eaten in the United States dropped in recent years?

Discussion and Analysis Questions

1. Do you think cattle represent a major world problem? Support your answer.
2. Should there be laws governing what kinds of food can be grown and eaten? Why or why not?
3. According to the author of this article, what is the major threat to the planet? Do you agree? Why or why not?

Group Activity

-fication is a productive suffix in English. It can be added to words to create new words. For example, *desertification* means "the process of becoming like a desert." In pairs, determine the meaning of each word below. What conclusions can you draw about the meanings of *-fication*?

magnification	purification
falsification	mummification
notification	calcification
electrification	certification

Individual Work

Copy the four statements printed in bold in the article. These statements criticize the use of cattle. Then write four statements that present a different view of each topic. Give substantive information; do not just change the sentences from affirmative to negative.

Science & Technology

1 ASK A SATELLITE FOR DIRECTIONS

BEFORE YOU READ

Preview

Travelers on Earth can get navigational help from space.

Getting Started

1. How did travelers find their way before the twentieth century? What devices did they use?
2. When you travel, what do you use to help you find your way?

Culture

Boy Scout troop ['bɔɪ skɑut ˌtrup]   a local group that is part of a national organization for boys. The Boy Scouts teach citizenship and self-reliance. Their motto is "be prepared."

Operation Desert Storm [ˌɑpɚeʃən 'dɛzɚt 'storm]   the multinational military effort conducted in 1991 to recapture Kuwait from Iraq. Iraq invaded Kuwait in August of 1990.

tracking collar ['trækɪŋ 'kɑlɚ]   a collar placed on a wild animal for the purpose of following its movements. The collar sends electronic signals that scientists can monitor.

Vocabulary

dashboard ['dæʃˌbord]   the interior front panel of a car or truck, where instruments are located. It is also called the "dash."

(to) fix [fɪks]   to identify; to locate, as on a map

gadget ['gædzət]   a useful object; a device

loran ['loræn]   a system of navigation that uses radio signals

(to) make a wrong turn ['mek ə ˌrɔŋ 'tɚn]   to go in a direction that one should not have gone

steep [stip]   very high; too high

tow truck ['to trək]   a kind of truck used to pull disabled vehicles

Culture and Vocabulary Activities

1. Select any five of the Culture and Vocabulary items. Use each one in a sentence.
2. In the first sentence of the article, *well* and a hyphen have been added to the adjective *prepared* to describe a Boy Scout troop (*well-prepared*). Create other phrases by adding *well* to an adjective (for example, a *well-made meal*).

Ask a Satellite for Directions

Hand-held gadgets that receive signals from space make it hard to get lost

NO WELL-PREPARED BOY SCOUT TROOP would wander into the wilderness without a compass. But Scouts may soon have a more sophisticated way to keep from getting lost, using a technology that the Army made famous during Operation Desert Storm. To find their bearings in the desert landscape, soldiers relied on hand-held electronic gadgets called Global Positioning System receivers. The devices, which pick up signals from a $10 billion network of U.S. satellites, can pinpoint a location instantly anywhere on the earth.

Civilians can buy similar products from electronics companies. GPS receivers steer boaters around dangerous reefs, track schools of bait for fishermen and help pilots avoid midair collisions. The price of a receiver—$1,500 to $3,800—is steep for Scout troops but falling rapidly.

The concept of the Global Positioning System is simple. With the help of an onboard atomic clock, each satellite in the network continuously broadcasts a signal indicating the time and the spacecraft's exact position. (A total of 16 satellites are now aloft; there will be 24, including three spares, when the system is complete.) A GPS receiver uses simultaneous readings from three different satellites to "fix" the user's longitude and latitude.

Relying on satellites rather than ground stations makes the system far more precise than conventional navigation technology. The loran systems commonly found on boats and airplanes, for example, are accurate only to within 100 m (330 ft.), compared with 15 m (49 ft.) for GPS.

California's department of transportation is testing a GPS dispatching system on a tow-truck fleet in the San Francisco Bay area. University of Wyoming scientists plan to use GPS technology in a tracking collar for studying the migration patterns of elk. And by combining GPS with computerized maps, engineers are developing electronic road atlases that, installed in car dashboards, could one day enable a visiting motorist to negotiate Los Angeles' freeways without ever making a wrong turn. ∎

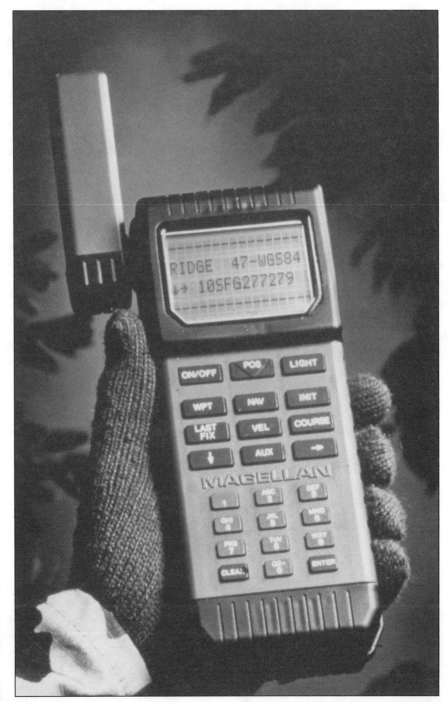

AFTER YOU READ

Comprehension Questions

1. What is the Global Positioning System? How does it work?
2. How was GPS used in Operation Desert Storm?
3. What are some civilian uses for the system?
4. How much does a GPS receiver cost?

Discussion and Analysis Questions

1. Do you think many people will buy GPS receivers? Why or why not?
2. Do you think you would ever have use for a GPS receiver? If so, describe when and how you would use it.
3. This article is very brief. Do you think the writer explained the Global Positioning System thoroughly enough? Do you think the writer included enough examples of potential uses for GPS? If you think the article should be longer, what other information would you include?
4. Do you think the photo that accompanies the article is necessary? Why or why not?

Group Activity

In groups of five or six, review the uses for GPS presented in the article. Then develop a list of other potential uses. Be as creative as possible. Select your best idea to present to the class.

Individual Work

Imagine that you must explain the Global Positioning System to a group of students who have never heard of it. You have only one minute to do so. Write the explanation you would give. You may wish to use the following form to begin: "The Global Positioning System is a ——————— that ———————."

THE BIG BLOWUP—ON VENUS

BEFORE YOU READ

Preview

Scientists are gaining new information about the planet Venus.

Getting Started

1. Who was Magellan?
2. What, if anything, do you know about the planet Venus?
3. Look at the picture and explain what you see. What words would you use to describe the landscape of Venus?

Culture

greenhouse effect ['grinhɑʊs iˌfɛkt]   the warming of a planet's atmosphere, caused by gases that prevent the sun's radiation from escaping

NASA [næsə]   the National Aeronautics and Space Administration. NASA is the federal agency in charge of U.S. missions to space.

Stealth bomber ['stɛlθ 'bɑmɚ]   a military aircraft that is difficult to detect with radar

Vocabulary

blowup ['bloəp]   an explosion

cauldron ['kɔldrən]   a container filled with bubbling liquid; a place of great activity

cratering [kredɚɪŋ]   the process by which a crater (a hole in the ground) is formed on a planet's surface. Many craters are caused by meteors.

faulting ['fɔltɪŋ]   the process by which a fault (a crack or break) is formed on a planet's surface

lava ['lɑvə]   hot liquid rock that bursts out of a volcano

probe [prob]   a satellite whose purpose is to explore space and send information back to Earth

run-away ['rən əˌwe]   out-of-control

Culture and Vocabulary Activity

The -ing ending on *cratering* and *faulting* adds the meaning of "a process by which _____ is formed." Add the -ing ending to the following words: *fissure, river, mountain, volcano*. Do the words you created exist in English? Could they?

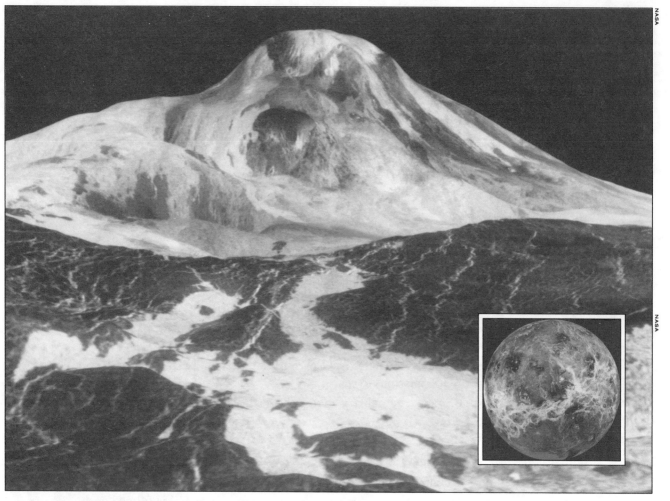

Peering under the Venusian cloud cover, the spacecraft spots an apparent lava flow from Maat Mons, the planet's second highest mountain

SCIENCE & TECHNOLOGY

The Big Blowup—on Venus

New images from the Magellan probe suggest that the planet orbiting closest to Earth is alive with volcanoes

By **MICHAEL D. LEMONICK**

THE SURFACE OF VENUS HAS NEVER seemed very hospitable. Temperatures hover around 470°C (900°F), the result of a runaway greenhouse effect, and the pressure of its atmosphere, thick with carbon dioxide and sulfuric acid, is some 90 times that of Earth's. Lead would flow like water on Venus, and water cannot have existed in liquid form for perhaps a billion years.

Now NASA's Magellan spacecraft seems to have found one more horror in the nasty landscape: active volcanoes. Last week the space agency released the first detailed map of Venus and the most spectacular images ever made of its surface.

The pictures offer the best evidence to date that a planet once presumed dead is actually a lively cauldron of geological change.

The most stunning image is of Venus' second tallest mountain, Maat Mons, which rises 8 km (5 miles). Most of the planet's many peaks, including 9.5-km- (6-mile-) high Maxwell Montes, look bright in the radar pictures Magellan takes from its orbit above the perpetual cloud cover. That means they are strong reflectors of radar waves. But Maat Mons is dark; like the Stealth bomber, it absorbs much of the radar falling on it.

This intriguing fact, say project scientists, is a strong hint that the mountain has recently been covered with lava. Rock that sits on the surface of mountaintops appears to weather quickly in the hot, chemically reactive atmosphere, creating a soil that is rich in iron sulfide. It is this mineral, the scientists believe, that shows up easily on radar. If Maat Mons doesn't have any, it has presumably been resurfaced, perhaps within the past few years.

Such resurfacing has undoubtedly taken place in Venus' lowlands: earlier images of the planet showed vast areas that are remarkably free of craters. That would be easy to explain on a planet like Earth, where cratering from meteor strikes is erased by steady erosion. But while there is some evidence of wind erosion on Venus, the best explanation for the lack of cratering is periodic lava flows. Magellan has found direct evidence of such flows, including domelike upwellings and hardened streams of rock trailing down the sides of Venusian peaks. There are also signs of other geologic activity, including dramatic faulting and several distinct episodes of mountain building. But until last week the evidence didn't indicate whether the activity was still going on or had ceased millions of years ago. The case for active Venusian volcanoes is not yet proved, but Magellan, which is now well into its second complete survey of the planet's surface, may eventually settle the issue. ■

AFTER YOU READ

Comprehension Questions

1. Prior to the voyage of the Magellan, what was known about the surface of Venus?
2. What is the highest mountain on Venus? What is the second highest mountain? How are they different?
3. What explains the lack of craters on Earth? What may explain the lack of craters on Venus?
4. What other evidence of geologic activity has Magellan found on Venus?

Discussion and Analysis Questions

1. Based on the information in the article, do you think volcanoes are active on Venus? Support your answer.
2. The spacecraft Magellan is named for a famous explorer. If you could name other space probes, after which explorers would you name them?
3. All writers make assumptions about their readers. What do you think this writer assumes about his readers?

Group Activity

Many people believe that space exploration is important. Others believe that the money would be better spent for projects on Earth. In groups of four to six, select one of these positions to defend. (Be sure that the same number of groups defends each position.) Develop an argument to support your position and present it to the class.

Individual Work

Write a one-paragraph summary of your group's position. (See the Group Activity above.) You may wish to begin in the following way: "Space exploration should (not) be continued because _____ ."

3

THE OFFICE GOES AIRBORNE

BEFORE YOU READ

Preview

Modern technology makes it impossible for anyone to be truly away from the office.

Getting Started

1. Make a list of things you might want to do with a telephone on an airplane (for example, call the office).
2. Read the list under the heading "Seat-Back Central." Do any of these items appear on the list you made for question 1? Are you surprised by any of the services the new airphones can provide?
3. How common do you think airphones will become? Do you think they will become popular with passengers? Why or why not?

Culture

fax machine ['fæks mə‚ʃin]   a machine that transmits documents electronically. "Fax" is a shortening of *facsimile* (a likeness).

laptop computer ['læptɑp kəm'pjutɚ]   a very small, portable word processor

Nintendo [nɪn'tɛndo]   the brand name of a popular series of video games for children

PC ['pi 'si]   a *p*ersonal *c*omputer

Vocabulary

aft [æft]   near the back of a boat or plane

doodad ['dudæd]   a thing; an object

fair game ['fɛr 'gem]   something that is acceptable according to the rules of play

fore [for]   near the front of a boat or plane

out of pocket [‚ɑut əv 'pɑkət]   out of reach; away from contact

(to) punch out ['pəntʃ ɑut]   to type

snoozer ['snuzɚ]   one who is sleeping

(to) wane [wen]   to get smaller or become less intense

(to) wax [wæks]   to grow or become more intense

Culture and Vocabulary Activities

1. Which words on the Culture and Vocabulary lists do you think are relatively new to the language? Why do you think so?
2. Find two sets of *antonyms* (words with opposite meanings) on the Vocabulary list.

The Office Goes Airborne

Traditional airline seatbacks are about to become full-service communications centers

By **BRUCE VAN VOORST** WASHINGTON

MICHAEL L. ABRAMSON/TIME MAGAZINE

FIRST IT WAS THE HOME. PHONES, FAX machines and PCs made it impossible to leave work at the office. Then the cellular phone made the car, even the golf course, fair game. In 1984 Airfone Inc., a GTE subsidiary, began installing telephones on airplanes. But their old-fashioned analog circuitry, vulnerable to interference, made many calls sound as if they came from Mars. Moreover, plane phones were usually scarce, located either fore or aft or shared, one to a three-seat complex, leaving travelers a reasonable excuse for staying blissfully out of pocket.

Soon even this partial sanctuary will be lost. In-Flight Phone Corp. of Oak Brook, Ill., a newcomer to the field, has begun installing advanced digital telephone systems in each and every seat, complete with video screens and ground data links that will revolutionize service in the sky. Each passenger will have a handset stowed in the armrest and a 4.5-in. by 6-in. screen mounted in the seat ahead, just above the tray table.

As they take their seats, passengers will find their names and WELCOME ABOARD already on their screens. News and weather data will scroll past as they settle in, followed by the ineluctable buckle-up-for-safety sermon. Next will come a menu with instructions (in four languages) on how to swipe any credit card through the electronic reader on the handset to pay the costs of a phone call.

What will impress telephone users aloft most, however, is the marked improvement in voice quality. The digital system, which represents and transmits information in strings of 0s and 1s that ensure accuracy, also comes equipped with a built-in computerized noise suppressor. Analog systems, which translate sound waves captured by microphones into electronic representations—or analogs—amplify the background noise along with the voice, and wax and wane depending on atmospheric conditions. Using digital technology, the new phones achieve quality equal to what earthlings get calling across town, even with the faintest signal.

For the first time, thanks to a Federal Communications Commission decision, passengers can receive incoming calls in flight—routed through a central switchboard and wordlessly announced on the video screen so as not to disturb snoozers. More important, passengers will be able to transmit high-quality computer or telefax data from their seats. Travelers carrying laptop computers need simply plug into the standard AT&T RJ-11 connector in the armrest; laptopless passengers can use the system's built-in keypad to punch out a message, displayed on the video screen, and send it.

The telephone and screen at each seat will transform the airplane armchair into a shopping and entertainment center, granting passengers access to everything from the boss's latest memo to computerized shopping catalogs to Nintendo. The difference is digital. The new FCC-approved system allows for safe and continuous operation even on takeoffs and landings. The high-tech electronic gear on the airplanes connects to a series of 80 ground centers scattered strategically across the U.S. and Canada. Whereas now lengthy calls must often be redialed when the plane leaves one area, continuous phone connections will soon be available. Nego-

tiations are under way to link up with similar systems being designed in Europe and the Far East.

Market analysts predict a huge growth in the service. Currently some 1,700 U.S. commercial airliners carry telephones, a number that will double by 1995. Passenger volume, hence potential customers, will soar from 452 million to nearly 800 million by 1999. Airfone president Robert Calafell predicts a "half a billion-dollar" industry by 1996. In addition to In-Flight—whose system American, USAir and Northwest have already agreed to test—four other companies have won FCC approval to offer digital service. One of them is Airfone, which is playing technological catch-up, and will go digital later this year. Its system will be distinguished from In-Flight's by having a small screen in the handset rather than on the seatback. "It's a communications and entertainment profit center for us all," says David Shipley, assistant vice president at USAir, which is installing In-Flight in its new Boeing 757s. "If you want to compete with the majors, you better have digital phones."

Passengers can only benefit from the competition. In-Flight is proposing to undercut Airfone's $8 three-minute tariff at $6. Spokesman Joe Hopkins of United Airlines, an Airfone customer that plans to switch to the advanced digital system, says, "Onboard telephone service has evolved from a unique feature to an everyday necessity. We now hear complaints when it's *not* available."

There may be some wishful thinking in all this marketing optimism. The rapid introduction of hi-tech doodads in the past has often met with consumer resistance that lasts until people figure out how the technology can actually improve their lives. And there are plenty of traditionalists who will regret this triumph of technology over privacy. For them, the outlook will get steadily worse. Motorola Inc. hopes soon to begin deploying its $3.5 billion Iridium global cellular communications system. The Iridium network—77 automobile-size communications satellites in orbits 500 miles high—should be in place by 1997. By then, with home and hearth violated, automobile, restaurant and airplane no longer consecrated, skiers on Zermatt's slopes and explorers at the South Pole will be susceptible to being overtaken by the message "The office calling." ■

SEAT-BACK CENTRAL

At the touch of a button, passengers can:

■ Tune in to live news and sports events

■ Order catalog merchandise

■ Phone from one seat to another inside the plane and set up conference calls with colleagues on the ground

■ Monitor the status of connecting flights

■ Access real-time stock-market quotations

■ Pick from a choice of movies and video games

AFTER YOU READ

Comprehension Questions

1. What were two problems with earlier airphones?
2. What technology has improved the voice quality of newer phones? What technology did earlier phones use?
3. What will be the main difference between the In-Flight phone and the new Airfone?
4. How will passengers benefit from the competition between In-Flight, Airfone, and other companies?

Discussion and Analysis Questions

1. Do you think the services described in the article are needed, or do you think they are unnecessary? Explain your answer.
2. If you traveled a lot for business or pleasure, which onboard telephone services might you use?
3. Do you think the projections described in the seventh paragraph are accurate? Why or why not?
4. The writer uses many examples to show how impressive the new airphones are. Is this approach effective? Support your answer.
5. How does the final quotation relate to the title of the article?

Group Activities

1. In groups of four to six, discuss the advantages and the possible disadvantages of communication by airphone. (See the ninth paragraph for an idea about the disadvantages.)
2. In groups of four to six, discuss whether competition between companies is desirable or undesirable.

Individual Work

Interview ten people. Ask them: "Do you think telephones in airplanes are a good idea? Why or why not?" Record their answers and summarize your findings. Be prepared to report your findings to the class.

4 ECHOES OF THE BIG BANG

BEFORE YOU READ

Preview

Recent discoveries support the Big Bang theory of the origin of the universe.

Getting Started

1. How many explanations of the origin of the universe do you know of? Discuss scientific, religious, and folk explanations.
2. Look at the graphic that accompanies the article. According to it, how many periods have there been in the development of the universe? How old is the universe? What was its original size?

Culture

Big Crunch ['bɪg 'krʌntʃ]   the collapse of the universe. The name is a somewhat humorous variation of the Big Bang.

great wall [gret 'wɔl]   a large formation that serves as a barrier. The term comes from the Great Wall of China.

missing link ['mɪsɪŋ 'lɪŋk]   the final piece to a puzzle; the needed information

NASA ['næsə]   the National Aeronautics and Space Administration. NASA is the federal agency in charge of U.S. missions to space.

Vocabulary

(to) congeal [kən'dʒil]   to harden; to become solid

probe [prob]   a satellite whose purpose is to explore space and send information back to Earth

(to) take shape ['tek 'ʃep]   to become formed

(to) weed out ['wid 'aʊt]   to remove; to take away

Culture and Vocabulary Activities

1. Look again at the graphic. The first two periods have names—the Inflationary period and the Plasma period. Read the descriptions of the next three periods. What names would you give to them?
2. As you read the article, write down any scientific terms whose meanings you are unsure of. Then compare your list with those of your classmates. Share information about the terms with each other.

By peering back into the beginning of time, a satellite finds the largest and oldest structures ever observed—evidence of how the universe took shape 15 billion years ago

ECHOES OF THE
BIG BANG

Big bang

Inflationary period
10^{-35} sec. old to
10^{-33} sec. old
The universe expands from less than the size of an atom to about the size of a grapefruit.

By **MICHAEL D. LEMONICK** WASHINGTON

THEY WERE, BY FAR, THE LARGEST AND most distant objects that scientists had ever detected: a swath of gargantuan cosmic clouds some 15 billion light-years from earth. But even more important, it was the farthest that scientists had ever been able to peer into the past, for what they were seeing were the patterns and structures that existed 15 billion years ago. That was just about the moment—or more precisely, an infinitesimal 300,000 years after the moment—that the universe was born. What the researchers found was at once both amazing and expected: NASA's Cosmic Background Explorer satellite—COBE—had discovered landmark evidence that the universe did in fact begin with the primeval explosion that has become known as the Big Bang.

In anticipation of the announcement, an overflow crowd had crammed into the meeting of the American Physical Society in Washington last week, and they were not disappointed. "If you're religious, it's like looking at God," proclaimed the leader of the research team, George Smoot, an astrophysicist at the University of California, Berkeley. Princeton astrophysicist David Spergel, who had recently co-authored a theory that was demolished by the COBE results, cheerily admitted, "We're dead. But this is great stuff . . . It's the most important discovery in cosmology in the past 20 years."

The existence of the giant clouds was virtually required for the Big Bang, first postulated in the 1920s, to maintain its reign as the dominant explanation of the cosmos. According to the theory, the universe burst into being as a submicroscopic, unimaginably dense knot of pure energy that flew outward in all directions, spewing radiation as it went, congealing into particles and then into atoms of gas. Over billions of years, the gas was compressed by gravity into galaxies, stars, planets and, eventually, even humans.

The first evidence of this scenario was established in 1964, when astronomers discovered the cosmic microwave background, the original radiation from the Big Bang. The second part, though, was much trickier. In order for gravity to make galaxies out of atoms, it needed something to work with—some chunks of space in which the atoms were closer together, a region of greater than average density, so that they could draw surrounding matter in. The excess densities need not have been very large, but they had to be there if matter was to congeal. And if they were present, they

Will the cosmos expand forever?

IT IS THE ULTIMATE QUESTION CONCERNING OUR FATE, BUT THE ANSWER COMES DOWN TO A simple issue. If there is enough matter out there in space, gravity will slow and then finally reverse the expansion of the universe; the cosmos will collapse. If, on the other hand, matter is spread too thin, the expansion will continue unchecked forever. But if the amount of matter is just right and the universe is at "critical density," the cosmos will continue to expand, but ever more slowly, until eons from now its growth will be barely perceptible.

So which will it be? The news from NASA's Cosmic Background Explorer satellite is reassuring. By supporting the theory of inflation, COBE also affirms the mathematical consequence that the universe is exactly at critical density. But since all the stars and galaxies add up to only 1% of that density, there must be some sort of "dark matter" that makes up the rest. Where and what is this matter? Astronomers think it might be hard-to-detect particles called neutrinos or still theoretical particles known as WIMPS. Searches are under way for both kinds of dark matter. But don't lose any sleep. Even if physicists are wrong and the universe ends up collapsing, it will be tens of billions of years before the Big Crunch. ■

Plasma period 3 min. old to about 300,000 years old
The universe is a fog of free-moving charged particles that light cannot penetrate.

About 300,000 years old
The expanding cosmos cools and the particles combine into atoms; the universe becomes transparent to light. Theoretically, some areas are denser than others and thus are warmer and emit more light. These areas later form gargantuan gas clouds.

Peering at ancient radiation from the 300,000-year-old universe, the COBE satellite detects tiny variations in temperature—confirming the big bang theory and providing the earliest glimpse of structure in the universe.

300,000 to 2 billion years old
Under the influence of gravity, the colossal clouds gradually break up into smaller, galaxy-size structures.

2 billion years old to 15 billion years old (present day)
Stars form in galaxies, and the universe continues to expand.

should be visible to a sensitive enough probe in the form of warm and cool spots mottling the microwave background.

The COBE satellite was designed to be sensitive enough, but the first maps of the microwave sky it beamed down showed nothing. That was a not a big problem. The research team knew that the cosmic microwaves are polluted with local microwaves from the Milky Way galaxy and that it would take months of computer analysis to weed out the unwanted signals.

In the end, it took more than a year. What finally appeared on the computer screens at the Goddard Space Flight Center in Maryland was a map with blotches of all sizes indicating regions of the sky where the microwaves are a minuscule 30 millionths of a degree warmer or cooler than average—almost imperceptible, but enough to save the Big Bang theory. Says University of California, Berkeley, astronomer Joseph Silk: "They've found the missing link. This removes the biggest remaining objection to the Big Bang."

Because the microwaves have been traveling for 15 billion years to get to the COBE sensors, the warm patches have long since evolved into groups of galaxies. Even the smallest patch observed by COBE is by far the largest area ever surveyed. The structures dwarf the "great wall" of galaxies discovered in 1990. The largest spans one-third of the known universe, or 10 billion light-years, which is 60 billion trillion (60 followed by 21 zeros) miles.

COBE is designed to see just the biggest structures, but astronomers would like to see much smaller hot spots as well, the seeds of local objects like clusters and superclusters of galaxies. They shouldn't have long to wait. Astrophysicists working with ground-based detectors at the South Pole and balloon-borne instruments in the stratosphere are closing in on such structures, and may report their findings soon.

If the small hot spots look as expected, that will be a triumph for yet another scientific idea, a refinement of the Big Bang called the inflationary universe theory. Inflation says that very early on, the universe expanded in size by more than a trillion trillion trillion trillionfold in much less than a second, propelled by a sort of antigravity. Bizarre though it sounds, cosmic inflation is a scientifically plausible consequence of some respected ideas in elementary-particle physics, and many astrophysicists have been convinced for the better part of a decade that it is true.

One prediction that comes out of the theory of inflation is that the mix of big and small hot spots in the early universe should follow a characteristic pattern. The spots COBE found conform to that pattern, and scientists like Smoot expect that the smaller hot spots will too. Another prediction of inflation is the surprising notion that everything astronomers can see, including all the stars and galaxies, constitutes just 1% of existing matter. The other 99% of the universe is dark and invisible.

There is already strong evidence that at least some dark matter must exist. The Milky Way and virtually all other galaxies rotate so fast that they should literally fly apart—unless the gravity from invisible halos of dark matter is holding them together. The halos still fall short of what inflation requires, but bolstered by the latest results, theorists are sure the rest will be found. Says Paul Steinhardt, a University of Pennsylvania physicist who helped develop inflation: "We were confident in our theory, of course, but it's always nice to know that Nature is cooperating." ■

AFTER YOU READ

Comprehension Questions

1. When was the Big Bang theory created?
2. What was the first evidence found to support the Big Bang theory?
3. What did the COBE satellite find? Why is this finding important?
4. What is the inflationary universe theory? What are two of its predictions?

Discussion and Analysis Questions

1. Do you think there is enough scientific evidence to support the Big Bang theory? Why or why not?
2. Read the inset entitled "Will the cosmos expand forever?" What is the answer to this question? Why do you think the writer includes this information separately?
3. Look at the list of scientific terms you made for Culture and Vocabulary Activity 2. How many terms are on your list? Obviously, the writer uses many scientific terms in this article. Must a reader understand each term completely in order to understand the article? Why or why not?

Group Activity

In groups of five or six, discuss the following question: Does acceptance of the Big Bang theory contradict any religious explanation of the origin of the universe? Is there agreement in your group? Is there agreement in the class?

Individual Work

Look at the final quotation in the article. Explain its meaning. Do you find any humor in it? If so, what? Be prepared to present your answer to the class.

5 READ A GOOD POWERBOOK LATELY?

BEFORE YOU READ

Preview

There has been a revolution in the book publishing industry, but readers may not be interested.

Getting Started

1. Do you read for pleasure? If so, what kinds of publications do you read?
2. Where is your favorite place to read for pleasure?

Culture

cash machine ['kæʃ məˌʃin]   a machine that dispenses money from one's bank account. A card and identification number must be used to obtain the money.

laptop ['læptɑp]   a very small, portable word processor

Macintosh ['mækɪnˌtɑʃ]   a brand of computer made by Apple Computer company. It is widely used in the United States, especially in schools.

reader-friendly [ˌridɚ 'frɛndli]   easy to read. The phrase comes from the term *user-friendly,* which describes a software program that is easy to use.

trade magazine ['tred mægəˌzin]   a publication that focuses on a single industry or profession. For example, there are trade magazines for publishing, for fashion design, and for the theater.

Vocabulary

(to) curl up ['kɚl 'əp]   to curl, twist, or bend; to sit or lie in a comfortable position

(to) dog-ear ['dɔg ɪr]   to bend the corner of a page in order to mark one's place in a book

(to) flip through ['flɪp 'θru]   to look quickly through (something) by turning the pieces or pages

software ['sɔftwɛr]   operating programs for computers. The computer equipment itself is called *hardware.*

start-up ['stɑrt əp]   a new company or business

touch-sensitive [ˌtətʃ 'sɛnsətɪv]   able to respond or react to touch

(to) zap [zæp]   to transmit or send quickly

Culture and Vocabulary Activity

Make up five different sentences. In each sentence, use one term from the Culture list and one from the Vocabulary list. For example: *The cash machine at my bank zaps money to me in seconds.*

Read a Good PowerBook Lately?

Publishers are discovering the virtues of paperless novels. But will readers curl up to a computer screen?

By PHILIP ELMER-DEWITT

THE HARD-COVER BOOK IS A PRETTY VENERable piece of technology. The letters on the page are descended from movable type pioneered by Johanes Gutenberg in the 1400s. The paper is not all that different from papyrus used by the Pharaohs. Books today may be written with word processors, but they are still printed in ink, bound with thread and delivered essentially by hand.

Computer enthusiasts have long predicted that the digital revolution would soon liberate the word from the printed page and put it directly on the screen. In the past decade, hundreds of reference books—including such well-known titles as Bartlett's *Familiar Quotations* and *Roget's Thesaurus*—have appeared in electronic form. But when it comes to literature, the electronic-publishing movement has run into resistance from both readers and publishers. As inevitable as the paperless book may seem, neither group could quite imagine sitting down to read Faulkner, Fielding or Flaubert on a computer.

So it was something of a breakthrough last week when Harold Evans, president of Random House, and John Sculley, chairman of Apple Computer, met in a New York City boardroom and announced that titles from one of America's most famous book series, the Modern Library, will be published in electronic form. Among the first to be issued on disk are Faulkner's *The Sound and the Fury*, Melville's *Moby Dick* and Dickens' *David Copperfield*. The disks, priced below $25, are designed to run on Apple's portable PowerBook computers, which are widely considered to be more reader-friendly than IBM-type laptops.

The PowerBook packs the features of a Macintosh into a machine the size and weight of a dictionary. But driving the new venture is a bit of magic performed by programmers at Voyager, a Santa Monica,

Calif., software company, that makes the experience of reading a book on a screen amazingly close to reading it on paper. "It's the first thing I've seen that I could curl up in bed with," says Nora Rawlinson, editor in chief of the trade magazine *Publishers Weekly*.

Voyager's software displays the text on clean white pages that replicate the de-

A new way of viewing *The Picture of Dorian Gray*

sign of the hardback rather than using the scrolling strings of text so familiar to computer users. A touch of a button turns the page or allows the reader to flip back and forth. Users can dog-ear the corner of a page to mark their place, or attach an electronic paper clip for easy reference. Passages can be underscored or marked on the side, and there are generous margins for putting down notes.

The computer also brings benefits not offered by ordinary books: a backlit screen that permits reading in a darkened bedroom without disturbing a spouse, the option of enlarging the type to reduce eyestrain, the ability to copy passages onto a "notebook" page, and a search feature that displays occurrences of any cho-

sen word, name or phrase. This last option could prove handy for, say, recalling the identity of an obscure Dostoyevsky character who suddenly reappears after 100 pages.

Other firms are working on similar products. Microsoft has published dozens of electronic reference books for IBM-compatible computers. The Slate Corp., an Arizona-based software vendor, has developed software that lets people flip through the pages of an electronic book by flicking a stylus across a touch-sensitive screen. And Booklink, a Florida-based start-up, is designing a notebook-size reading device that could be loaded with digitized books from a cash machine–type dispenser that would serve as an electronic library. By eliminating distribution and warehousing costs, Booklink's backers think they can make classics available for as little as $1 or $2 a title.

Elegant as these products may be, there is no guarantee that even those readers who own the necessary equipment will want to use it for reading novels. If anything, the new paperless books are reminders of how good real books are. As Denise Caruso, editor of the newsletter *Digital Media*, points out, books are everything that everyone wants the new electronic media to be: portable, intensely personal and highly interactive.

Will readers give up the feel of paper and the smell of ink for a machine whose batteries have to be recharged every three hours? "The great power of the printed book is that it requires no technology; it is accessible to anyone who can read," admits Daniel Boorstin, the former Librarian of Congress and a member of the Modern Library editorial board. Initially at least, the market for computer books will probably be among students and scholars, who can use the electronic features to do productive work, rather than those simply reading for pleasure.

Ultimately, it may be the economics of publishing, not the aesthetics, that determine what shape literature will take. Fiber-optic wires and data-compression techniques make it possible to deliver books—as well as magazines and newspapers—over telephone or cable-TV lines. In the future, readers may select what they want to read from a menu of titles and have their choices zapped almost instantly to their portable machines. Old-fashioned books will probably never be entirely displaced, but as the cost of digital information continues to fall, and the environmental and production costs of paper keep rising, the pleasure of buying and reading a new hardbound volume may someday be limited to the few who can still afford it. ■

AFTER YOU READ

Comprehension Questions

1. How much do literary disks for PowerBook computers cost?
2. What features does Voyager's software offer?
3. What features does the PowerBook computer have?
4. What technology is Booklink developing?

Discussion and Analysis Questions

1. Why might some people be reluctant to use the PowerBook for pleasure reading?
2. Would you enjoy reading a novel using the PowerBook? Why or why not?
3. The writer describes books as "intensely personal and highly interactive." What do you think he means by this? Do you agree with him? Do you think electronic books can be personal and interactive? Explain your answers.

Group Activity

The third paragraph mentions several well-known books that are available on disk. In groups of three, develop a list of ten literary classics that you think should be available in electronic form. Compare your group's list with those of other groups.

Individual Work

In approximately one-half page, identify your favorite piece of literature, explain why you enjoy it, and tell whether you think reading it electronically would change your feeling for it.

6 ADVENTURES IN LILLIPUT

BEFORE YOU READ

Preview

Scientists are now able to see things never before seen by the human eye.

Getting Started

1. Read the title and the short description of the article. Which two words have similar meanings?
2. Look at the smaller picture. What do you think the object is? Now read the caption. Were you right?
3. Have you ever used a microscope? If so, what have you observed?

Culture

AT&T ['e 'ti ən 'ti]   American Telephone and Telegraph, a major U.S. communications company

Braille [brel]   a writing system for the blind. The letters and numbers are represented by raised dots.

DNA ['di 'ɛn 'e]   deoxyribonucleic acid, the material in all living cells that controls genetics

IBM ['aɪ 'bi 'ɛm]   International Business Machines, a major U.S. company that makes computers and other high-tech products

Lilliput ['lɪlə,pʊt]   an island described in the book *Gulliver's Travels* by Jonathan Swift. The island's inhabitants are only six inches tall.

magic wand ['mædʒɪk 'wɑnd]   a rod or stick used by a magician; an instrument with special powers

Vocabulary

drag [dræg]   a force that slows motion

free fall ['fri fɔl]   a situation in which an object falls without any opposing force. A parachute jumper is in free fall before the parachute opens.

laser ['lezɚ]   a device that makes beams of light stronger. *Laser* is an acronym for "*l*ight *a*mplification by *s*timulated *e*mission of *r*adiation."

micro- ['maɪkro]   very small

molasses [mə'læsəz]   a dark, thick syrup that is produced during the manufacturing of sugar. An old-fashioned phrase describes some people as "slow as molasses in January."

snapshot ['snæpʃɑt]   a photograph

strobe [strob]   a bright flash of light

whimsical ['wɪmzɪkəl]   filled with fanciful ideas

Culture and Vocabulary Activity

The prefix *micro-* can be added to nouns in English to change their meanings. Read the brief description of the article. In which words is the prefix *micro-* used? Invent ten other English words using *micro-*. What do they mean? For example, a *microskirt* is a very short skirt.

Adventures in Lilliput

Extraordinary new laser tools and microscopes are enabling researchers to observe and manipulate a breathtaking microworld

By **J. MADELEINE NASH** CHICAGO

THINK SMALL. NOW THINK SMALLER still. For in the lilliputian wonderland that scientists have begun to explore, a grain of rice looms as large as an asteroid, a droplet of water as wide as an inland sea.

Using powerful new tools, biologists at the University of Chicago have gently sliced through a red blood cell to peer at individual protein molecules clinging to its inner membrane. At the California Institute of Technology, chemists have watched in wonder as a hydrogen atom romances an oxygen away from a carbon dioxide molecule. And at Stanford University, physicist Steven Chu has mastered techniques for levitating millions of sodium atoms inside a stainless-steel canister and releasing them all at once in luminescent fountains. Of late, Chu and his colleagues have amused themselves by stretching a double-stranded DNA molecule as taut as a tent rope. When they release one end, the molecule recoils like a miniature rubber band. *Boing!*

Just as improvements in navigational tools opened the oceans to sailing ships, so a new generation of precision instruments has exposed a breathtaking microworld to scientific exploration. Aided by computers that convert blizzards of data

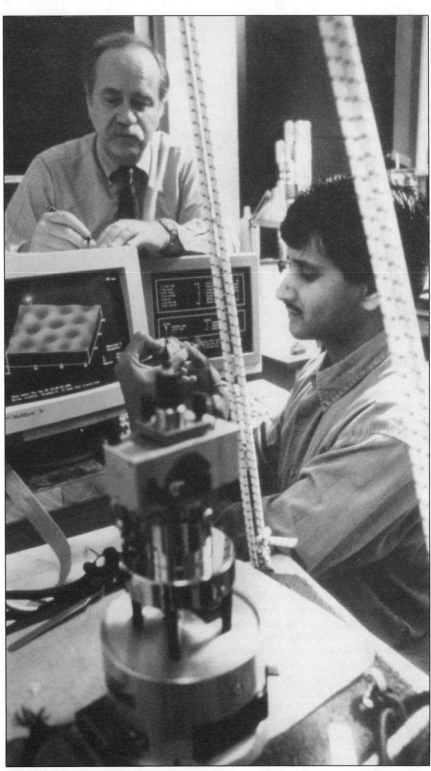

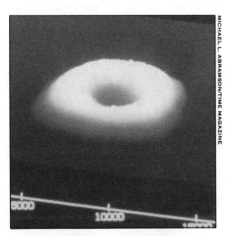

THE ATOMIC FORCE MICROSCOPE probes the structure of matter one atom at a time, generating detailed computer images such as this view of a red blood cell. The AFM can even slice through the cell to reveal proteins inside.

into images on a screen, these instruments are helping scientists see—and even tinker with—everything from living cells to individual atoms. "This technology is still pretty crude," marvels Chu. "Who knows what we may be able to do with it in a few years' time."

Among the instruments generating excitement:

FEMTOSECOND LASERS.
Like strobes flickering across a submicroscopic dance floor, these devices can freeze the gyrations of atoms and molecules with flashes of light. The lasers are being used to study everything from how sodium joins with other atoms to form salts to how plants convert sunlight into energy through the process of photosynthesis. Physicists from California's Lawrence Berkeley Laboratory reported that they used such a laser to take a "snapshot" of the chemical reaction that is the first step in visual perception. This reaction, triggered when light hits the retina of the eye, had never before been directly observed. And with good reason. The reaction was clocked by the L.B.L. team at 200 femtoseconds, which are millionths of a billionth of a second. How fast is that? Well, in little more than a second, light can travel all the way from the moon to the earth, but in a femtosecond it traverses a distance that is but one hundredth of the width of a human hair. "This sort of time scale is almost impossible to imagine," exclaims L.B.L. director Charles Shank, who helped pioneer the technology.

LASER TRAPS.
Beams of laser light can also be used to ensnare groups of atoms, which can then be moved around at will. But because atoms at room temperature zoom about at supersonic speed, they first have to be slowed down. In 1985 the invention of "optical molasses" by a research team at AT&T Bell Laboratories provided an ingenious solution to the problem. As its name implies, optical molasses uses light to create enough electromagnetic "drag" to bring wildly careering atoms to a screeching halt. Because the atoms lose virtually all their kinetic energy, they approach the perfect stillness of absolute zero, the frozen state at which motion ceases.

At such supercold temperatures, scientists believe, matter may start to exhibit bizarre and interesting new properties. Certainly, cold atoms can be trapped and manipulated in a variety of cunning ways. The fountains created by Chu, for example, are enabling scientists to ob-serve atoms in free fall and thus measure gravitational forces with unprecedented accuracy. Fountains are also helping scientists measure the oscillations of cesium atoms more precisely than ever before, and cesium atoms are to atomic clocks—the world's most precise timepieces—what quartz crystals are to wristwatches.

OPTICAL TWEEZERS.
With a single beam of infrared laser light, scientists can seize and manipulate everything from DNA molecules to bacteria and yeast without harming them. Among other things, optical tweezers can keep a tiny organism swimming in place while scientists study its paddling flagella under a microscope. Optical tweezers can also reach right through cell membranes to grab specialized structures known as organelles and twirl them around. Currently, researchers are using the technology to measure the mechanical force exerted by a single molecule of myosin, one of the muscle proteins responsible for motion. Scientists are also examining the swimming skill of an individual sperm. "One day," imagines Michael Berns, director of the Beckman Laser Institute and Medical Clinic at the University of California at Irvine, "we may be able to pick up a live sperm and stuff it right into an egg."

SCANNING TUNNELING MICROSCOPES.
Invented only 10 years ago, these extraordinary instruments probe surfaces with a metallic tip only a few atoms wide. At very short distances, electrons can traverse the gap between the tip and the surface, a phenomenon known as tunneling. This generates a tiny current that can be used to move atoms and molecules around with pinpoint precision. Thus last year physicists from IBM's Almaden Research Center manipulated 35 xenon atoms on a nickel surface to spell out their company's logo. They have also fashioned seven atoms into a minuscule beaker in which they can observe chemical reactions at an atomic level, and they devised a working version of a single-atom electronic switch that, in theory, could replace the transistor. Though some of the achievements seem whimsical—constructing a miniature map of the western hemisphere out of gold atoms, for instance—such stunts demonstrate a technique that may eventually be used to store computer data on unimaginably small devices.

ATOMIC FORCE MICROSCOPES.
Like STMs, these instruments possess an atomically small tip that resembles a phonograph needle. An AFM reads a surface by touching it, tracing the outlines of individual atoms in much the same way a blind person reads Braille. Because the electromagnetic force applied by the tip is so small, an AFM can delicately probe a wide range of surfaces, including the membranes of living cells. Even more astounding, by applying slightly more pressure, scientists can use an AFM tip as a dissecting tool that lets them scrape off the top of cells without destroying their interior structures. Scientists have used an AFM to detail the biochemical cascade that results in blood clotting; to examine the atomic structure of seashells; and to uncover the tiny communication channels that link one cell to another. "We're looking at scales so small," says University of Chicago physiologist Morton Arnsdorf, "they almost defy comprehension."

Without question, these recent additions to the scientific tool kit hold tremendous practical promise. A more accurate atomic clock, for instance, is not just a curiosity. "If we can put better clocks into orbit," notes William Phillips, a physicist at the National Institute of Standards and Technology, "we might improve the global positioning system enough to land airplanes in pea-soup fog." Even now it is not difficult to imagine that STMs might be employed by the semiconductor industry to produce minuscule electronic devices, that optical tweezers might be used by surgeons to correct defects in a single cell or that femtosecond lasers might eventually be harnessed to control, as well as monitor, chemical reactions. Speculates University of Chicago chemical physicist Steven Sibener: "In the future, combinations of these magic wands may become much more powerful than using them one by one."

Such marvels, of course, will not materialize overnight. Cautions IBM physicist Donald Eigler: "The single-atom switch looks small until you realize it took a whole roomful of equipment to make it work." Still, computer chips the size of bacteria and motors as small as molecules of myosin are rapidly moving out of the world of fantasy and into the realm of possibility. "For years, scientists have been taking atoms and molecules apart in order to understand them," says futurist K. Eric Drexler, president of the Foresight Institute in Palo Alto, Calif. "Now it's time to start figuring out how to put them together to make useful things." With such powerful instruments to help them, scientists and engineers may finally be getting ready to do just that. ∎

AFTER YOU READ

Comprehension Questions

1. What does a femtosecond laser do?
2. What is the purpose of a laser trap?
3. What do optical tweezers consist of?
4. What are some humorous things that scientists have done with a scanning tunneling microscope (STM)?
5. How is the atomic force microscope (ATF) similar to the STM? What additional things can it do?

Discussion and Analysis Questions

1. What is your reaction to the "tools" described in this article?
2. Do you think "Adventures in Lilliput" is a good title for this article? Support your answer.
3. Do you think that readers who are not usually interested in science would enjoy this article? Why or why not?

Group Activity

The suffix *-ian* can be added to certain nouns in English. For example, a Lilliputian is a person who lives in Lilliput. In groups of three, analyze the folowing lists. Which words in the second list are formed similarly? Can you develop rules to explain the word formation? Are there any words that don't fit the patterns?

State	Resident
Georgia	Georgian
Florida	Floridian
Texas	Texan
California	Californian
Oregon	Oregonian
Arkansas	Arkansan
Kansas	Kansan
Alaska	Alaskan
Minnesota	Minnesotan
Kentucky	Kentuckian
South Carolina	South Carolinian

Individual Work

In the first paragraph of the article, the writer describes a tiny world in which a grain of rice would look like an asteroid and a drop of water would look like a sea. Write a half-page description of how other common items would look in a Lilliputian world. Use your imagination.

Health & Medicine

A LESSON IN COMPASSION

BEFORE YOU READ

Preview

Some medical centers want doctors to learn what it's like to be a patient.

Getting Started

1. What qualities do you think are important for a doctor to have?
2. Have you ever done any role playing? If so, what role did you take? How did it make you feel?

Culture

bedside manner [ˈbɛdsɑɪd ˈmænɚ]   the way in which a doctor relates to patients. Some doctors are said to have a good bedside manner; others are said to have none.

family practice [ˈfæm(ə)li ˈpræktəs]   general medical practice; an area of medicine that focuses on general care for all ages

Medicare [ˈmɛdəˌkɛr]   government-supported health care for Americans aged sixty-five and over

resident [ˈrɛzəˌdɛnt]   a doctor who has graduated from medical school and is undergoing more training in a special area

Vocabulary

(to) blow one's top [ˈblo wənz ˈtɑp]   to become very angry

burnout [ˈbɚnˌɑʊt]   exhaustion and discouragement resulting from overwork

crash course [ˈkræʃ ˈkors]   a very fast lesson

(to) deal with [ˈdil wɪθ]   to manage; to handle

(to) do labs [ˈdu ˈlæbz]   to take blood and urine samples for medical testing

(to) go through [ˈgo ˈθru]   to experience; to endure (something unpleasant)

(to) role-play [ˈrol ˌple]   to pretend to be another person

stirrup [ˈstɚəp]   a metal support on an examining table used to position a patient's foot

tough [təf]   difficult

(to) wind up [ˈwɑɪnd ˈəp]   to end up; to finish or conclude

Culture and Vocabulary Activities

1. Review the Culture and Vocabulary lists. Which words and phrases are medical terms? As you read the article, look for other medical terminology.
2. Find two synonyms for *illnesses* in the article.

A Lesson in Compassion

What's it like to be a patient? For more and more aspiring doctors, there's only one way to find out.

By ANASTASIA TOUFEXIS

ELLEN WEISS CAN HARDLY SEE. DAVID Schmitt can barely hear. Together, the elderly woman, who suffers from diabetes, congestive heart failure and arthritis, and the widower, who is recovering from a hip fracture, slowly shift through the halls of Hunterdon Medical Center in Flemington, N.J. Typical victims of aging's cruelest blows? Not really. Weiss is actually a resident in family practice, age 30, and Schmitt a medical student, 26. They have been assigned roles, ages and infirmities as an innovative part of their medical training.

Introduced in only a few medical centers so far, such role playing is designed to expose doctors to the anguish endured by the infirm. It is just one of several techniques being tried at U.S. medical schools and hospitals in an attempt to deal with the most universal complaint about doctors: lack of compassion. "Residents are usually young, healthy, privileged," says Dr. Stephen Brunton of Long Beach Memorial Medical Center in Long Beach, Calif. "They've not really had a chance to understand what patients go through."

Role-playing programs give them a crash course. At Hunterdon, students' faces are instantly aged with cornstarch and makeup. Next the disabilities are laid on: yellow goggles smeared with Vaseline distort vision, wax plugs dampen hearing, gloves and splints cripple fingers, and peas inside shoes impair walking. Then the ersatz invalids are asked to perform common tasks: purchasing medication at the pharmacy, undressing for X rays, filling out a Medicare form and, most humiliating, using the bathroom.

At Long Beach, new residents in family practice assume fabricated maladies and check into the hospital for an overnight stay—incognito. The staff treats them as they would any other patient, even sending them a bill. The entire entering class of medical students at the Uniformed Services University of the Health Sciences in Bethesda, Md., are issued bedpans and told to use them. They spend part of the

first day of school as hobbled patients. A few male students are even subjected to an indignity familiar to women: waiting in the stirrups for a doctor to arrive.

Instant patients start out peppy and joking. "But by the end of a few hours, most say, 'I'm exhausted,'" observes nurse Linda Bryant at Hunterdon. Schmitt discovered that "a major accomplishment

A student is prepped to experience hospital life—as an invalid

was doing up my collar." And, to his surprise, "I wound up resenting physicians who didn't realize how much medication would cost and how hard it was to go and pick it up." Weiss also had an epiphany: "I realized how little I talk to patients. I might ask them about chest pains but not 'Can you get dressed, eat O.K., take your medicine?'" At Long Beach, Jeffrey Ortiz thought he was in for a quiet rest when he was sent to the intensive care unit, suffering from "chest pains." Instead he spent a sleepless night: "People were coming in to do labs, the man in the next bed was groaning, and the heart monitor was bleeping. It was noisy and scary."

Any patient could have told him so, but many educators believe the direct experience of such miseries will leave an enduring sense of sympathy. Doctors have long defended taking a cool, dispassionate approach to patient care, arguing that it helps preserve objective judgment and

protect against burnout. But critics disagree. "By concentrating on symptoms and lab data, we ignore a wealth of information that can affect patients' well-being," observes Dr. Simon Auster at the Uniformed Services medical school. Moreover, he says, "it takes less energy to get close to a patient than to maintain a distance." Auster warns, however, that caring should not be confused with wallowing in soppy feelings with patients or adopting an appealing bedside manner. "That's superficial charm," he declares, as opposed to the more difficult task of grappling with the painful emotional issues in medicine.

To lure more caring individuals to the field, schools are seeking older students as well as non-science majors. Reformers are also revising the curriculum to place more emphasis on how to relate to patients. Some schools have engaged actors to portray patients—some of them ornery or withdrawn—whom students must then interview and counsel. At Duke University's medical school in North Carolina, Melanie Wellington had a tough time with "Tom Brown," a black man in his 50s, whose dietary habits were contributing to high blood pressure. "Brown" said he didn't want to be treated with drugs because medication had ruined his brother's sex life. Says Wellington: "The biggest problem was my own discomfort," particularly when it came to asking him about his sexual history and possible drug abuse, which drew hostile responses. "Now I preface my interviews with 'These are questions we ask everyone. We need the answers to take the best care of you.'"

Such educational experiments are not a panacea, but already they are yielding some symptomatic relief for patients. At Long Beach, the residents' experiences as patients-for-a-day have prompted administrators to accelerate the hospital's admissions process: it now takes 15 minutes or less. Other results are harder to measure but just as significant. Robert Stambaugh admits that he felt "self-conscious and silly" during his brief stint impersonating a patient at Uniformed Services. But two years later, he drew on the experience to summon up sympathy for an obstreperous patient whose brain had been injured in a car accident. "He'd throw bedpans, pull out catheters and verbally abuse everyone," Stambaugh recalls. As the student doctor who had to repeatedly replace the catheters, he was tempted to blow his own top. "On reflection, though," he says, "I recognized that the patient was scared to death, confused and had lost a great deal of his dignity. That was what made me able to deal with him." ∎

AFTER YOU READ

Comprehension Questions

1. What complaint do patients often have about doctors?
2. What may be the cause of this problem?
3. How do some doctors defend their behavior?
4. What kinds of things do doctors do in their role plays?
5. Have the role-play experiences been successful?

Discussion and Analysis Questions

1. What is your reaction to medical role playing? Do you think it should be required for all doctors in training?
2. If you were a doctor, would you enjoy such role playing? Why or why not?
3. Do you think the writer did a good job of presenting a variety of doctors' reactions? Support your answer.

Group Activity

In the United States, doctors hold prestigious positions in society. Is this true in other cultures that you are familiar with? In groups of six, discuss the role of doctors in other countries.

Individual Work

In a half-page paper, agree or disagree with the following statement: *Role-playing patients is a valuable use of doctors' time.* Be sure to support your position.

2 HEALING BY WIRE

BEFORE YOU READ

Preview

New technology can connect medical specialists with patients far away.

Getting Started

Have you ever heard of *telemedicine?* What do you think the word means? If you're not sure, reread the Preview and read the brief description of the article. What do these statements tell you about telemedicine?

Culture

acute-care [əˈkjut ˈkɛr]   having facilities to treat very serious medical conditions

CAT scan [ˈkæt skæn]   *c*omputerized *a*xial *t*omography; an X-ray procedure in which results are analyzed by computer

medically underserved [ˈmɛdɪkli ˌəndərˈsərvd]   having relatively few doctors or medical facilities. Most rural areas in the United States are medically underserved compared to urban areas.

post-traumatic-stress disorder [ˈpost trəˈmædɪk ˈstrɛs dɪsˈordər]   a disorder caused by experiencing a disaster such as a war or an earthquake. Symptoms often appear years after the event.

Vocabulary

awful lot [ˈɔwfəl ˈlɑt]   a great deal; a large quantity

(to) book [bʊk]   to schedule

(to) clone [klon]   to copy exactly; to make an exact replica

(to) crop up [ˈkrɑp ˈəp]   to appear without warning

drawback [ˈdrɔbæk]   a disadvantage; a negative aspect

hybrid [ˈhaɪbrəd]   a mixture of different varieties of things

linkup[ˈlɪŋkəp]   a hookup; a connection

(to) run through [ˈrən ˈθru]   to review; to go over

Culture and Vocabulary Activities

1. In this article, the words *book, crop* (in *crop up*), and *run* (in *run through*) have slightly different meanings from their usual meanings. Discuss the connection between the basic meanings and the changed meanings of these words.
2. Paragraph five discusses radiology, cardiology, and neonatology. What does the suffix *-logy* mean? Make a list of other English words that end in *-logy*.

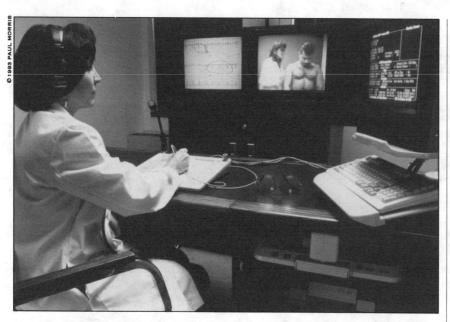

© 1993 PAUL MORRIS

A radiologist in Miami can study X rays and discuss treatment with a patient in Manila

Healing by Wire

With videophones and satellite linkups, an examination by the world's top specialists can be a phone call away

By ANDREW PURVIS

A NEURORADIOLOGIST IN IOWA STUDIES the swirling contours of his patient's CAT scan and immediately books the man for surgery. An Atlanta cardiologist, glancing at an untouched bottle of heart pills, looks his patient in the eye and urges him to take his medicine. A psychiatrist notes the pallor on the face of an earthquake survivor in Armenia and counsels her on post-traumatic-stress disorder.

Typical encounters between doctor and patient? Perhaps. But in each case the doctor and the patient are not seated knee to knee in an examining room: they are hundreds—in one case thousands—of miles apart. The physicians are practicing telemedicine, an emerging hybrid of telecommunications and patient care in which people in medically underserved areas use ordinary telephone lines to consult with highly trained specialists whom they could not otherwise afford to see.

In the past two years, two-way video telemedicine projects have been launched in Texas, Georgia and West Virginia, while less sophisticated methods relying on still photography have cropped up in Iowa, North Carolina and Nevada, among other states. U.S. doctors via satellite have diagnosed conditions in patients in Armenia,

the Philippines and Belize. "It's a way of cloning the specialist and sending him out to locations around the world," says Dr. Jay Sanders, a telemedicine pioneer now teaching at the University of Miami.

Since the first videophone was unveiled at the New York World's Fair in 1964, doctors have dreamed of healing by wire. But the reality of transmitting a detailed picture over a 1-mm-thick (.04 in.) copper cable proved elusive. Then in the 1980s engineers working with a technique called digital signal compression managed to boost the data-carrying capacity of ordinary phone lines 30-fold.

Specialists in radiology, cardiology and neonatology, whose high-priced services are in great demand in rural areas, have been quick to take advantage of the new technology. These doctors do much of their diagnosing with tests such as echocardiograms, CAT scans and fetal monitoring, which can be displayed electronically and sent over the wires with ease.

For towns like Indianola, Miss. (pop. 12,000), the technology arrived just in time. One evening last month, the physician on duty at the South Sunflower County Hospital admitted a five-year-old girl who had miraculously survived a brutal car wreck. Apart from cuts and bruises, she seemed O.K., although tests showed that she had lost some blood. A year ago, a

doctor might simply have kept her under observation. But the hospital had recently hired Teleradiology Associates, a group of radiologists based in Durham, N.C. Just to be safe, the doctor sent them a CAT scan of the child.

Viewing the image on a TV screen in his dimly lighted office three states away, Dr. David Forsberg noticed that something was wrong. "You could see a rupture in the integrity of the spleen." He immediately recommended surgery; her bleeding organ was removed and her life saved. "In the middle of the night, it's reassuring to know that you're bringing your patients the best care available," says Dr. Tony Kusek, a country doctor—and teleradiology enthusiast—in Albion, Neb.

Outfitted with new data-compression technology, telephone lines can also carry primitive video. Networks that allow doctor and patient to sit down face to face, so to speak, and run through symptoms, diagnosis and treatment have been set up in Texas, West Virginia, Georgia and Florida (where the system is used to treat state-prison inmates). Images are still jerky, but consulting specialists can guide the doctor or nurse on site through a physical exam and discuss the results. "It's like learning to fly a plane with the pilot at your shoulder," observes Dr. Charles Driscoll, a family practitioner at the University of Iowa.

The future of telemedicine can be glimpsed in an experiment combining satellite transmission and high-definition television. Last December doctors in Boston used these technologies to study patients in Belize suffering from cutaneous leishmaniasis, a parasitic skin disease. The quality of the images was "amazing," says Dr. Linda Brinck. Doctors could clearly see the changes in skin texture and coloration that characterize the ailment.

The drawback: satellites and HDTV cost millions, and even the more modest telemedicine networks that use ordinary phone lines and two-way video are priced at $500,000. "For community hospitals, that's an awful lot of money," notes Dr. Tony Franken, head of radiology at the University of Iowa.

Still, the costs of fiber optics and digital compression are shrinking. Eventually, the projected savings from telemedicine—up to $1,500 for every patient who does not have to be transported to an acute-care hospital—are likely to outweigh the price. For enthusiasts like Dr. Brinck, the possibilities are limitless. She envisions U.S. specialists teaching the latest diagnostic techniques to isolated medics in Central Africa who, in turn, can inform American colleagues of emerging health crises in their regions. Satellite ties with doctors in Africa in the 1960s, she points out, might have drawn attention to AIDS long before it exploded in the bathhouses of San Francisco 20 years later. This is one way, at least, in which a smaller world may become a healthier world. ■

AFTER YOU READ

Comprehension Questions

1. What technology has made "healing by wire" possible?
2. Which medical fields are currently benefiting most from this technology?
3. What are the advantages of telemedicine for patients?
4. What is the main disadvantage of telemedicine?

Discussion and Analysis Questions

1. What do you think will be the future of "healing by wire"? What needs to happen for it to become widely used?
2. Do you think the writer is implying that doctors in rural areas or in other countries are not knowledgeable? Support your answer with examples from the article.

Group Activity

In the article, Dr. Charles Driscoll uses an *analogy* (a comparison between two things) to explain the advantages of telemedicine. He says, "It's like learning to fly a plane with the pilot at your shoulder." In groups of four or five, discuss whether you think this is an effective analogy. Then as a group develop analogies for the following:

    a. being a doctor
    b. being a student
    c. being a teacher
    d. learning a second language
    e. speaking English

Share your analogies with the rest of the class.

Individual Work

Think of three possible titles for this article (instead of "Healing by Wire"). Share your ideas with the class.

3 WHEN YOUR DOCTOR HAS AIDS

BEFORE YOU READ

Preview

Should HIV-infected health-care workers be required to tell patients about their condition? Federal and state health officials disagree.

Getting Started

As a class, discuss what you know about AIDS and how it is transmitted.

Culture

AIDS [edz]   *a*cquired *i*mmune *d*eficiency *s*yndrome; a deadly disease caused by HIV

Centers for Disease Control (CDC) ['sɛntɚz fɔr dɪ'ziz kən,trol]   federally supported medical research facilities located in Atlanta, Georgia

fed [fɛd]   an official of the federal government. The word is slang, usually plural, and sometimes has a negative connotation.

HIV ['etʃ ɑɪ 'vi]   *h*uman *i*mmunodeficiency *v*irus; the virus that causes AIDS

witch hunt ['wɪtʃ hənt]   an extremely emotional investigation in which innocent people are harmed and/or harassed. The phrase refers to the Salem (Massachusetts) witch trials of the 1600s, in which women were accused of being witches.

Vocabulary

(to) backfire ['bækfɑɪr]   to end in the opposite way of what was planned

(to) buck [bək]   to resist or go against something

case-by-case ['kes bɑɪ 'kes]   one-by-one; one at a time

(to) chart a course ['tʃɑrt ə 'kors]   to make a plan of action; to choose a direction

incentive [in'sɛntɪv]   a motive; a reason to do something

(to) part company ['pɑrt 'kəmpə,ni]   to disagree

(to) set (something) back ['sɛt ,səmθɪŋ 'bæk]   to make something go backwards; to reverse or defeat something

(to) spark [spɑrk]   to begin

(to) track down ['træk 'dɑʊn]   to search for and find

Culture and Vocabulary Activities

1. Why do you think people use *acronyms* like AIDS and *abbreviations* like HIV and CDC? What is the difference between an *acronym* and an *abbreviation?*
2. Make up sentences using the verbs *backfire, set (something) back,* and *track down.*

When Your Doctor Has AIDS

Bucking an emotional national crusade, New York decides not to force physicians to tell their patients

By CHRISTINE GORMAN

SURELY THERE ARE ONLY A HANDFUL OF people in the U.S. who have not heard about or witnessed on television the suffering of Kimberly Bergalis—the 23-year-old Floridian who contracted AIDS from her dentist. Her anguished letters and poignant testimony before Congress have sparked a nationwide campaign, endorsed by the Centers for Disease Control (CDC) to test health-care workers for HIV and inform their patients if they are infected.

But last week the New York State health department decided to put Bergalis' plight into perspective. She is but one of 1 million HIV-infected Americans and one of only five ever to have been infected by a health-care worker—all five by the same dentist. These facts, state health officials concluded, did not merit what they saw as a witch hunt to track down and expose every health-care worker who carries the deadly virus.

Rejecting the emotionalism surrounding the Bergalis case as well as the Federal Government's response to her highly unusual predicament, New York proposed its own set of guidelines governing the lives of infected doctors and their patients. By charting an independent course, the state, which leads the nation in AIDS cases, could lose tens of millions of dollars in federal health-care funds if authorities in the national government determine that New York's rules depart too radically from its own.

In most respects, the state's proposed policy matches that set forth last summer by the CDC. Both urge health-care workers to undergo voluntary HIV tests. Both recommend setting up expert panels to determine, on a case-by-case basis, whether infected health-care workers should continue practicing medicine and what procedures they may safely perform. Where the feds and state part company is over the issue of informing patients about their doctor's health status. Under CDC guidelines, an infected health professional may continue to perform invasive procedures, such as cardiac or abdominal surgery, if he or she informs patients; New York makes no such demand.

Why? Because state health officials are convinced the CDC's requirement will backfire. The state has discovered that

Infected by a patient, Dr. Aoun objects to the witch hunt

hospitals, worried about their liability under the CDC guidelines, have begun to force the resignations of HIV-infected workers, regardless of whether or not they perform invasive procedures. With their livelihoods thus threatened, argues the state, infected doctors have a big incentive to hide their condition from hospital colleagues as well as patients. That, say state officials, will be far more dangerous than protecting the doctors' privacy while formally advising them to refrain from invasive procedures.

Furthermore, state health officials argue, the best way to minimize the remote chance of patients getting HIV from a medical worker is to make sure that strict infection controls are followed. New York is now requiring all health professionals who perform invasive procedures to undergo mandatory training in the latest sterile techniques. Such measures not only

protect patients from an infected doctor, they also protect patients from one another by ensuring that instruments are thoroughly decontaminated between uses. Infection control also protects the doctor. In New York City, where 1 in 50 people carries the AIDS virus, and in most other places, doctors have far more to fear from their patients than vice versa.

Dr. Hacib Aoun of Baltimore is one of 40 U.S. health workers known to have become infected with AIDS on the job. Like many doctors, he deplores the CDC recommendations and prefers New York State's approach. "The CDC guidelines mean that hospitals will just get rid of their infected doctors no matter what," says Dr. Aoun. "I understand the Bergalis family's pain. I understand it better than anybody else. But their efforts have set AIDS education and treatment in this country back by many years." ■

AFTER YOU READ

Comprehension Questions

1. How did Kimberly Bergalis contract AIDS? How many Americans have gotten HIV from health-care workers?
2. What are the CDC guidelines regarding health-care workers with HIV?
3. How do New York's guidelines differ from those of the CDC?
4. According to health officials in New York, what is the best way to avoid spreading HIV from health-care workers to patients?

Discussion and Analysis Questions

1. Do you think New York should lose federal funds because its guidelines are different from the CDC guidelines? Explain your answer.
2. New York officials say that health-care workers with HIV may lie if they are forced to tell patients about their condition. Do you agree? Why or why not?
3. This topic is obviously very controversial. Do you think the writer did a good job of presenting both sides of the issue? Give examples to support your opinion.

Group Activity

In groups of five or six, discuss the following statement: *Health-care workers with HIV must inform patients of their condition.* Discuss the advantages and disadvantages of such a policy. Do the members of your group agree about the best policy?

Individual Work

Write a half-page paper stating your position on the issue discussed in the Group Activity. Be sure to give reasons for your position.

WHEN PATIENTS CALL THE SHOTS

BEFORE YOU READ

Preview

Living wills are becoming more widespread.

Getting Started

1. What is a will? Do you have a will? Why or why not?
2. What is a living will? Read paragraph two of the article and the section called "The Two Basic Types of Living Wills." What do these sections tell you about living wills?

Culture

hospice ['hɑspəs]   a medical facility for terminally ill patients. The facility is more like a home than a hospital; its main purpose is to make patients as comfortable as possible.

persistent vegetative state [pɚ'sɪstənt 'vɛdʒə,tetɪv 'stet]   an irreversible condition in which a comatose patient is being kept alive by artificial means

Vocabulary

bureaucratic [,bjurə'krædək]   overly complicated; characteristic of a bureaucracy. The word usually has negative connotations.

(to) call the shots ['kɔl ðə 'ʃɑts]   to make the decisions

chronic ['krɑnɪk]   lasting a long time or occurring frequently

comatose ['komətos]   deeply unconscious; in a coma

(to) fall short ['fɔl 'ʃort]   to lack something; to fail to achieve a goal

jarring ['dʒɑrɪŋ]   disturbing; unsettling

nudge [nədʒ]   a push; a force

(to) steel oneself ['stil wən,sɛlf]   to brace oneself; to get ready for something unpleasant

surrogate ['sɚəgət]   a replacement; someone who represents another person

(to) wind up ['wɑɪnd 'əp]   to end up; to finish or conclude

Culture and Vocabulary Activities

1. A *euphemism* is a gentle or polite way of saying something. Which of the Culture terms is a euphemism? What would be a more direct way of saying the same thing?
2. The following are other euphemisms: *to pass away, the dearly departed one,* and *to be no longer with us.* What do you think they mean?

When Patients Call the Shots

The next time you go into a hospital, prepare to be presented with a living will

By ANDREW PURVIS

THERE IS NOTHING THERAPEUTIC ABOUT the somber process of checking into a hospital. Already ailing and disoriented, incoming patients must fill out endless forms, produce insurance cards and steel themselves for the inevitable probes, cuts, needle pricks and medications that mark a modern hospital stay. The last thing patients want to think about is the possibility that they will never leave—that their illness or a medical mistake will leave them comatose and thus incapable of making life-and-death decisions for themselves.

Yet that prospect is what most Americans will now be asked to consider every time they enter a hospital, whether it is to undergo heart bypass surgery or to get a hernia repaired. A new law that goes into effect this week requires all federally funded hospitals, nursing homes and hospices to tell incoming patients of their right to fill out a living will, a document that specifies that if something goes wrong, they will not be kept alive against their wishes. Although the rule is long overdue, experts wonder whether hospitals are up to the bureaucratic task and whether jarring questions—if not properly handled—may stir needless fear and anxiety.

The concept of a living will has been around for decades. Moved by the tragic stories of comatose patients like Nancy Cruzan, the Missouri woman who was kept alive for seven years against her parents' wishes, more than 40 state legislatures have enacted laws aimed at encouraging patients to make their treatment preferences known beforehand. Some of the newest laws authorize people to appoint a surrogate, or proxy, who can make medical decisions for them when necessary. Widespread use of such measures could reduce the extraordinary expense of keeping terminal patients on life-support systems that neither they nor their family desires.

Yet so far, just 15% of Americans have made out living wills, and the new federal rule is an attempt to encourage their use. At Chicago's Rush-Presbyterian—St. Luke's Medical Center the admitting clerk reads a little speech to incoming patients: "Do you have a living will? Can we have a copy of it?" Those who answer no are handed a pamphlet that goes over the Illinois law on the topic. A California health-care group has prepared special booklets describing the basics of living wills in 10 languages, including Chinese and Farsi.

Unfortunately, the law falls short of ensuring that patients will get what they want if and when the critical time comes. Many states allow the withdrawal of treatment or feeding tubes only under limited conditions, regardless of a patient's preferences. Removal may be permitted when death is imminent but not when a patient is suffering from a chronic condition like "persistent vegetative state." Even now, the decision on what is best for a particular patient often winds up in court.

At best, the new law is a mild nudge in the right direction. "It urges people to get their affairs in order," says the American Hospital Association's Fredric Entin. Like many medicines, the measures may at first be hard to swallow, but the consequences of not taking them could be incalculably worse.   —*Reported by Lynn Emmerman/Chicago and Jeanne McDowell/Los Angeles*

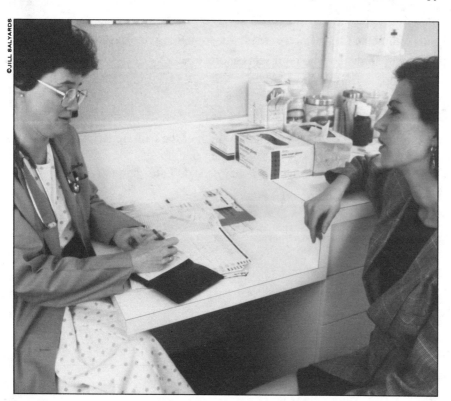

©JILL SALYARDS

THE TWO BASIC TYPES OF LIVING WILLS

1 *The patient decides whether he wants to prohibit doctors from performing life-prolonging procedures such as tube feeding and artificial respiration.*

2 *The patient names someone else—a friend, family member or doctor—to make that decision for him. The surrogates can withhold care, hire and fire doctors, and discharge the patient from the hospital or nursing home.*

AFTER YOU READ

Comprehension Questions

1. What is the new federal law regarding living wills?
2. How many states have passed laws regarding living wills?
3. How many Americans have living wills?
4. What may be some problems with living wills?

Discussion and Analysis Questions

1. Did you know about living wills before you read this article? Do you think they are a good idea? Explain your answer.
2. Do living wills truly allow patients to "call the shots"? Why or why not?
3. If the writer were to make this article longer, what information do you think he should add? Why?

Group Activity

In groups of four to six, discuss the benefits of having a living will. How many can you identify? Why might some people choose not to have a living will?

Individual Work

Write a brief summary (one-half page maximum) of your group's discussion about the pros and cons of having a living will.

5 NOW HEAR THIS—IF YOU CAN

BEFORE YOU READ

Preview

Hearing loss is a serious health problem, but it can often be avoided.

Getting Started

1. What are some of your daily activities? What sounds do you usually hear during a day?
2. Do you frequently hear loud or very loud sounds? If so, what are they?

Culture

House [haʊs]   the U.S. House of Representatives, one of two elected federal legislative bodies in the United States. The other is the U.S. Senate.

Walkman ['wɔkmən]   the brand name of a lightweight portable radio and cassette recorder used with headphones. Walkmans are extremely popular with joggers and bike riders.

Vocabulary

barrage [bə'rɑʒ]   a steady attack; a concentrated outpouring

cacophony [kə'kɔfə,ni]   harsh sounds; discordant sounds

cap gun ['kæp gən]   a toy gun that makes a loud snapping noise

(to) confiscate ['kɑnfə,sket]   to seize or take away property

decibel ['dɛsə,bɛl]   a unit for measuring sound

(to) hit [hɪt]   to reach

insidious [ɪn'sɪdiəs]   developing gradually and without notice, but resulting in great harm

(to) make noise about [mek 'nɔɪz ə,baʊt]   to complain about; to draw attention to

racket ['rækət]   a lot of noise

Culture and Vocabulary Activities

1. Read the first paragraph of the article. How many words can you find that mean "a very loud noise"?
2. As you read the article, make a list of other words used for various kinds of loud noises.

Now Hear This—If You Can

Americans are amazingly tolerant of the noise that engulfs them at work and play. They shouldn't be. The din causes millions to lose their hearing, slowly but surely.

By ANASTASIA TOUFEXIS

DIANE RUSS OF EVANSTON, ILL., NEVER stays in the kitchen when the dishwasher is running. She wouldn't think of using power tools without wearing earplugs. And on weekends she keeps her windows closed. "Some mornings you can't walk outside because so many people are using their power mowers," she laments. "It's very noisy out there." Who would dispute it? From the roar of airplanes to the wail of sirens, the blast of stereos to the blare of movie sound tracks, noise is a constant part of American life. But few go to the lengths Russ does to avoid it. Noise is annoying and frustrating—and accepted.

That tolerant attitude needs to change—and fast. Increasingly, the racket that surrounds us is being recognized not only as an environmental nuisance but also as a severe health hazard. About 28 million Americans, or 11%, suffer serious hearing loss, and more than a third of the cases result from too much exposure to loud noise. Last week specialists testifying before a House committee documented an alarming new trend: more and more of the victims of noise-induced deafness are

adolescents and even younger children. "We need to get people thinking the same way about protecting their ears as they now do about protecting their eyes," says Dr. James Snow Jr., director of the National Institute on Deafness and Other Communication Disorders. "There is so much noise we're exposed to that we tend to become complacent about it."

Much of the clamor is unavoidable because it fills work sites or public places. As many as 10 million Americans are exposed daily to on-the-job noise that could gradually cause some degree of permanent hearing loss. Sixty million Americans endure other noise, including the cacophony of city traffic, that is louder than the level the Federal Government deems safe, and 15 million live close to busy airports or beneath heavily traveled air routes. In some neighborhoods of northern New Jersey, more than 1,000 flights thunder overhead each day.

Much of the punishment, though, is voluntary. "Unfortunately," says Russ, an audiologist at Northwestern University's hearing clinic, "most of us unnecessarily increase the burden of noise we put ourselves under in our private lives." Homeowners endure the steady whine of

everything from chain saws and power lawn mowers to vacuum cleaners and dishwashers. And the din of leisure activities can be just as dangerous as the roar from the factory floor. "We have laws to protect the hearing of workers in noisy workplaces," says senior scientist William Clark of the Central Institute for the Deaf in St. Louis. "But there are no laws covering recreational noises." The most hazardous pastimes by far are hunting and target shooting—enjoyed by nearly 13% of the population. A single crack of gunfire can hit 130 decibels or more, easily exceeding the danger level of 85 decibels.

Children lead some of the most raucous lives of all. Noisy activities range from playing with cap guns to practicing with school bands to riding the school bus. Of greatest concern, however, is youngsters' devotion to amplified music. Rock concerts can surpass 110 decibels, though they are more of a threat to musicians than to audience members, who endure the punishing pounding for only an hour or two.

The most endangered kids are those who wander around with cassette players blaring music into their skulls for hours. These personal stereos can funnel blasts

© WILLIAM R. SALLAZ/GAMMA LIAISON

Jet Takeoff 130

of 110 decibels or more into the ear. "If you can hear the music from a Walkman someone next to you is wearing, they are damaging their ears," declares Dr. Jerome Goldstein of the American Academy of Otolaryngology. After years of such assaults, notes audiologist Dean Garstecki, head of the hearing-impairment program

OUCH! Prolonged exposure to noises of 85 decibels produces gradual hearing loss. Above 100 decibels, even brief exposure can cause permanent damage.

at Northwestern University, "we've got 21-year-olds walking around with hearing-loss patterns of people 40 years their senior."

The ear is an amazingly flexible organ, but it simply was not designed to withstand the strain of modern living. Hearing naturally deteriorates with advancing years, but not by much. Mabaan tribesmen in the Sudan, for example, who have never been exposed to industrial sounds, maintain their hearing into old age. Sudden intense noise, like a gunshot or dynamite blast, can damage hearing instantly by tearing the tissue in the delicate inner ear. Sustained noise from a jackhammer or disco music is more insidious. The prolonged barrage flattens the tiny hair cells in the inner ear that transmit sound to the nerves. As the hairs wilt, people often feel a fullness or pressure in the ears or a buzzing or ringing, known as tinnitus.

Such symptoms soon subside and the hairs regain their upright posture—if the ear gets some rest. But unrelenting noisy

assaults can eventually cause the hair cells to lose their resilience and die. They do not regenerate, and the result is a gradual loss of hearing.

Those who cannot escape exposure to loud or prolonged noise should wear ear protectors, which can muffle sound by about 35 decibels. National Institute on Deafness director Snow contends that such protective gear should be as commonplace for children as bicycle helmets and infant car seats. His institute and other organizations are launching programs to educate children about hazards to hearing. And musicians who have suffered hearing loss, including Pete Townshend of the Who, are helping spread the message about the price of high-decibel rock. "We teach kids to keep their hands off the hot stove," says Jeff Baxter of the Doobie Brothers. "Let's do the same with their hearing."

EFFORTS ARE ALSO BEGINNING TO BE made to attack unavoidable noise pollution. John Wayne International Airport in Orange County, Calif., boasts the toughest runway noise standards in the country. Observers can stand on the field and carry on conversations in normal tones, even as jets take off and land. Los Angeles International Airport has pledged to be equally quiet by the end of the decade.

Some communities are starting to enforce antinoise ordinances more vigorously. New York City, arguably the noisiest urban center in the country, issued 1,000 citations last year, primarily targeting air-conditioning equipment, discos, street construction machinery and horn blowing. In Southern California, police in National City and Redondo Beach have been empowered to confiscate big speakers installed in autos to make them what are known as "boom cars." Says officer Michael Harlan of National City: "If we hear a boom car 50 ft. or more away on a public street, we can cite the driver."

Noise is a low priority of the U.S. government. In fact, the Reagan Administration closed the Environmental Protection Agency's noise-control office in 1982 and dropped noise-emission labeling on such items as power tools and lawn mowers. Hearing experts call for a return of noise-emission information as well as new warning labels on audio equipment that can produce dangerously high decibel levels.

The ultimate hope, says Dr. Patrick Brookhouser of Boys Town National Research Hospital in Omaha, is that people will realize "when you lose hearing you lose, to some degree, one of our most vital attributes, the ability to interact with our environment." In other words, Americans should be making the most noise about noise itself. *—Reported by Barbara Dolan/ Chicago, with other bureaus*

©SPOONER/GAMMA LIAISON

Rock Concert 110

AFTER YOU READ

Comprehension Questions

1. How many Americans suffer serious hearing loss? How many cases have been caused by exposure to loud noise?
2. What are some of the loud noises Americans are exposed to every day?
3. What are the most dangerous leisure activities with respect to noise?
4. What is *tinnitus?* What causes it?
5. What should people do if they can't avoid long exposure to loud noises?

Discussion and Analysis Questions

1. Have you ever thought of noise as an environmental nuisance? as a health hazard? Do you think many people are aware of the problems noise can cause? Explain your answer.
2. Are loud noises a problem where you live? If so, what are the sources of the noise?
3. Do you think the writer does a good job of explaining that noise is a serious problem? Give examples to support your answer.

Group Activity

In groups of three, develop two lists: one of common recreational noises and one of common non-recreational noises. Compare your lists with those of other groups. Discuss ways to avoid or reduce the level of each kind of noise.

Individual Work

Write a half-page description of your favorite pleasant sound(s).

6 IS THERE A METHOD TO MANIPULATION?

BEFORE YOU READ

Preview

The public and the medical community now view chiropractic more favorably than they did in the past.

Getting Started

1. What is chiropractic? Does it exist in your home culture? If so, is it viewed as "real" medicine or as alternative medicine?
2. Have you ever gone to a chiropractor? Do you know anyone who has? If so, describe the results.

Culture

American Medical Association [ə'mɛrə,kən 'mɛdɪ,kəl ə,sosi'eʃən]   a very large and influential professional organization of doctors. It is often called the A.M.A.

chiropractic [,kaɪro'præktɪk]   a method of treating pain and disease by manually adjusting parts of the body, especially bones in the back and neck

clinical trial ['klɪnə,kəl 'traɪəl]   a controlled scientific experiment

cult [kəlt]   a group of people following a certain trend, belief, or leader. The word usually has negative connotations.

internist [ɪn'tɚnəst]   a doctor who diagnoses and treats infectious diseases; a specialist in internal medicine

Vocabulary

bunk [bəŋk]   nonsense

cachet [kæ'ʃe]   prestige; social value

crushed [krəʃt]   demoralized; devastated

(to) get cracking ['gɛt 'krækɪŋ]   to get moving

holistic [ho'lɪstɪk]   pertaining to the whole of something

mainstream ['menstrim]   belonging to the majority group

manipulation [mə,nɪpju'leʃən]   skillful control or adjustment with one's hands

quackery ['kwækɚi]   the pretended practice of medicine by an unqualified and dishonest person

(to) refer a patient [rə'fɚ ə 'peʃənt]   to send a patient to see another doctor, often a specialist

(to) spring up ['sprɪŋ 'əp]   to appear

Culture and Vocabulary Activities

1. In the first paragraph of the article, find two words that refer to someone or something that is *fake*.
2. As you read the article, look for the names of various medical specialists (e.g., *rheumatologist*). Try to figure out what each specialist does.

Is There a Method to Manipulation?

Once scorned as quackery, chiropractic is winning adherents and respect

By ANDREW PURVIS

WHEN INTERNIST PAUL SHEKELLE was in medical school in the 1970s, the gentle art of chiropractic was widely viewed as bunk: heir to the tradition of bloodletting and rattlesnake oil. The American Medical Association's committee on quackery had branded the practice an "unscientific cult," and medical-school professors had obediently followed suit. The reluctance of the so-called back-crackers to submit their technique to the scrutiny of hard science served only to reinforce the official scorn. Recalls Shekelle: "They were seen as hucksters and charlatans trying to dupe the public into paying for useless care."

The public, meanwhile, seemed happy to be duped. Millions of Americans remained devoted to the healers' manipulative ways. And in recent years that enthusiasm has blossomed. About 1 in 20 Americans now sees a chiropractor during the course of a year. The number of U.S. practitioners jumped from 32,000 in the 1970s to 45,000 in 1990.

Chiropractic has even achieved a certain celebrity cachet. Quarterback Joe Montana got his brawny back manipulated on national TV (during the Superbowl pregame show). Cybill Shepherd grew so attached to her practitioner that she married him. Overseas, where chiropractic is both more popular and more widely accepted by doctors, Princess Di regularly gets her regal back cracked. And Russian ballet stars Vadim Pisarev and Marina Bogdanova reportedly would not risk an arabesque without a periodic adjustment.

Now, almost despite itself, mainstream medicine has started to take notice. Several authoritative studies have confirmed that chiropractic-style spinal manipulation is effective for the treatment of lower-back pain. Leading physicians now openly discuss the technique, and some are even referring their own patients to these once scorned colleagues. Concedes Dr. Shekelle, who directed one of the recent studies: "Their philosophy of disease is totally foreign to us. But for some conditions it sure seems to work."

A Palmerton, Pa., chiropractor gives a hands-on prescription

About 1 in 20 Americans now sees a chiropractor in the course of a year. Most of them seek help for back trouble.

The growing acceptance was apparent at this year's meeting of the American Academy of Orthopedic Surgeons, where for the first time a symposium was held on back manipulation, and about one-third of surgeons present admitted referring patients for the technique. Some 30 hospitals around the country now have chiropractors on staff, and multidisciplinary clinics that offer both medical and chiropractic care have sprung up in several urban centers. In addition, a small band of "research" chiropractors has begun testing the method in carefully designed clinical trials. "Manipulative medicine," declares Dr. Nortin Hadler, a rheumatologist at the University of North Carolina, "is no longer a taboo topic."

One reason for turnabout is that spinal manipulation has held up under study, at least for some conditions. In a report released this July by the Rand Corp., a prestigious research organization in Santa Monica, Calif., a panel of leading physicians, osteopaths and chiropractors found that chiropractic-style manipulation was helpful for a major category of patients with lower-back pain: people who are generally healthy but who have developed back trouble within the preceding two or three weeks. Another important study published last summer in the *British Medical Journal* compared chiropractic treatment with outpatient hospital care that included traction and various kinds of physical therapy. Its conclusion: spinal manipulation was more effective for relieving low-back aches for up to three years after diagnosis.

Such positive findings come despite the fact that no one is entirely sure how chiropractic manipulation works. Practitioners assert that they are correcting spinal "subluxations," which they describe as misalignments of vertebrae that result in damaging and often painful pressure on nerves in the spinal cord. Because nerves in the cord connect to every organ and body part, such misalignments, they say, can cause problems in the feet, hands and internal organs as well as the back.

Most doctors are skeptical of this theory. "Chiropractors may sound very authoritative," says Chicago rheumatologist Robert Katz, "but their basic understanding of the pathophysiology of the spine is simply not there." Chiropractors respond that they spend at least four years studying the subtleties of the spine, including exhaustive courses in anatomy, pathology, biochemistry and microbiology, and are in fact far more knowledgeable than many medical doctors about this anatomical region.

Whatever the benefits of manipulation and massage, many chiropractors admit that at least some of their success stems from their attentive manner and holistic approach to disease. Practitioners tend to discuss a patient's entire life-style, emphasizing stress reduction, a healthful diet, exercise and maybe even a change in work habits. Patients love it, especially after experiencing the sometimes narrow approach of medical specialists, who may thoroughly examine a body part without a hint of interest in the human being.

New York social worker Shoshana Shonfeld, 40, for instance, was crushed when an orthopedic surgeon told her she would either have to live with chronic back pain or undergo radical disk surgery, with no guarantee of success. Then she found a chiropractor who, she recalls, "did all kinds of wonderful things." In addition to spinal manipulation, the practitioner served up a potpourri of health-care advice on everything from diet to correct posture and toning up muscles in the stomach and lower back. Now, she says, "my back is almost perfect. My body feels aligned; it feels straight."

ONE STUDY IN WASHINGTON STATE found that patients were significantly more satisfied with their chiropractor's manner than with their medical doctor's. Patients may even be too satisfied. One frequent complaint about chiropractors is that treatment goes on for too long. Patients become dependent on regular manipulation, and their therapists are all too happy to accommodate them. Alan Adams of the Los Angeles College of Chiropractors estimates that perhaps 10% to 15% of his colleagues are guilty of this.

While the vast majority of chiropractic patients are treated for back, neck and shoulder complaints as well as minor headaches, some 10% seek help for organic diseases of all sorts. Can manipulation help them? The chiropractic literature is replete with examples of astonishing cures of ulcers, hypertension, childhood asthma, blindness and even paraplegia. But individual case histories prove nothing, and organized studies are few and far between. Spinal manipulation has been shown to alter the heartbeat and the acidity of the stomach, says Peter Curtis, a medical professor at the University of North Carolina, who studied the technique, "but whether you can cure a peptic ulcer or angina is another question entirely." The A.M.A. withdrew its earlier condemnation of chiropractic as a cult in 1988—after federal courts ruled it an unfair restraint of trade—but it remains adamantly opposed to broad application of chiropractic therapy.

Of course, chiropractic could restrict itself to relieving back pain and still have its hands full. By some estimates, 75% of all Americans will suffer from low-back aches at some point in their lifetime. The annual cost to U.S. society of treating the ubiquitous ailment was recently tallied at a crippling $24 billion, compared with $6 billion for AIDS and $4 billion for lung cancer. If spinal manipulation could ease even a fraction of that financial burden, remaining skeptics might be forced to stifle their misgivings or get cracking themselves. ■

AFTER YOU READ

Comprehension Questions

1. What did the American Medical Association think about chiropractic in the past?
2. How many Americans see a chiropractor each year?
3. How many chiropractors were there in the United States in 1990?
4. What has caused some medical experts to change their minds about chiropractic?
5. What is one complaint that patients sometimes have about chiropractors?

Discussion and Analysis Questions

1. In your opinion, is chiropractic a legitimate field of medicine? Explain your answer.
2. The article contains examples of famous people who use chiropractic. Why do you think the author includes these examples?

Group Activity

In groups of three or four, discuss other kinds of healers or medical treatment that you know about from other cultures. How many can you think of? Share your information with the class.

Individual Work

Would you go to a chiropractor? In a brief statement, tell why or why not.

Entertainment & Sports

1 COUNTRY MUSIC'S NEW MECCA

BEFORE YOU READ

Preview

Branson, Missouri, is becoming a new home for country music performances.

Getting Started

1. Are you familiar with country music? Can you name any country singers? Do you know the traditional center of country music?
2. Find the state of Missouri on the map at the back of this book. Does it seem to be a likely place for an entertainment center? Why or why not?

Culture

Broadway ['brɔdwe]   a street in New York City that is famous for its theaters, especially its musical theaters

flag-waving ['flæg ˌwevɪŋ]   patriotic; referring to a love of and respect for the American flag

gold rush ['gold rəʃ]   a situation in which many people try to get quickly to a source of wealth. The famous Gold Rush in California began in 1848.

gospel ['gɑspəl]   a kind of popular religious music. Gospel music is often associated with the southern United States.

Las Vegas [lɑs 'vegəs]   a city in Nevada known for its gambling casinos and adult-oriented entertainment

mecca ['mɛkə]   a center of attraction; a place sought by many people. As the birthplace of Muhammad, Mecca in Saudi Arabia is a holy Islamic city to which people make pilgrimages.

Vocabulary

blue [blu]   obscene; vulgar; dirty

boomtown ['bumtɑʊn]   a town characterized by rapid expansion or development

burned out ['bɚnd 'ɑʊt]   exhausted and discouraged as the result of overwork

(to) downplay ['dɑʊnple]   to make less important or less noticeable

draw [drɔ]   an attraction

glitz [glɪts]   flashiness and glamour

(to) go heavy on ['go 'hɛvi ɔn]   to emphasize; to make more important

honest-to-goodness ['ɑnəst tə 'gʊdnəs]   true; real

(to) pick up ['pɪk 'əp]   to go faster; to begin to move

Culture and Vocabulary Activities

1. Which two Vocabulary items are antonyms?
2. As you read the article, make a list of words you aren't familiar with. Discuss these words and their meanings with the class.

Bright lights, boomtown: Nashville may be the capital of country, but Branson, Mo., is its Broadway

ENTERTAINMENT & SPORTS

Country Music's New Mecca

Why 5 million people a year spend $1.5 billion in a tiny but tuneful town nestled in the Ozarks

By ELIZABETH L. BLAND

IT IS 200 MILES SOUTH OF KANSAS CITY, near the center of the U.S. but isolated from everything. You reach it by a two-lane highway that snakes through the Ozark Mountains with nothing but oak trees for company. You round a corner and—*Look!*—there is a line of campers and cars stretching to the horizon, crawling along a five-mile strip of neon lights that flash from theaters, motels and miniature golf courses.

Welcome to Branson, Mo. (pop. 3,706). This hardscrabble town attracts 5 million tourists a year, who drop an estimated $1.5 billion into local pockets. And in a recession-slowed summer when many travelers are staying close to home and spending less, business in Branson is up 5% from last year.

The draw: big-time country-music shows, enough to fill 24 theaters every afternoon and evening, with stars such as Mickey Gilley, Loretta Lynn, Conway Twitty, Mel Tillis and Reba McEntire, several of whom have moved to the area and own the theaters in which they perform. Nashville may still be the capital of country music, its recording and publishing hub, but Branson has become its Broadway. Says Mel Tillis (*Heart Healer*), who moved to Branson two years ago: "You go to Nashville, you see the stars' homes. You come to Branson, you see the stars."

Down-home hospitality keeps the audiences coming—mostly from a 300-mile radius that takes in St. Louis, Memphis and Wichita, but increasingly from all across the U.S. Patrons can meet the stars' families in theater lobbies; Tillis' wife, for one, sells candy. Most of the performers sit onstage at intermission to sign autographs, and violinist Shoji Tabuchi heads to the parking lot after his show to wave goodbye to the tour buses. Prices are right too. You can still get a motel room for $40, and there are 6,000 campsites in town. Says Mary Nell King of Pocahontas, Ark.: "I've seen one Broadway show in the past 10 years. But we can get to Branson two or three times a year."

The appeal of the rolling Ozarks is not lost on the entertainers, most of whom have settled there after long, exhausting runs on the road. Even with 12 shows a week, Tillis considers life in Branson "a vacation." Says resident singer-comedian Jim Stafford, whose witty, whimsical show is in its second year: "It is easy to get burned out on the road. But here I live on the lake. I just drive in, play and go home."

Branson, too rocky to grow anything but "kids and tomatoes," has long been a tourist town. It drew its early visitors as the setting of the sentimental 1907 best seller *The Shepherd of the Hills,* now re-enacted nightly in the amphitheater. Things picked up around 1960 with the opening of Silver Dollar City, a turn-of-the-century theme park, and Table Rock Lake, a fish-rich creation of the Army Corps of Engineers. At about the same time came a country jamboree called the *Baldknobbers,* named for a legendary vigilante group, and still a top attraction. But it was not until 1983, when Roy Clark's Celebrity Theater began to bring big names to town, that the strip began its growth spurt.

Next spring will see the strongest surge yet: new theaters from Johnny Cash, Silver Dollar City and, perhaps, Andy Williams. Country is still king, but the newer shows have broader ambitions. Violinist Tabuchi's variety show, perhaps the most popular in town, downplays country and goes heavy on glitz. Says Ben Bush, a businessman who plans a two-theater complex next spring: "People want to be entertained. If that means less country music, then that is what it will take."

But city fathers have no intention of turning their town into another Las Vegas. Branson sees itself as a family attraction: almost every production has a flag-waving number, and there are several gospel shows. Jack Herschend, president of Silver Dollar City, points out that no blue shows have succeeded. "This is such a family place that anyone who tried to capture the off-color niche wouldn't work."

Some locals are less than thrilled by the heavy traffic—and by the half-percent increase in sales tax passed last week to pay for new roads. Many more jobs are available than in the past, but most are seasonal and pay at or near minimum wage. "In the winter everyone sits around on unemployment," says Gary Evans, a vending-machine salesman. "Mostly, though, the attitude is, 'Don't bite the hand that feeds you.'"

But there is no turning back the clock. Too many tourists have found a friendly, affordable mecca in Branson; too many nationally known performers, some of whose hits are behind them, have found appreciative audiences. "It is an honest-to-goodness boomtown," says Stafford. "There are other places where this could be happening, but it's not. The gold rush is here." Spoken like a true pioneer. ∎

AFTER YOU READ

Comprehension Questions

1. Why do tourists like to come to Branson?
2. Why do entertainers like to perform in Branson?
3. Why don't city officials want Branson to become like Las Vegas?
4. What do residents think of Branson's popularity?

Discussion and Analysis Questions

1. Would you like to visit Branson? Why or why not?
2. Does Branson sound like a passing fad, or do you think it will continue to attract tourists?
3. Read the next-to-last paragraph again. What do you think the saying "Don't bite the hand that feeds you" means?

Group Activity

In pairs, discuss the possible meanings of the following sayings:

a. Don't look a gift horse in the mouth.
b. Don't cry over spilled milk.
c. Look before you leap.
d. Better safe than sorry.
e. A stitch in time saves nine.

Do you know other similar sayings in English or in another language? Share them with your partner and then with the class.

Individual Work

Alliteration is the repetition of consonant sounds, usually at the beginning of words. Most often used in poetry, it is sometimes used in prose as well. Two examples in this article are "the *c*apital of *c*ountry music" and "a *t*iny but *t*uneful *t*own." Choose any five Culture or Vocabulary items and write one sentence for each that displays alliteration.

2 THE TACTICS OF TANTRUMS

BEFORE YOU READ

Preview

Some famous athletes use anger to improve their performance.

Getting Started

1. What is your favorite professional sport to watch? Who are its star athletes? Are they temperamental or even-tempered?
2. Do you ever lose your temper (become angry) when playing sports? If so, how does losing your temper affect your play?

Culture

spoiled brat ['spɔɪld 'bræt]   a child whose poor behavior is supposedly due to receiving too much attention or having too many possessions

sports psychologist ['sports saɪ'kɑlə,dʒəst]   a specialist in the mental and behavioral characteristics of athletes

Vocabulary

double-edged ['dəbəl 'ɛdʒd]   having two sides; having good and bad aspects

(to) draw on ['drɔ 'ɔn]   to make use of; to use

(to) flare up ['flɛr 'əp]   to grow intense for a brief period

(to) get even ['gɛt 'ivən]   to repay someone's bad deed; to take revenge

(to) power up ['pɑʊɚ 'əp]   to make stronger; to give energy to

(to) step up ['stɛp 'əp]   to increase

(to) take [tek]   to win; to defeat someone

(to) turn on ['tɚn 'ɔn]   to start; to cause to flow

Culture and Vocabulary Activity

Many two-word verbs in English are created by adding *up* to a verb. Find three examples of two-word verbs using *up* in the Vocabulary list. As you read the article, look for more examples. Compare the meanings of the two-word verbs using *up*. How are they similar?

The Tactics of Tantrums

For some athletes, getting mad is a way to do better than get even

By ANASTASIA TOUFEXIS

OVER THE YEARS, JIMMY CONNORS HAS treated spectators to phenomenal displays of tennis and temper—and at the U.S. Open last week, he exhibited both again. In the second set of a match against Aaron Krickstein, Connors flared up when the umpire overruled a linesman and called one of his passing shots wide. In a one-minute tantrum, the 39-year-old, five-time Open winner called the offending official "a bum," as well as several more colorful names. From then on, Connors played brilliantly, and he took the 4-hr. 41-min. match in a tempestuous tie breaker, before advancing again three days later.

The abuse, though it drew no penalty from Open officials, appalled many onlookers. Some longtime Connors watchers, however, recognized that such displays may be an integral, even calculated, part of Connors' game. "The world may see a spoiled brat," observes David Pargman, a sports psychologist at Florida State University, in Tallahassee, "but some élite athletes turn on the anger strategically."

In sports ranging from baseball to football to hockey, agrees Cal Botterill, a psychologist who works with the Chicago Blackhawks, "the very best athletes can use their emotions—and anger is one of them—to push their performance up." In fact, a baseball adage has it that managers prefer players who get mad. Anger steps up the body's pitch: blood pressure rises, heart and respiration rates quicken, and adrenaline surges. That may sharpen performance by heightening alertness, boosting energy and speeding up reactions.

Some athletes use hostile emotions to catapult themselves into fiercer play. Toronto Blue Jays pitcher Dave Stieb is one. "It might allow me to throw my next pitch harder or concentrate harder," he says. Others cultivate anger as part of their game preparation. Sports psychologist Bruce Ogilvie of Los Gatos, Calif., recalls that one great football defensive end, now retired, worked himself up for Sunday competition by starting to fantasize on Thursday that his opponent had raped his wife.

Men more than women seem to draw on anger as a tool, but it is decidedly double-edged. In a sport like golf, which depends on fine motor control, rage can

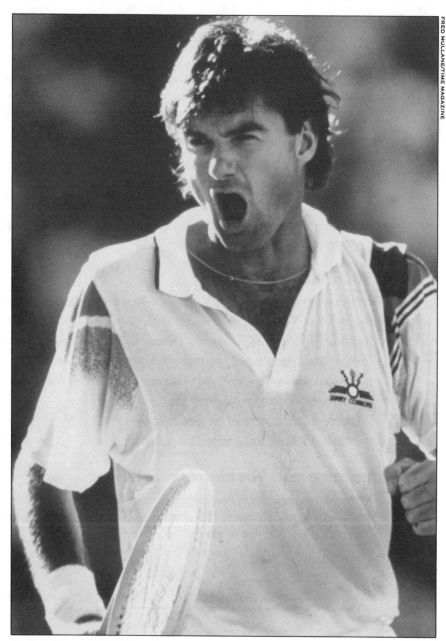

Connors flares up at the Open

spell disaster. In football, anger may help power up a blitzing lineman, but it can impair a quarterback's judgment.

Some experts believe anger is a vastly overrated asset. Says Jerry May of the University of Nevada at Reno: "It leads to inconsistent results. Anger can tighten muscles and increase the risk of injury." May, who chairs the U.S. Olympic Sports Psychology Committee, makes an analogy

with sex. "To respond optimally, you must be excited but relaxed. You need that feeling to excel in sports as well." St. Louis Cardinals pitcher Bob Tewksbury agrees. "The more I try to have fun and laugh about situations, the better I perform," he says. So far this year, Tewksbury has won nine games and lost ten. —**With reporting by Ratu Kamlani/New York and Elizabeth Taylor/Chicago**

AFTER YOU READ

Comprehension Questions

1. According to some sports psychologists, how and why do certain athletes use anger?
2. How does anger affect the body's functions?
3. What positive effects can anger have on athletic performance?
4. What negative effects can anger have on athletic performance?

Discussion and Analysis Questions

1. In your opinion, does anger usually help or hinder an athlete's performance?
2. The writer uses many direct quotations in this article. What is their role? How effective do you think they are?

Group Activity

In groups of four to six, discuss one of the following questions:

a. Should athletes who have extreme displays of anger during competition receive penalties?
b. Do you think society allows famous athletes to behave differently than ordinary citizens?

Individual Work

Attend a sports event or watch one on television. Watch carefully to see if any of the players displays anger. If so, is it verbal or physical? Does it appear to be planned or spontaneous? Report to the class.

3 MS. KIDVID CALLS IT QUITS

BEFORE YOU READ

Preview

A major activist group ends its fight on behalf of children's television.

Getting Started

1. Did you watch television as a child? If so, what were your favorite shows? What effect do you think they had on you?
2. What are some shows children watch today? Have you seen them? What is your opinion of them?

Culture

FCC ['ɛf 'si 'si]   the Federal Communications Commission, a federal agency that governs the operations of radio and television stations

FTC ['ɛf 'ti 'si]   the Federal Trade Commission, a federal agency that governs the buying and selling of merchandise

kidvid ['kɪdvɪd]   television shows for children

Ms. [mɪz]   a title used for women in place of *Miss* or *Mrs.* It does not indicate a woman's marital status. The use of *Ms.* often connotes a belief in women's rights.

Vocabulary

activist ['æktə,vəst]   a person who actively supports a cause or ideal

ceiling ['silɪŋ]   a limit; a restriction

gullible ['gələ,bəl]   easily convinced; easily fooled

(to) hawk [hɔk]   to sell

insidious [ɪn'sɪdiəs]   developing gradually and without notice, but resulting in great harm

knack [næk]   a talent; a special ability

logo ['logo]   a design or symbol used to identify a particular product or company

(to) make a buck ['mek ə 'bək]   to earn money. *Buck* is slang for a dollar.

snowball effect ['snobɔl ə'fɛkt]   an increasing rate of growth; growing influence

Culture and Vocabulary Activities

1. Does your native language or a language that you have studied have words for *Mrs.* and *Miss?* for *Ms.?* Does it have words that indicate the marital status of men?
2. Look at the meaning of *snowball effect* in the Vocabulary list. Can you explain why the effect got this name?

Ms. Kidvid Calls It Quits

Activist Peggy Charren disbands her group, saying its job is done. But is children's TV really any better?

By RICHARD ZOGLIN

FEW PEOPLE IN ANY FIELD HAVE DEMONstrated the power of a single impassioned voice as well as Peggy Charren. As head of Action for Children's Television, the activist group she founded 23 years ago in the living room of her suburban Boston home, Charren has been a tireless fighter for better children's TV. Because of her efforts, commercials aimed at kids are less manipulative than they once were; the hosts of children's shows, for example, can no longer hawk products to gullible young viewers. Even when she failed to bring about change, her constant, nagging presence—and a knack for the pithy quote—kept network programmers mindful that their responsibility to children went beyond simply making a buck from them.

Last week Charren announced that ACT would disband at the end of the year. Her reason: the passage of the 1990 Children's Television Act, which sets advertising limits on children's programming and requires TV stations to air at least some fare that serves the educational needs of kids. "For more than 20 years, ACT has tried to get the public-interest laws that govern broadcasting to apply to children," said Charren. "With the passage of the 1990 Children's Television Act, this goal has been achieved. People who want better TV for kids now have Congress on their side."

Other organizations will carry on the kidvid cause, and Charren herself will not disappear. But the demise of ACT leaves a void and raises a question: For all Charren's efforts, has children's TV got any better? In some ways, as Charren readily admits, it is worse. In the 1970s, partly because of Charren's lobbying, the networks added a host of informational shows for children, from ABC's *Afterschool Specials* to CBS's newsmagazine for kids, *30 Minutes.* During the Reagan years, however, government regulation eased, and most of those shows were canceled or scaled back. Though PBS and cable have added greatly to the diversity of programming for children, network and syndicated fare, which still accounts for the bulk of kids' TV viewing, is largely a ghetto of interchangeable cartoons.

Nor has the commercialization of children's TV abated. In the late '70s, ACT was one of the groups that pressed for an FTC inquiry into whether commercials directed at kids ought to be banned or restricted. But after extensive hearings, the FTC took no action, and commercials are still an inextricable part of the economics of children's television.

The '80s gave rise to an even more insidious phenomenon: cartoon shows based on popular toys. Charren sought to ban programs like *G.I. Joe* and *My Little Pony* as little more than program-length commercials. Most have since expired from low ratings, but a fresh wave may be on the way: several new shows in development feature snack-food characters like Chester Cheetah, who hawks Cheetos. "It's nauseating," says Charren. "Having turned all the toys into programs in the '80s, now they're going to turn all the logos into programs in the '90s."

The Children's Television Act will hardly solve all the problems. Its ceilings on kidvid advertising—12 minutes an hour on weekdays, 10½ minutes on weekends—are higher than what the networks currently run. Still, Charren sees the law as a breakthrough, mainly because it threatens stations with the loss of their license if they don't air some educational fare for kids. Says Charren: "That has much more power behind it than the noise of Peggy Charren and ACT."

That remains to be seen. The law is so vaguely worded that its impact depends almost entirely on how it is enforced. The key question is, What constitutes educational fare? (A documentary on rock music? A "pro-social" cartoon like *Captain Planet*?) Squire Rushnell, the former head of children's programming at ABC and now a producer of kids' shows, is pessimistic. "Until there is an impetus from the White House that would create a snowball effect with the FCC and on down, nothing is going to really happen."

Charren had an impact, not just because of the causes she championed but because of the ones she didn't. Despite her concern for children, she refused to ally herself with conservative groups fighting to purge TV of excessive sex and violence. "I believe that censorship is worse than any kind of junk on TV," she maintained. Her primary thrust was not for quality (that overused term) so much as for diversity: to give parents and kids more choice. Children's TV may still be a long way from her goal, but it is a lot closer than it would have been without her.

—*Reported by William Tynan/New York*

The founder of ACT has fought for diversity in children's TV

AFTER YOU READ

Comprehension Questions

1. What positive effects did Peggy Charren and ACT have on children's television?
2. Why did Charren decide to disband ACT?
3. What happened to the informational children's shows of the 1970s?
4. What kinds of shows is Charren worried about now?
5. Why didn't Charren join conservative groups opposed to sex and violence on television?

Discussion and Analysis Questions

1. What is your opinion of Peggy Charren and ACT?
2. In paragraph three, the writer asks, "For all Charren's efforts, has children's TV got any better?" What do you think his opinion is? Use examples from the article to support your answer.

Group Activity

In groups of three or four, discuss the following questions:

a. Should there be limits on the number, length, and kind of advertisements shown during children's shows?
b. Should there be regulations concerning the content of children's shows?

Individual Work

1. Watch a children's television show. Note how many commercials there are, how long the commercials are, and what products are being sold. Report your findings to the class.
2. Ask several children what their favorite shows are and why. Report what you learn to the class.

4 HOT HOUSE OF CHAMPIONS

BEFORE YOU READ

Preview

California leads the nation in producing championship athletes.

Getting Started

1. Is participation in sports emphasized in your culture?
2. Are there sports facilities in your hometown? If so, are they public or private? What age groups use them?

Culture

Dorado [dor'ɑdo]   a Spanish word meaning "golden land"

Golden State ['goldən ˌstet]   California. Each state has a nickname—for example, New Jersey is the Garden State.

Hall of Fame ['hɔl əv 'fem]   a museum that honors the best players of a particular sport; the group of players who have been selected for this honor

infrastructure ['ɪnfrəˌstrəktʃɚ]   the support system for an organization

upward mobility ['əpwɚd mo'bɪləˌti]   the ability to move to a higher social class

Vocabulary

boom state ['bum 'stet]   a state characterized by rapid expansion or development

crunch [krəntʃ]   a crisis; a time of pressure or tightness

edge [ɛdʒ]   an advantage; a favorable position

(to) hamstring ['hæmstrɪŋ]   to make powerless; to cause to become ineffective

homegrown ['hom'gron]   made or produced locally

hot house ['hɑt ˌhaʊs]   a greenhouse; a place where things (usually plants) are nurtured and grown in a consistently warm environment

mentor ['mɛntor]   a friend and teacher; a trusted counselor

rec center ['rɛk ˌsɛntɚ]   a recreation center; a gathering place that has facilities for sports and other leisure-time activities

(to) vie [vɑɪ]   to compete; to contend

Culture and Vocabulary Activities

1. A large part of what is now the United States was settled by the Spanish. Look at the map at the back of the book. Which states have Spanish names?
2. Can you guess which state belongs to each of the following nicknames?
   a. the Grand Canyon State
   b. the Empire State
   c. the Land of Lincoln
   d. the Sunshine State
   e. the Peach State
   f. the Aloha State

Hot House of Champions

Climate, cash and culture give California athletes a winning edge

By SALLY B. DONNELLY

WHEN O.J. SIMPSON REFLECTS ON his childhood in San Francisco, it is not the house on the hill he remembers most but the football field up the street. Simpson grew up in a low-income housing project, but he lived on the fields and in the gym of the public sports park nearby, honing the skills that would take him to the pro-football Hall of Fame. The well-maintained facility was home to leagues in virtually every sport. "For the gangs of those days, the rec center was the focus of activity," Simpson recalls. "There was always room, and there were always opportunities."

For legions of élite athletes like Simpson, California remains the land of upward mobility. The state has produced legions of homegrown sports stars (sprinter Florence Griffith Joyner, high diver Greg Louganis, slugger Darryl Strawberry) and has polished the skills of legions more who moved to California to train (swimmer Janet Evans, decathlete Jackie Joyner-Kersee, volleyball player Karch Kiraly). From title-winning ice skaters (Debi Thomas) to record-setting long jumpers (Mike Powell), from Olympic champion swimmers (Matt Biondi) to gold-medal skiers (Bill Johnson), California is the American sports machine.

Some of the reasons for the dominance of California athletes are obvious. First is nearly ideal year-round weather; in much of the state, the idea of a rain delay is a foreign concept. "It was just natural that we played sports anywhere, anytime," says Cheryl Miller, a Los Angeles native who developed into one of the best women basketball players of all time and a 1984 Olympic gold medalist. "I certainly wouldn't have been the player I was if I grew up somewhere else."

Then there is the state's unparalleled sports infrastructure. California boasts some of the world's best sporting mentors, among them UCLA volleyball coach Al Scates, Stanford University swimming coach Skip Kenney, ice-skating coach Frank Carroll of the Ice Castles Training Center in Lake Arrowhead and gymnastics coach Don Peters of the Southern California Acrobatic Team in Huntington Beach. A vast network of facilities, leagues, coaches and clubs crisscrosses the state.

Add to those factors the leisure-time culture made possible by the state's past prosperity. California has been a boom state for most of the past 30 years, but with their dedication to work, people brought a devotion to play. "Middle-class values about work have combined with an affluent attitude toward sport and leisure. And unlike in any other state, here it was

Long jumper Mike Powell practices at track in Rancho Cucamonga

possible," says Peters, who has turned out 40 members of the U.S. women's national volleyball team and 13 Olympians since 1963.

More abstract—even spiritual—ingredients also help put California first. "This is still 'Land's End,'" says sociologist Harry Edwards, a professor at the University of California, Berkeley. "California continues to offer a sense of hope and opportunity that other parts of the country do not and cannot." Speed and strength are available anywhere, but in few places are they as prized as in the Golden State. As author Herbert Gold observed, "This Dorado of escapees from elsewhere has produced a new race—the Californian. So much athletic grace is almost unnatural."

But others are now vying with California. Sunbelt states like Texas and Florida already have topflight sports systems at the high school and university levels. Recent research supporting the benefits of high-altitude training will continue to attract athletes to mountainous states like Colorado and Utah.

The state's fiscal crunch could also threaten its sports supremacy. Since 1989, the nation's troubled economy has reached into California with a vengeance. With nearly 8% of its population unemployed and budget deficits hamstringing state and local governments, sports facilities are sure to be hit. Especially threatened are programs for poor urban neighborhoods, where sports are a vital diversion and sometimes a way out.

"The funding is drying up, and the inner cities are going to suffer the most," asserts Ed Fox, publisher of *Track & Field News*. "We've already seen a significant drop-off of athletes from places like Oakland, which used to be rich in young talent." Brooks Johnson, former athletic director at Stanford, says some fundamental economic choices must be made if California is to continue producing sports stars at its usual rate. "It's volleyball or vandalism. Either we invest in our youth, or we are going to ruin whole segments of the population."

For now, California remains the national champion. But if financial problems are not addressed, the state's climate and coaching will mean little when game time comes. The question will not be who wins or loses, but who gets a chance to play. ■

AFTER YOU READ

Comprehension Questions

1. Why has California been able to produce so many excellent athletes?
2. What states are now competing with California in athletics?
3. What may negatively affect the sports programs in California?

Discussion and Analysis Questions

1. Do you think sports are an important part of life? Why or why not?
2. In the next-to-last paragraph, one California athletic director states, "It's volleyball or vandalism." What does he mean? Do you think he is being realistic or too dramatic?

Group Activity

Imagine that you are a member of a group planning a recreation center for your community. Imagine also that your budget is unlimited. In groups of six, decide what facilities should be available at the center. Describe your center to the class.

Individual Work

Write a half-page statement explaining the role that sports play in your life.

5 FRANKLY, IT'S NOT WORTH A DAMN

BEFORE YOU READ

Preview

Scarlett, the sequel to *Gone With the Wind,* rates low in comparison.

Getting Started

1. Have you read *Gone With the Wind* or seen the movie? If so, what did you like/dislike about it? What do you remember about the story and the characters?
2. Do you think book or movie sequels are ever as good as the original? Explain your answer.

Culture

Klansman ['klænzmən]   a member of the Ku Klux Klan, a secret white supremacist group that began in the South after the Civil War

Material Girl [mə'tɪriəl 'gɚl]   a female who is more interested in possessions than in relationships. The phrase comes from a song recorded by the pop star Madonna and is used as a nickname for Madonna herself.

minstrel-show ['mɪnstrəl 'ʃo]   resembling a minstrel show, a performance of African-American songs and jokes put on by white performers wearing black facial makeup. The civil-rights movement of the 1960s ended the popularity of such shows.

Old Sod [old 'sɑd]   Ireland. Large numbers of immigrants to the United States came from Ireland.

political correctness [pə'lɪdɪˌkəl kə'rɛktnəs]   a social and intellectual movement that focuses on the rights of minority groups

War Between the States ['wor bəˌtwin ðə 'stets]   the U.S. Civil War (1861–1865), in which the Confederate States of the South seceded from the Union

Vocabulary

(to) back up ['bæk 'əp]   to support

(to) bear watching ['bɛr 'watʃɪŋ]   to need watching; to deserve observation or monitoring

free-lance ['fri læns]   independent; having no long-term commitment to a single employer

hard act to follow [ˌhɑrd 'ækt tə 'fɑlo]   an outstanding presentation or performance, one that future efforts will be compared to (probably unfavorably)

lost cause ['lɔst 'kɔz]   a project or plan with no hope of success. Many people referred to the Civil War as the Lost Cause for the South.

roots [ruts]   one's origins; one's cultural heritage

(to) spring from ['sprɪŋ 'frəm]   to develop from; to come from

(to) throw in ['θro 'ɪn]   to add

Culture and Vocabulary Activity

The verb *bear* as in *bear watching* is used in several English phrases. Make sentences with the following: *bear remembering, bear doing, bear repeating.*

Frankly, It's Not Worth a Damn

In the sequel to Gone With the Wind, Rhett and Scarlett reunite, she heads for Ireland, has a baby and leaves the reader wondering why tomorrow ever came

By R.Z. SHEPPARD

GONE WITH THE WIND, BOOK AND movie, may be as close to a perpetual-motion machine as the entertainment business is likely to get. Margaret Mitchell's 1936 best seller and David O. Selznick's Technicolor extravaganza have sustained each other for more than 50 years. Readers beget viewers, and countless moviegoers

for Mitchell, who died in 1949 after she was struck by a car on Peachtree Street. She had steadfastly refused to write a sequel, preferring the icy finality of Rhett's, "My dear, I don't give a damn" (Gable threw in the "Frankly"). Yet Scarlett's final aria, "Tomorrow is another day," left the door open.

Where it has remained on rusting hinges until last week. *Scarlett* (Warner Books; 823 pages; $24.95), the carefully

The Continuation of Margaret Mitchell's Gone With the Wind. It was to be the basis for a joint film venture by Universal Pictures and MGM. When the deal soured, Edwards was left with an unpublishable manuscript, since its copyright was linked to the release of the film.

Here is a publishing phenomenon that bears watching: the book conceived, produced and marketed like a theatrical property. The deal came first, the writer came second, and then the publicity machine passed them all. The project was draped in a gauze of secrecy that, now removed, reveals no great surprise. The book is a tease. Rhett and Scarlett remain rascals and opportunists. He continues to profit from the defeat of the Confederacy; she shrewdly expands her Atlanta business interests and plots her slippery husband's recapture. For those who were on Mars last week, the most famous bickerers in literature since Petruchio and Katharina get back together again. Although her contract with Mitchell's estate provides for a sequel to the sequel, Ripley says she will not write it. But tomorrow is another day.

Once again publicity foreplay is more exciting than what goes on between the covers. The managed anticipation that preceded *Scarlett's* publication was

YOU HAVEN'T *AGED* A BIT. BUT IT TOOK A $4.9 MILLION ADVANCE FOR ME TO SAY I LOVE YOU THE SECOND TIME AROUND.

FOR *THAT* KIND OF MONEY, YOU CAN *LEAVE* AND *COME BACK* AGAIN.

S.S./SHOOTING STAR

have been seduced at the bookstore. All this adds up to 28 million copies sold and still counting. The 3¾-hour movie, owned by Ted Turner since he bought the MGM film library in 1985, has become the eternal flame of popular culture. It is a safe bet that somewhere in the world, day and night, Clark Gable's Rhett Butler and Vivien Leigh's Scarlett O'Hara flicker across a screen.

It is no mystery. The newspaper feature writer from Atlanta had an energetic style and a story that mated the War Between the States with the War Between the Sexes. It was a hard act to follow, even

prepared, shrewdly promoted novel by Alexandra Ripley, is finally out in the U.S. and 40 other countries. Warner Books paid $4.9 million for the American rights and has backed up its bet with print orders totaling nearly 1 million copies. The William Morris Agency, representing Ripley and the Margaret Mitchell estate, sold the foreign rights for $5 million more. William Morris' Robert Gottlieb believes film rights could sell in the "high seven figures." *Scarlett* is the first published sequel to *Gone With the Wind,* though it is not the first one written. Fifteen years ago, Leigh's biographer Anne Edwards wrote *Tara:*

enlivened by the intricacies of copyright law and the persistent, though unconfirmed, rumor that Sidney Sheldon had been a candidate before the Mitchell estate settled on Ripley, 57, a native of Charleston, S.C., and author of three solid historical romances. There was also the confirmed rumor that Ripley threatened to quit when told by her editor that the first draft of *Scarlett* was not commercial enough. Finally, there was the author's disarming candor. "Margaret Mitchell is a better writer," Ripley said. "But she's dead."

Despite the helping hand of Jeanne Bernkopf, one of Manhattan's most experienced free-lance editors, *Scarlett* still needs a story stronger than girl chases boy. The excessive number of extended and inconclusive family gatherings recalls Mitchell's comment in *Gone With the Wind:* "When a Southerner took the trouble to pack a trunk and travel 20 miles for a visit, the visit was seldom of shorter duration than a month." *Scarlett* could also use a dose of Joyce Carol Oates' gothic intensity.

It takes the reader only a few pages to realize that Ripley has had to forfeit the novelist's right to create her own characters. Rhett Butler and Scarlett O'Hara sprang from everything Mitchell knew and felt about a time that was still fresh in her region's memory. Ripley's self-imposed handicap shows in the dialogue. Mitchell gave her sardonic hero the best lines, hardbitten and vivid in the Raymond Chandler style. "I've seen eyes like yours above a dueling pistol," he says to Scarlett. "They evoke no ardor in the male breast." Ripley's Rhett is frequently wordy and inelegant: "You're dead weight—unlettered, uncivilized, Catholic, and an exile from every-

thing decent in Atlanta. You could blow up in my face any minute."

More fireworks would be welcome. *Gone With the Wind* played against the most important event in American history, the war that swept away the feudal South and laid the foundations for the modern nation-state. *Scarlett* begins in 1873, during the late Reconstruction. It is not a romantic period. The first half of the novel finds America's original Material Girl, now 30, shopping and socializing in Atlanta, Savannah and Charleston, where she bumps into Rhett Butler, a wealthy scalawag. She still wants what she cannot have: him. He still plays the can't-live-with-'em, can't-live-without-'em game. Following a sailing mishap, they make impetuous love on a beach. He lowers his mizzen and rejects her once again. She soon discovers she is pregnant and goes to Ireland.

Why? Scarlett wants to get in touch with her Irish roots, and Ripley wants to get her away from the freed slaves and budding Klansmen of the Reconstruction South. Pushing a complex reality under the Old Sod solves the problem of having to create

substantial roles for black characters. When hired to write the book, Ripley insisted on a contemporary treatment of race, specifically the avoidance of dialect. Her method is to retain speech patterns while providing elocution lessons.

The result is an Eddie Murphy parody: "What this little girl need, I say, is a hot brick in her bed and a mustard plaster on her chest and old Rebekah rubbing out the chill from her bones, with a milk toddy and a talk with Jesus to finish the cure. I done talk with Jesus while I rub, and He bring you back like I knowed He would. Lord, I tell Him, this ain't no real work like Lazarus, this here is just a little girl feeling poorly."

While *Scarlett* errs on the side of political correctness, *Gone With the Wind*—its minstrel-show dialogue intact—still sells like buttermilk biscuits. The irony does not seem to disturb the Mitchell estate. Ripley, a seasoned professional, apparently understood what she was getting paid so well to do: write the book that was doomed from conception to be endlessly compared to the original. *Scarlett* is the South's new Lost Cause. ■

AFTER YOU READ

Comprehension Questions

1. When was *Gone With the Wind* written? Who was the author?
2. How many copies of the book have been sold?
3. What happened to the first sequel to *Gone With the Wind*?
4. Who wrote *Scarlett*?
5. What criticisms does the writer of this article have about *Scarlett?*

Discussion and Analysis Questions

1. Do you think a sequel to *Gone With the Wind* should have been written? Why or why not?
2. Does the writer say anything positive about *Scarlett*? Do you think this is a balanced review of the book? Support your answer.
3. Would you like to read *Scarlett*? Why or why not?

Group Activity

In groups of three, discuss your favorite books. Explain why the book you selected is your favorite. Is there a sequel to your favorite book? Could there be? Why or why not?

Individual Work

Think about your group's discussion in the Group Activity. What elements make a book memorable (for example, characters, plot, writing style, etc.)? Identify these elements in a half-page paper.

6 REAL-LIFE DAVIDS VS. GOLIATHS

BEFORE YOU READ

Preview

Modern gladiators compete on a popular television show.

Getting Started

1. What is a gladiator? Do you know who the original gladiators were? Share what you know about them.
2. Do you enjoy watching athletic competitions? Why or why not?

Culture

blue-collar ['blu 'kɑlɚ]   working-class. The term *blue-collar* refers to the work clothes often worn by workers in this category. *White-collar* workers are generally managers and office employees who wear dress clothes to work.

bungee cord ['bəndʒi ‚kord]   a long elastic rope used in bungee jumping. In this sport, a person jumps off a high platform while attached to a bungee cord.

campiness ['kæmpi‚nəs]   a state of overacting and obvious exaggeration

David and Goliath ['devəd ænd go'lɑɪəθ]   two Biblical characters. David killed the giant Goliath with a slingshot and later became ruler of Israel.

Elvis ['ɛlvəs]   Elvis Presley, a popular American rock-and-roll star who died in 1977

jock [dʒɑk]   an athlete. The word is slang and sometimes derogatory.

Walter Mitty ['wɔltɚ 'mɪdi]   the main character of James Thurber's short story "The Secret Life of Walter Mitty." Mitty is an ordinary man who fantasizes a variety of roles for himself.

pilot ['pɑɪlət]   a trial show; a single TV program created to determine if a similar TV series will be successful

Rocky ['rɑki]   the main character of the *Rocky* movies, portrayed by Sylvester Stallone. Rocky is a working-class man who becomes a boxing champion.

upscale ['əpskel]   associated with higher socioeconomic levels

wannabe ['wɑnə‚bi]   a person who "wants to be" like someone else or to have what someone else has

Vocabulary

armchair ['ɑrmtʃɛr]   remote; vicariously experiencing something through others' actions

(to) hit the road ['hɪt ðə 'rod]   to leave; to begin a trip

hybrid ['hɑɪbrəd]   a mixture of different varieties of things

tug-of-war [‚təg əv 'wor]   a game in which two teams pull at opposite ends of a rope to determine which team is stronger

Culture and Vocabulary Activities

1. In paragraph two, find a phrase that means *to cheer on.*
2. An *armchair athlete* is mentioned in paragraph five. Add *armchair* to other nouns to describe people who experience other things from afar (for example, *armchair traveler*).

Real-Life Davids vs. Goliaths

When amateurs take on the American Gladiators, it makes for a TV show, toys and—who knows?—maybe even a movie

By JANICE C. SIMPSON

Contenders put their agility and tenacity on the line (here, in the Swingshot) as they struggle to outperform one another and to survive against challenges from gladiators

WE DON'T KNOW ABOUT ELVIS, BUT Walter Mitty lives. You can find him poised atop a 7-ft. platform swinging a big stick at a muscle-bound giant with a name like Laser or Nitro. Or swooping through the air on a bungee cord 15 ft. above the ground, trying to master a kind of aerial basketball. Sound like Mitty's fantasies have got a little outrageous? Obviously, you haven't seen *American Gladiators,* the syndicated television show on which ordinary, albeit very physically fit, people compete in athletic events against a squad of professional male and female athletes and body builders.

A wacky hybrid of sporting event, game show and Roman circus, *American Gladiators* has developed a strong cult following among both adults (who root for the amateur challengers) and kids (who cheer on the cartoonlike gladiators). Ratings have nearly doubled since the show debuted two years ago, making it one of the top five weekly hours currently in syndication. Says gladiator Dan Clark, better known as Nitro: "For the spellers, you've got *Wheel of Fortune;* for the guys who go shopping, you've got *The Price Is Right;* for the athlete, you've got *American Gladiators.*"

This month the gladiators are hitting the road for a 100-city cross-country tour in which local jocks will have a chance to take on the titans. "The main attraction of *Gladiators* is that you can come down and be in the show," says Michael Horton, who portrays the gladiator team leader Gemini. "We give the everyday blue-collar person who's kept himself or herself in shape a chance to show what he or she can do." So far, 25,000 have tried out for the television show, and legions more are expected to compete for a slot in the live contests. Just as on the television show, competitors

will try to win points by completing tasks such as scaling a 30-ft. wall in 60 sec., while the gladiators try to thwart their efforts.

Only the strongest survive. The very first round of the tryouts, in which men are required to do 25 pull-ups, and women eight, in 30 sec., eliminates up to 90% of all challengers. The field is further winnowed by subsequent requirements: running the 40-yd. dash in under 6 sec., winning a one-on-one game of tug-of-war, and playing a round of Powerball, a brutal version of tag.

The Top Ten point winners to emerge from the national tour will meet in Atlantic City next May to compete for $50,000 in prizes. But the major attraction seems to be the chance for the average guy or gal to be more than an armchair athlete. "I've always been pretty athletic, but competition is new to me," says Joseph Mauro, 25, a Brooklyn baker who made it through the trials in New York City. "I'm excited about this because I want to meet those guys in the ring."

Kids love the gladiators because their shows are like real-life video games with living heroes. "I like the way the gladiators make it seem so easy," says Braxton Winston, 8, a Brooklyn fan who watches the

TV show with his brother Brandon, 7. The boys' mother Stella is in favor too. "I like them liking the gladiators," she says. "They're good role models. They don't do drugs, they eat the right foods, they take pride in their bodies. They give the children something to strive for."

Merchandisers are racing to cash in on what is shaping up as the next popculture craze after the Teenage Mutant Ninja Turtles. A Nintendo video-game version of *Gladiators* is being readied for release this month. Topps is planning to come out with trading cards of the 10 gladiators. Newhall Merchandising Concepts, Inc., is whipping up American Gladiators Juniors vitamins for young gladiator wannabes. And Mattel is introducing a line of toys that includes miniature gladiator action figures and small-scale models of events such as the obstacle course, known as the Eliminator. In Hollywood fevered brains are at work, of course, trying to think of a way to develop an animated cartoon series and a movie from all this. "We haven't figured out how to do that yet," confesses Samuel Goldwyn Jr., whose company owns the rights to the show. "Just guys in gladiator suits solving crimes won't do it."

The idea for these latter-day gladiatorial games originated with iron-workers in Erie, Pa. "I wanted a workingman's Olympics," says Dann Carr, a five-time national arm-wrestling champ, who created the contests 20 years ago as entertainment for the annual Erie Iron Workers Union picnic, "but I never thought it would take off like it did."

In 1983 Carr asked his buddy Johnny Ferraro, a one-time Elvis impersonator and a relentless promoter, to help him turn the games into a charity benefit to raise money for a local youth center. When 3,000 people showed up for the event, Ferraro recognized the mass-appeal potential and took the idea to Hollywood. "This was real-life Rocky," he says. It took five years and scores of rejections before the Goldwyn company finally agreed to develop a television series.

The pilot was a disaster. Actors were recruited to play the gladiators and were directed to adopt fake personalities. The costumes were tacky, and the overall style was uncomfortably close to the campiness

A video game and toys are muscling their way into stores

of pro wrestling. "It was a schlock job," says Ferraro. "Out of a diamond, they gave you a piece of coal."

The concept was reworked to focus on the David-and-Goliath aspects of the competition. New gladiators with backgrounds as professional football players and Olympic competitors were hired. The costumes were redesigned for a sportier look. And, most important, both gladiators and contenders were directed to play for real. "It's now pure competition," says Horton, a former lineman with the Philadelphia

Eagles and Boston Patriots who is the only one of the gladiators from the original pilot still with the show. The authenticity of the competition is driven home by the injuries among gladiators as well as contenders. "We've had broken collar bones, torn up knees and neck damage," says Horton.

Critics initially dismissed the show as "crash television." But viewers liked what they saw: good-looking people, fast action and high drama. Nowadays the producers keep the show fresh by regularly adding new games emphasizing agility and tenacity over brute strength. Sports magazine-style features, such as locker-room interviews with the gladiators and taped profiles of the contenders, have been incorporated for a more upscale look.

Behind the scenes, a delighted Ferraro has trimmed his sideburns and got out of the Elvis business so that he can devote all his energy to *Gladiators.* "Danny and me have invented the nuclear bomb," he says. "And now it's exploding." ∎

AFTER YOU READ

Comprehension Questions

1. Who are the gladiators on "American Gladiators"?
2. What must amateur contestants do to qualify to be on the show?
3. Who invented these games? Why?
4. What do audiences like about the show?
5. How has the show affected children's toys and games?

Discussion and Analysis Questions

1. Would you like to watch "American Gladiators"? Would you like to be a contestant? Why or why not?
2. Would a show like "American Gladiators" be popular in other countries? Explain your answer.
3. Do you think "Real-Life Davids vs. Goliaths" is an appropriate title for this article? Why or why not?

Group Activity

In groups of four or five, describe and discuss games of competition that are popular in your culture or a culture that you are familiar with. Tell the class about unique or unusual ones.

Individual Work

Competitive games are part of the history of many cultures. Write a one-page paper explaining why you think this is so.

Fads & Fashions

1 TOOLS WITH INTELLIGENCE

BEFORE YOU READ

Preview

Sophisticated versions of many simple tools are now available.

Getting Started

1. What kinds of tools do you have in your home? Do you do your own household work and repairs? If not, who does this work?
2. Do you ever use any electric tools? Do you ever use any electronic tools? If so, tell the class about them.

Culture

computer age [kəm'pjudɚ ,edʒ]   the period of time since the invention of the computer

crabgrass ['kræbgræs]   a type of creeping grass generally considered to be a weed. Many Americans try to eliminate crabgrass from their lawns.

Iron Age ['aɪɚn 'edʒ]   the period of human history that began around 1000 B.C., when iron was first smelted and used

Phillips-head ['fɪləps ,hɛd]   a kind of screw that has a crossed (+) indentation on its head. A Phillips-head screw can be turned only with a Phillips screwdriver.

Vocabulary

high-tech ['haɪ 'tɛk]   very advanced; having the latest in technology

(to) kick in ['kɪk 'ɪn]   to contribute; to add to an amount

putting green ['pədɪŋ ,grin]   a smooth, grassy area on a golf course that surrounds the hole into which the ball must be played

router ['raʊdɚ]   a machine that cuts narrow channels in wood

(to) run into [,rən 'ɪntu]   to encounter; to come upon

savvy ['sævi]   knowledgeable

too smart for one's own good ['tu 'smart for ,wənz on 'gʊd]   more intelligent than is necessary or appropriate

top-of-the-line [,tap əv ðə 'laɪn]   the best of a category of items; the best of what is available

torque [tork]   a force that turns or twists

(to) turn up ['tɚn 'əp]   to increase; to make larger

(to) zap [zæp]   to transmit or send quickly

Culture and Vocabulary Activities

1. Look at the tools pictured with the article. Can you guess what each one is? Try to give a one-sentence statement of the purpose of each tool (for example, *A lawn mower cuts grass*).
2. Now read the descriptions beside the pictures. Were your one-sentence statements accurate?

Tools with Intelligence

A new wave of do-it-yourself gadgets brings the benefits of the computer age to those who are handy around the house

By PHILIP ELMER-DEWITT

CONSIDER THE SCREWDRIVER. SIMPLE. Utilitarian. And hopelessly out of date. Few people who have put together a cabinet with a cordless screw turner will ever happily go back to driving Phillips-heads by hand. The most advanced power screwdrivers even come with built-in computer systems that sense when a screw is running into resistance and turn up the torque accordingly.

Having infiltrated every nook, cranny and copy machine in the modern office, the electronics revolution is starting to work its magic in the workshop. Tools that date back to the Iron Age can now take advantage of two decades of technological advances, including lightweight rechargeable batteries, custom-made computer chips, liquid-crystal readouts and semiconductor sensors. Result: a new generation of smart tools that promise to bring the benefits of the computer age to those who like to work with their hands.

The first tools to go high-tech were top-of-the-line industrial workhorses: saws with electric brakes that "knew" when to stop; routers with electronic feedback to control their cutting speeds; laser-guided graders that raised and lowered themselves automatically and could make the bumpiest construction sites as level as a putting green.

Now those same technologies—and a few new ones—are finding their way into tools used by weekend do-it-yourselfers, a group swelled by large numbers of electronics-savvy baby boomers. Some of these tools, like the electronic tire gauge, may be too smart for their own good, and will probably go the way of most overpriced gimmicks. But a few, including the digital level and the electromagnetic stud finder, actually make tough jobs easier to do. And if a smart tool can do that, there will always be people smart enough to buy it. ∎

Electronic lawn mower: Black & Decker's $269 Lawnforce mower features a sophisticated, computer-controlled power-monitoring system that senses when the grass is getting too thick and kicks in extra power to keep the cut consistent. Now if the mower only had a way to kill crabgrass...

Electromagnetic stud finder: Where should you drive that nail? Zircon's Studsensor ($14.95), the first popular entry in the smart-tool category, senses minute electromagnetic disturbances caused by changes in density to locate the position of wooden studs and beams behind walls. More than 11 million have been sold.

Tapeless tape measure: By zapping an ultrasound beam where it's pointed, Seiko's Home Contractor ($50) can measure distances from 2 ft. to 30 ft. with 99% accuracy. It can also calculate area and volume and tell how many tiles you will need to cover a floor or ceiling. Sonin makes a $170 version that measures distances up to 250 ft.

Computerized level: Most levels use bubbles trapped in thin glass vials, which tell you only when a surface is level or plumb. But Wedge Innovation's SmartLevel ($50) uses a gravity-seeking electronic sensor to measure those and all angles in between. It's accurate to one-tenth of a degree.

Digital tire gauge: With the low-profile tires found on today's high-performance cars, proper inflation is too critical to rely on standard pencil-type tire gauges. At least that's what the folks at Measurement Specialties say. Their $25 AccuTire uses solid-state electronics to measure tire pressure within $1/2$ lb. per sq. in.

JAMES KEYSER/TIME MAGAZINE

AFTER YOU READ

Comprehension Questions

1. In addition to the tools pictured, what other tools are named in the article? What does each one do?
2. What has caused the recent changes in tools?
3. How would you explain a "smart tool" to someone?

Discussion and Analysis Questions

1. Which of the tools pictured or discussed do you think will become popular? Be sure to look at the prices when you consider your answer.
2. The writer begins this article with words and phrases, not with complete sentences. What does this technique accomplish? Do you like it?
3. In the third paragraph, the writer puts the word *knew* in quotation marks. Why does he do this?

Group Activity

In groups of five or six, select one of the following to do:
   a. "Invent" a household tool or appliance that would make life easier (for example, a robot that makes beds).
   b. Think of ways to improve an existing tool or appliance.

Then choose one person in your group to present your product to the class.

Individual Work

Write a one-paragraph description of your group's product. Be sure to include its name and purpose, as well as reasons why every household should have one.

2 LOOK WHO'S LISTENING TOO

BEFORE YOU READ

Preview

Some women read to their unborn babies; others play classical music. A new device may provide even more stimulation for unborn children.

Getting Started

1. What kinds of things should a pregnant woman do to take care of her unborn child?
2. Do you think that unborn children can be influenced by sounds in the environment? Explain your answer.

Culture

ultrasound test [ˈəltrəˌsɑʊnd ˈtɛst]   a physical examination of a fetus using sound waves. The test checks the development of the fetus.

yuppie [ˈjəpi]   having to do with a "*y*oung *u*rban *p*rofessional"; pertaining to someone whose career and salary allow a comfortable lifestyle in or near a large city. The word is sometimes used in a negative way.

Vocabulary

(to) dub [dəb]   to nickname; to provide another name for

(to) get away [ˈgɛt əˈwe]   to escape; to go to a different place

head start [ˈhɛd ˈstɑrt]   an early beginning that places one ahead of others; an advantage

(to) market [ˈmɑrkɪt]   to sell; to put up for sale

motor-skills [ˈmotɚ ˌskɪlz]   referring to physical, not intellectual, abilities. Eye-hand coordination is one example of a fine motor skill.

norm [nɔrm]   the average score on a test

(to) pick up on [ˈpɪk ˈəp ɔn]   to learn; to understand

risky [ˈrɪski]   dangerous

Culture and Vocabulary Activities

1. As you read the article, make note of the different terms used to refer to a child who is not yet born. Discuss the connotations of each term.
2. As you read, also make note of the different phrases used to describe the belt. Which of the phrases do you think the creator would use in marketing the belt? Why?

Look Who's Listening Too

**Mothers have long tried to stimulate their unborn children.
Now a "cardiac curriculum" does the same thing.**

By EMILY MITCHELL

SOMETIMES NEW PARENTS CAN'T WAIT TO give their children a head start in life. They begin before the baby is even born. In hopes that sounds will somehow influence the fetus in their womb, zealous moms-to-be have attended classical concerts or kept tunes playing constantly at home. Now there is an updated, high-tech version of that technique: a contraption that delivers complex sonic patterns to unborn children, to excite the fetal nervous system and exercise the baby's brain.

The essence of the $250 system is simple: a belt, with two speakers in a pouch, to be fastened around the mother's abdomen. A series of 16 audiotapes, dubbed the "cardiac curriculum," plays an increasingly complicated pattern of heartbeat-like sounds (one mother describes them as African drumbeats) to the unborn infant.

Some users swear by the tapes. Melissa Farrell of Lake Wallenpaupack, Pa., had always thought that reading aloud would affect the unborn. When she became pregnant, the electronic fetal-improvement system seemed a good way to give daughter Muryah Elizabeth "as much of an opportunity as possible and see if it would stimulate her thought process." Though only 21 months old, Muryah plays with toys designed for youngsters twice her age, Farrell says. In Kirkland, Wash., Lisa Altig is using the tapes for a third time. Her two children, Natalie, 3, and Richie, 18 months, were relaxed babies who now "seem to pick up on things fast," says their mom. "They have an energy for learning."

The baby tapes are the creation of Seattle developmental psychologist Brent Logan, founder of Prelearning, Inc., a prenatal-education research institute. "This is not a yuppie toy," says its inventor. "We have barely literate families who are using the tapes." To date, 1,200 children—the oldest of whom is now four—have "listened" to the recordings. Last year 50 of the youngsters, ranging in age from six months to 34 months, were given standardized language, social and motor-skills tests. Their overall score was 25% above the national norm.

Many medical experts, however, remain skeptical. Dr. Thomas Easterling, who teaches obstetrics at the University of Washington, believes the idea of fetal improvement is possible but doubts Logan's claims for his belt. Parents who try the tapes, says Dr. Kathryn Clark, a San Francisco obstetrician and mother of a one-year-old, are "highly motivated people who would have been doing some kind of nurturing anyway." Also, she points out, prenatals do respond to sound and become restless, but "we don't necessarily know that they like it. They might want to get away from it."

Although ultrasound tests are used almost routinely on fetuses, Dr. Curt Bennett, professor of pediatrics at the University of Washington, says there is a possibility that the baby tapes could be harmful. "Sound waves that are too intense might have fetal consequences," he says. The better-baby belt, he adds, "is an invention after all, and it does have the potential to be risky."

Early next year, Engenerics, a research company in Snohomish, Wash., will begin to market a smaller sonic-stimulation device for the baby-in-waiting. Logan has more prenatal improvement products in the works—as yet undisclosed—as well as some postnatal items for the sonic-belt kids. He predicts that one day pregnant women will be wearing devices that offer an even more sophisticated curriculum. What next? Violin lessons for the unborn?
—*With reporting by D. Blake Hallanan/San Francisco*

GARY BENSON

As son Richie looks on, Lisa Altig sends drumbeats within

AFTER YOU READ

Comprehension Questions

1. What is the purpose of the sonic belt? How much does it cost?
2. In the second paragraph, the tapes are called a "cardiac curriculum." Why?
3. What positive results do some users of the belt claim?
4. According to medical experts, what are some possible negative results?

Discussion and Analysis Questions

1. What is your opinion of the sonic belt?
2. All writing has a *tone* (the attitude of the writer toward the topic or toward the reader). What is the tone of this article? In other words, is the writer supportive of the product, critical of it, or neutral? Use examples from the article to support your answer.

Group Activity

In groups of four to six, discuss the following: If it is true that unborn children are affected by their environment, what do you think pregnant women should do? For example, what activities should they participate in? What music should they listen to?

Individual Work

Write a one-paragraph reaction to the sonic belt. Indicate whether you think it is basically harmless, helpful, or harmful. Give reasons to support your opinion.

3 FORGET VERDI, TRY CARMEN

BEFORE YOU READ

Preview

Sometimes games can be excellent learning activities.

Getting Started

1. Have you played any computer games? If so, which ones? Were they designed for entertainment or for learning?
2. Have you ever seen the television show "Where in the World Is Carmen Sandiego?" If so, what did you think about it?

Culture

game show ['gem ʃo]   a television program in which contestants can win prizes, often by correctly answering questions

multimedia [ˌməltɪ'midiə]   involving a variety of *media* or forms of communication. Some examples of media include books, newspapers, television, and radio.

PBS ['pi 'bi 'ɛs]   the *P*ublic *B*roadcasting *S*ystem, a public television channel

public television ['pəblɪk 'tɛlə,vɪʒən]   television channels that are not-for-profit and that carry no advertising. Public television is known for its high-quality programming.

Vocabulary

(to) blossom ['blɑsəm]   to develop; to become

brainstorm ['brenstorm]   a creative and unique idea; something thought of quite suddenly

(to) gush [gəʃ]   to praise enthusiastically

hottest ['hɑdəst]   most popular

light-fingered ['lɑɪt ˌfɪŋgɚd]   talented at stealing

(to) nab [næb]   to catch

software ['sɔftwɛr]   operating programs for computers. The computer equipment itself is called *hardware*.

Culture and Vocabulary Activities

1. As you read, find the Culture and Vocabulary items in the article. Is the meaning of each one clear when you view it in context?
2. In the second paragraph, find synonyms for the verbs *rob* and *travel*.

Forget Verdi, Try Carmen

A software program has blossomed into a multimedia success that kids love—and that makes them love to learn

By DAVID E. THIGPEN

WHAT IN THE WORLD IS CARMEN Sandiego? Answer: one of the hottest and most successful new tools in the childhood-learning market today. What began six years ago as a mystery-style computer program designed to coax youngsters into using reference books has blossomed into a public television game show, a best-selling set of computer video games, a series of adventure books and a collection of jigsaw puzzles, all popular with kids age eight and up. "It's addictive," says Jonathan Pray, 13, an eighth-grade student in Golden, Colo., who has been prodded by Carmen into memorizing all the world's countries and their capitals.

The notion behind the Carmen boom is no more complex than that old favorite, cops and robbers. Carmen is a glamorous ex-spy turned international thief, who leads a gang of wry rogues with names such as Clare d'Loon, Luke Warmwater and Justin Case. The light-fingered mob crisscrosses the globe and skips back and forth in history in search of national trea-

sures to smuggle. Carmen may steal away to ancient China to purloin the Great Wall, hop ahead to medieval England to snitch the Magna Carta, or foray to present-day Uganda to abscond with a rare mountain gorilla.

The object is to find and capture Carmen or one of her gang and restore the stolen treasures. In the version that is airing on PBS, player-detectives decipher a series of verbal clues, then use their knowledge of geography to score points. The top scorer gets to chase Carmen around a large, unmarked map. In the computer version—which is played with the help of books like the *World Almanac* or an atlas—competitors may be shown an image of Socrates and have to know when he lived in order to move to the next clue. Carmen's trail may lead a player from Kigali to Istanbul, from the Golden Gate Bridge to the Cowboy Hall of Fame, or from the Leaning Tower of Pisa to Mayan ruins. Some of the questions are far from easy: players may have to know the currency of a distant country, identify a South Pacific island tribe, or describe the significance of historical figures such as Frank-

ish King Clovis I (A.D. 466–511) in order to nab the thief.

The Carmen phenomenon began in San Rafael, Calif., in the workshop of the Broderbund Software Co. The co-founder of Broderbund, Gary Carlston, had the original brainstorm; software writers then wove geographical and historical facts into the clues. The program eventually grew into five different Carmen titles, selling 2 million copies. In September Golden Books began publishing a line of adventure books, including *Where in Time Is Carmen Sandiego?* and *Where in Europe Is Carmen Sandiego?* This fall the half-hour *Carmen* TV series debuted nationally on PBS.

Educators around the country positively gush about the series. "I'm teaching a lot more geography and problem solving," says Jon Bennett, a fourth-grade teacher in Blusston, Ind., who uses the Carmen computer games in his class. "Kids have a reason for finding out where the Golden Gate Bridge is. They love Carmen, and they don't realize they're learning." But maybe, just maybe, they are.

—Reported by Lois Gilman/New York

A competitor talks to a villain on the PBS version of the find-it game; the Broderbund Software program that led to it all

AFTER YOU READ

Comprehension Questions

1. What is Carmen Sandiego?
2. What is the basic notion behind Carmen Sandiego?
3. Why do educators like the game?
4. Why do children like the game?

Discussion and Analysis Questions

1. In the first paragraph, one boy says, "It's addictive." What does he mean?
2. Do you think you would enjoy using the Carmen Sandiego software? Why or why not?
3. In the third paragraph, the writer mentions numerous locations. What is his purpose in mentioning so many?

Group Activity

Divide the class into two groups (or four if the class is large). Each group should develop lists of ten international capitals and ten famous monuments (for example, the Eiffel Tower). Then the two groups take turns asking each other to name the country associated with each capital and monument. The group with the most correct answers "finds" Carmen Sandiego.

Individual Work

Develop a list of ten questions about the history and geography of your home country or a country that you are interested in. Be prepared to ask the class your questions.

4 IS THIS BIRD A TURKEY?

BEFORE YOU READ

Preview

In order to make money, some Americans are becoming ostrich farmers.

Getting Started

1. What is the most unusual animal you can think of that people raise for a profit?
2. Have you ever heard of people raising ostriches? What products do you think can be made from an ostrich?
3. Skim the first and last paragraphs of this article. What do you think the writer's opinion of ostrich farming is?

Culture

haute cuisine [ˌhot kwɪˈzin]   gourmet food

pyramid scheme [ˈpɪrəmɪd ˌskim]   an illegal business plan in which a few individuals profit at the expense of many others

Vocabulary

aficionado [əˌfɪʃɪəˈnɑdo]   a fan; a follower

(to) bag [bæg]   to put away (as if in a bag); to forget about

fad [fæd]   a very popular, but short-lived practice

(to) get one's head out of the sand [ˌɡɛt wənz ˈhɛd ɑut əv ðe ˈsænd]   to start paying attention to one's surrounding. This phrase refers to the common, but false, belief that ostriches hide their heads in the sand when frightened.

kidding [ˈkɪdɪŋ]   joking

landing [ˈlændɪŋ]   ending (to a flight)

scam [skæm]   a swindle; a deceptive act or plan

(to) spawn [spɔn]   to produce, especially in large quantity

(to) stick one's head in the sand [ˌstɪk wənz ˈhɛd ɪn ðə ˈsænd]   to ignore or hide from obvious signs of danger. *Bury* or *hide* may be substituted for *stick* in this expression.

(to) take off [ˈtek ˈɔf]   (for something) to start selling well

turkey [ˈtɚki]   a failure; a sham

white-hot [ˈwɑɪt hɑt]   very active; very intense

Culture and Vocabulary Activities

1. Which two words on the Culture and Vocabulary lists are borrowed from other languages? What languages are they from? What has happened to the pronunciation of these words?
2. What vowel sound appears most often in the Vocabulary words? Can you name another language in which this sound exists? Give some examples of words that have this sound.
3. Find the pair of antonyms on the Vocabulary list.

Is This Bird a TURKEY?

A market in, yes, ostriches has taken off. But investors may be in for a hard landing.

By **MICHAEL RILEY** ATLANTA

PSSST! WANT TO GET RICH QUICK? STOP buying gold bullion. Forget the stock market. Bag the racehorses. Just get your head out of the sand and buy some ostriches.

That's right, ostriches. Lured by the promise of doubling or even tripling their investment, Americans from Maine to California are flocking to buy the big birds, convinced that they're on to the hottest thing since the chinchilla craze of the 1950s. Suzanne Shingler, part owner of Fowler Farms near Albany, Ga., has discovered the magic of ostrich farming, and the gaze she directs at the large ivory-colored egg in her hands has all the gleam of a gold-rush prospector's. "In a few months," chirps Shingler, "this precious baby will be worth $6,000." It will take $20,000 this year alone for her to care for 20 ostriches and their offspring, but the farm stands to rake in between $300,000 and $500,000 selling the chicks to other investors.

Such success stories have created a white-hot market for ostriches, with some investors plopping down $100,000 or more to start farms. Today nearly 20,000 ostriches grace about 2,000 U.S. farms, up from a handful of farms a decade ago. Imports of live chicks have soared 500% in the past five years. Little wonder. A fertilized ostrich egg fetches $1,500, and a pair of breeding adults goes for around $40,000. With female ostriches laying upwards of 80 eggs a year, it takes just basic math to calculate astronomical returns.

Construction magnate Daisuke Mizutani in 1989 bought half the Bordelon Breeders farm in Texas, one of the largest in the U.S., and Louisiana's Pacesetter Ostrich Farm will be the first to go public this month. Even cautious bureaucrats are falling in love with this ungainly bird. The Texas department of agriculture, which recently hired a full-time ostrich expert, has already made more than $1.2 million in low-interest loans to farmers in the booming industry, and projects that ostrich farming will pump nearly 5,000 jobs and $170 million into the state's economy by the year 2000. Georgia's legislature plans to consider a $150,000 grant to the University of Georgia to find ways to increase the hatching rate (now 30%) and reduce chick mortality. "It's beyond the fad stage," claims Kenny Page, avian-medicine professor at the university. "It is where the chicken industry was 30 years ago."

Unlike its avian peers, the ostrich spawns a variety of luxury products. Start with the meat, which aficionados liken in taste to beef tenderloin. At about $20 per lb., there's a wealth of cuts to be had from the average 400-lb. bird. Ostrich meat is healthful as well: half the calories of beef, one-seventh the fat and considerably less cholesterol, and it even bests chicken and turkey in those categories. Huntington's, a posh eatery in Dallas' Galleria, serves, among other ostrich specialties, a blackened fillet, an ostrich tortilla pizza and a hibiscus-smoked ostrich salad. "Our customers thought we were kidding at first. Ostrich?" says restaurant manager Monika Cundiff. "But then they became fascinated by it." One out of four diners orders the lean meat. Even if ostriches don't become haute cuisine, investors are hoping the big birds achieve greater fame than a spot on *Sesame Street*. Ostrich eyelashes are used as paintbrush bristles, feathers for dusting and hats and coats, and the thick, tough hide is prized for everything from cowboy boots to sofas.

Despite all these potential products, ostrich farming, for the time being, still smells a little bit more like an investment scam than the producer of a legitimate cash crop. "In my opinion, it's a pyramid scheme," warns scientist Gary Davis of North Carolina State University in Raleigh. Ostriches remain largely the obsession of a rarefied breeders' market, where demand far outstrips supply and pushes prices through the barn roof. All the chicks hatched in the U.S. this year have been sold to investors hoping to cash in on the craze, but the good times are unlikely to last. As the number of ostriches soars, the high-flying prices will drop, unless a huge market for food and other products opens up. But that has yet to happen. Furthermore, observes Texas rancher Randy Reaves, who since 1988 has traded in most of his cattle for the more lucrative big birds, "people don't understand that they can't throw some of these birds in their backyard and expect to make $1 million and drive a Rolls-Royce. It's not that simple." If future investors choose to stick their heads in the sand, the ostrich may become an apt metaphor. —*Reported by Allan Holmes/Albany and Richard Woodbury/Dallas*

AFTER YOU READ

Comprehension Questions

1. What is the average cost of a fertilized ostrich egg? of a pair of adult ostriches?
2. What products does an ostrich yield? Compare the information in the article with your answer to question 2 in the Getting Started section. Did you guess correctly?
3. What may happen to ostrich prices if the number of ostriches grows?

Discussion and Analysis Questions

1. What is your opinion of ostrich farming? Is it a serious business or just a fad? What do you think its future will be?
2. Would you eat ostrich meat? Why or why not?
3. Explain the information given in the brief description of the article. Then recall your answer to question 3 in the Getting Started section. Do your two answers agree?
4. The writer includes the names of many people in this article. What is the advantage of including names?

Group Activity

In groups of four to six, make up two lists: one of the group members' favorite foods and one of foods that one or more people in the group would never eat. Does any item appear on both lists? Can you make any generalizations about either list? Compare your lists with those of the other groups.

Individual Work

Reread the article. Make a list of all the words and phrases associated with birds. Compare your list with those of your classmates. Be prepared to discuss the meanings of the words and phrases on your list.

5 A THIRST FOR COMPETITION

BEFORE YOU READ

Preview

In recent years, Americans have become very concerned with physical fitness. As a result, a billion-dollar industry has developed around athletic shoes, exercise clothing, fitness equipment, and other items associated with working out.

Getting Started

1. Have you ever heard of a sports drink? If so, what brand have you heard of? Why do you think people drink sports drinks?
2. Have you ever tasted a sports drink? If so, did you like its taste? Do you think it helped you?
3. Read the title of the photo section and the captions under the photos. Discuss how this information relates to the title of the article.

Culture

fast break ['fæst 'brek] a basketball maneuver in which players move quickly and surprise the opponents

jock [dʒɑk] an athlete. The word is slang and sometimes derogatory.

MVP ['ɛm 'vi 'pi] *m*ost *v*aluable *p*layer. To be named the most valuable player of a game is an honor.

N.B.A. ['ɛn 'bi 'e] the National Basketball Association

N.F.L. ['ɛn 'ɛf 'ɛl] the National Football League

Vocabulary

(to) brace [bres] to get ready; to prepare oneself

contender [kən'tɛndɚ] a competitor; one who participates in a contest or fight

fray [fre] a fight

gulpability [ˌɡəlpə'bɪlɪti] the ability to be drunk in large swallows (gulps). This is an invented word.

(to) knock [nɑk] to criticize

(to) make a (big) splash [ˌmek ə (bɪg) 'splæʃ] to attract attention; to have a big impact

(to) muscle in ['məsəl ˌɪn] to intrude; to forcefully make a place for oneself

power play ['pɑuɚ 'ple] a situation in which two competing groups or individuals try to defeat each other in order to gain power

qualified ['kwɑləˌfaɪd] limited; modified

worked up [wɚkt 'əp] excited; anxious; worried

Culture and Vocabulary Activities

1. Examine the Culture and Vocabulary lists. Which items are new to you? Which are associated with sports?
2. As you read the article, keep a list of words and phrases associated with sports.

A Thirst for Competition

Gatorade, the long-reigning champ of the billion-dollar sports-drink field, braces for a big-league challenge from Coke, Pepsi and other contenders

By LEON JAROFF

IN A FOUR-CITY FAST BREAK, THE COCA-COLA Co. has made the first move, flooding thousands of stores in the Southern U.S. with cans and bottles, displays and posters, backed by a TV ad campaign, to introduce its newest product, PowerAde. It's a drink made for athletes and, in the words of a Coke spokesman, "anyone who works up a sweat." At PepsiCo, Inc., plans are well under way for a summer rollout of its new drink for jocks and those who aspire to be: All Sport. Other large companies are entering the fray with similar products—Dr Pepper/Seven-Up with a drink called Nautilus, and A&W Brands, Inc., with a player yet to be named.

What they're all worked up about is the U.S. sports-drink market, a billion-dollar retail segment that has been growing about 10% annually. It will take world-class contenders like these to unseat the defending champion, Quaker Oats Co.'s Gatorade, which accounts for some 90% of nationwide sales. Like Kleenex in the tissue market and Xerox among copiers, Gatorade has become the generic word for sports drinks.

Simply defined, sports drinks replenish the fluid, minerals and energy lost during exercise. Long familiar to athletes, Gatorade has become highly visible to sports fans, in the form of the ubiquitous large green-and-orange vats of the drink in dugouts or near team benches at major league events. Hardly a postgame interview passes without a shot of the MVP taking a sip from a paper cup labeled "Gatorade," which is, after all, the official sports drink of major league baseball, the N.F.L., the N.B.A. and the National Hockey League. "Gatorade defines the category," says Jesse Meyers, publisher of *Beverage Digest,* an industry trade publication based in Old Greenwich, Conn. "There is not a beverage category in any country in the world that is so dominated by one producer."

With that kind of clout, Gatorade executives seem unperturbed by the new entries in their field. They note that 50 to 60 brands of competing sports drinks have been introduced—and have disappeared—during the past decade. "Competition has been great for us," says Peggy Dyer, Gatorade's vice president of marketing. "Competition makes us better."

Still, Gatorade cannot afford to be complacent; it will be hard-pressed to match the distribution reach of Coke and Pepsi. Besides its grocery- and convenience-store business, for example, Coke has 350,000 vending-machine and fountain outlets in the U.S. alone. And the vending machines, the company says, are perfect "sampling points" for customers to try a new product like PowerAde.

Ironically, Gatorade may be responsible for spawning one of its new heavyweight competitors. With an eye on expansion, especially overseas, Gatorade approached Coca-Cola last January about using Coke's distribution system. But the talks broke off in April, and the next thing Gatorade knew, Coke had pledged a "major commitment" to sports drinks.

PowerAde makes only oblique reference to its primary target, Gatorade, in its commercials. But Pepsi will take the champ head on. Touting "gulpability" (achieved by using wide-necked bottles), All Sport ads will knock Gatorade by stressing that, in the words of a Pepsi spokesman, "there is no reason a sports drink can't taste good." The commercials will also contrast 1960s black-and-white sports scenes with contemporary color action to emphasize that "our drink was formulated a generation after theirs."

A University of Florida nephrologist, Dr. Robert Cade, concocted Gatorade in 1965 to sustain the school's football team. The Stokely-Van Camp Co. acquired the formula and turned the drink into a moneymaker, before being acquired by Quaker in 1983. "Though it may have been developed a long time ago," says Gatorade's Dyer, "nobody has been able to come up with a way that will improve how the product works."

Competitors disagree. Still, while percentages of ingredients vary from brand to brand, all the drinks contain water (for fluid replacement), salt and potassium (to maintain the body's fluid-electrolyte balance), and sugar (for quick energy and flavor). Do they actually work? Manhattan internist Peter Bruno, the team doctor for basketball's New York Knicks, gives a qualified yes. "If you work out more than an hour, you must replace both water and sodium," says Bruno. "But when you exercise for less than an hour, you only need to replace the water." Most medical experts agree that for those who exercise moderately, plain water will do until the next meal, which usually replenishes the essential carbohydrates and minerals.

Even if the Cokes, Pepsis and others make marketing inroads into the champ's lead, as some analysts believe they will, you have to wonder if they will ever attain the mystical status Gatorade reached in 1987, when football's New York Giants began dousing coach Bill Parcells with a conspicuously labeled vat of the stuff near the end of every winning game. Since then, teams at many levels have adopted that ceremony, helping Gatorade make an ever bigger splash in the market. —*With reporting by Susanne Washburn/New York*

HERE COMES THE POWER PLAY

GATORADE: Still the generic word for sports drink

ALL SPORT: Pepsi's "gulpable" workout beverage

POWERADE: Coke muscles in with its own tonic

AFTER YOU READ

Comprehension Questions

1. Who invented Gatorade? When and why was it invented?
2. What ingredients are used to make Gatorade? What do these ingredients do?
3. What percentage of the U.S. sports-drink market does Gatorade have? Do Gatorade officials seem worried about new competition from Pepsi and Coke? Why or why not?
4. What advertising strategies will Pepsi and Coke use against Gatorade?
5. Are sports drinks useful for everyone? Why or why not?

Discussion and Analysis Questions

1. Do you think the new sports drinks from Pepsi and Coke will hurt the sales of Gatorade? Support your answer.
2. The seventh paragraph quotes All Sport advertisements that say "there is no reason a sports drink can't taste good" and "our drink was formulated a generation after theirs." What do these statements imply about Gatorade? Do you think such statements in advertising are fair? Why or why not?
3. Look at the list of sports terms you made for Culture and Vocabulary Activity 2. Why do you think the writer used so many sports terms? Is there a possible disadvantage in using so many sports terms?
4. The writer suggests that the competition between Gatorade, All Sport, and PowerAde is like the battle between opposing teams. Is this an accurate comparison? Explain your answer.

Group Activity

In groups of five or six, invent your own sports drink to market. What will you call it? What color will it be? What shape will the bottle have? Should the bottle be glass or plastic? What will the label look like? Once your group has decided these details, write a thirty-second television advertisement for your product. Choose someone from your group to present the ad to the class.

Individual Work

Write a brief reaction to the advertisements presented for the Group Activity. Which ad was the most effective? Why? You may wish to use the following form for your response: "I liked the _____ ad because _____ . In addition, it _____ ."

6 CALIFORNIA DREAMIN'

BEFORE YOU READ

Preview

The state of California is often the source of new styles and trends in the United States.

Getting Started

1. When you think of California, what do you think of?
2. What is your favorite make (brand) of car? What do you like about it?
3. Look at the photos. What is your reaction to these cars?

Culture

Afro ['æfro]   referring to someone of African-American heritage

Anglo ['æŋglo]   referring to a white person who is not Latino

bean counter ['bin ˌkɑʊntɚ]   a statistician; an accountant

Latino [læ'tino]   referring to someone of Spanish-speaking heritage

melting pot ['mɛltɪŋ ˌpɑt]   a place where different types of people mix. Many view the United States as a melting pot.

think tank ['θɪŋk tæŋk]   a group organized to develop ideas or to solve problems. In the United States, think tanks often focus on political issues.

Vocabulary

canonical [kə'nɑnəkəl]   following a general rule

cliché [kli'ʃe]   an overused phrase or statement

flivver ['flɪvɚ]   a small and inexpensive car

nips and tucks ['nɪps ən 'təks]   small changes

nugget ['nəgət]   a valuable piece or lump of something

proving ground ['pruvɪŋ ˌgrɑʊnd]   a place where new products, such as automobiles, are tested

slam-bang ['slæm bæŋ]   wild; exciting

stuffy ['stəfi]   conservative; boring; stifling

wellspring ['wɛlsprɪŋ]   a never-ending source

Culture and Vocabulary Activities

1. Several items on the lists above have negative *connotations* (meanings that are additional to the dictionary definition). Find these words and phrases.
2. Look at the two-word terms on the lists. (You may include *slam-bang* and *wellspring* in this group.) Make a generalization about where the stress (accent) goes in such phrases.

California Dreamin'

Ideas for the world's autos now come from design studios clustered around (where else?) trendsetting L.A.

By KURT ANDERSEN

CLICHÉS MAY BE CLICHÉS, BUT THEY are usually also true. The great nuggets of conventional wisdom about Southern California—the easy embrace of novelty, an approach to creative endeavors largely unencumbered by tradition, a profound attachment to cars—are not only apt; they have converged to form an extraordinary new center for automobile design.

Most cars are still dreamed up in Detroit and Turin, Wolfsburg and Tokyo. But virtually all the world's major automobile companies—18 to date—have established design departments within an hour or two of downtown Los Angeles. The Japanese were first. Then came special think tanks run by America's Big Three. So far, an estimated two dozen production-model cars have been shaped by the new California design colony, including, of course, the delicious, almost perfect, and instantly successful Miata, designed by four young Americans (and a Japanese) working for Mazda in Orange County. Now the influx has accelerated, and even the Germans have deigned to establish Southern California design studios—Mercedes last year, Audi last spring and, just last month, BMW.

Pleasant weather is only part of the attraction. There is a collective sense that to design for Americans requires understanding them viscerally, and a belief that Los Angeles is not just the wellspring of car culture but as close to Ur-America as any one place gets. More prosaically, Southern California represents the biggest automobile showroom anywhere: every year 3% of all new cars on the planet are registered in California, and most

of those in Southern California. If you're to succeed in the U.S., you must sell in Southern California. And to do that, observes Peter Fischer, a marketing vice president at Volkswagen, "you have to see, feel, smell what these customers want." Says Mark Jordan, who was Mazda's chief designer on the Miata: "If you can excite the people in California, the rest of the country will take care of itself." The world's car companies have been drawn to L.A. by the same giddy promise—a fresh start, anything goes—that has always pulled in immigrants. Detroit has been creating cars its own way for 75 years. In Europe and Japan the conventional wisdoms can be confining, even stultifying. "We selected a place like San Diego for our design studio," says Gerald Hirshberg, Nissan's chief U.S. designer, "because it had no track record, no history. It feels like almost anything is possible out here."

But the rationale is not simply the need to meet the demands of the American car market or harness the spirit of innovation. From the homogeneous van-

tage points of Japan and Germany, the exuberant free thinking seems to be a function of L.A.'s slam-bang Anglo-Afro-Latino-Asian ethnic mix—cultural democracy by default. "The Southern California area is like a melting pot—there are so many different races," says Mitsubishi vice present Satoru Tsujimoto. "From those different backgrounds, there are many different values. So there are many different designs." For companies acutely conscious of their need to sell cars all over the world to people of wildly disparate sensibilities and experiences, California seems like an unsurpassed multicultural proving ground.

The intellectual epicenter of this design cluster, which runs from Ventura down to San Diego, is the Art Center College of Design in Pasadena. Among car designers, no institution is more highly regarded. The Art Center exists in cozy symbiosis with the industry: working designers, such as Geza Loczi, who heads Volvo's studio in Camarillo, train students like Michael Ma, 26, a Vietnamese refugee

Fantasy flivvers: Mercedes' Michael Ma with his Tatanka, inspired by the American buffalo

> **How ideas take shape: An automotive designer creates a sketch for a new car design. Next, workers take his vision and transform it into a full-size clay model. Finally, technicians get measurements from a dummy version for use on the real thing.**

A reinterpretation of the sports car: the instantly popular Miata

who graduated this August and went directly to work for the Mercedes studio in Irvine. Ten of the 18 Southern California auto-design studios are run by Art Center alumni, and their staffs are dominated by fellow graduates, including Mazda's Mark Jordan.

The studios are small, usually consisting of 10 to 20 designers, most of them American (10 of 13 at Mazda, all 20 at Mitsubishi). Because their headquarters are thousands of miles away, the designers stationed in California exist in splendid—and creatively productive—isolation, relatively free from the kill-joy scrutiny of bean counters, marketing drones and engineers. "After a year in the U.S.," says Gerhard Steinle, chief of the Mercedes studio, "I see how important it is to be away from the factory."

The California design shops do seem blessedly free of the factory-like organization that prevails in Detroit and elsewhere. Designer Alberto Palma, 27, interned at General Motors in Detroit before coming to work for Toyota in Newport Beach. He found the GM experience "kind of stuffy. Everyone was divided into units for different aspects of design. Here we can sit down and talk about a project from ground up." Jack Stavana, Mazda's director of product planning and research who masterminded the marketing of the Miata, agrees. "Frankly," says Stavana, who worked for Chrysler for five years, "I needed to get out of Detroit, because there weren't fresh ideas there. We start with a fresh sheet of paper."

It is the Japanese companies that seem to take their Californians most seriously. Of the two dozen or so cars that have been largely or entirely designed in California over the past 15 years, most have been Japanese, notably the Miata, Honda's sporty CRX and Toyota's Celica. Mercedes, which set up shop only last October, plans to have a California prototype by the end

of next year. The other Europeans are proceeding more timidly. The sort of California innovations Audi expects in the near term, for instance, are tilt-down steering wheels and dashboard coffee-cup holders.

The American automakers opened their studios in 1983 and 1984, and Chrysler's brand new LH model—an intriguing would-be car with the wheels 10 in. farther back than standard to create more legroom and a stabler ride—is mostly a California creative product. But, in general, Detroit has been typically cautious in handing design responsibilities to the Californians. Ford's chief designer, Jack Telnack, allows that the recent Thunderbird and Escort models have only been "influenced" by notions from their people on the coast.

The Miata, with its convertible top and intense colors, is the only product of the Los Angeles studios that exudes a distinct regional pizazz—the first truly postmodern automobile, both a reinterpretation of and an improvement upon nostalgically recalled classic sports cars. Yet despite all the drafting tables suddenly clustered together, the Miata does not signal the emergence of a canonical L.A. style.

The Californians do seem inclined (or ordered) to develop cars of a certain general type—determinedly jaunty, self-consciously American. Having proved themselves unsurpassed at manufacturing and mass-marketing reliable, well-engineered

cars, the Japanese seem to have descended on Los Angeles specifically to master the improbable art of creating cars that thrill. The most successful California designs have been tough-but-smart, fun-but-practical Middle American vehicles (Toyota's Previa minivan, Nissan's Pathfinder, Isuzu's Trooper and Amigo) or else sports cars that temper the species' inherent sexiness with a certain grownup decorousness (the Celica, the Miata).

THE MOST INTERESTING, THOUGHTFULLY conceived new cars coming out of Southern California may, in the end, owe less to local free-spiritedness than to the simple wisdom of hiring a few talented people and allowing them to work, leaving their problem-solving sessions and reveries undisturbed by the anxious buzz of corporate headquarters.

Many of their fetching schemes—Toyota's inflatable car; Isuzu's moon-unit Expresso minivan; Michael Ma's Tatanka, a sort of 21st century Beetle—will prove too impractical, too expensive, too weird. But the great achievement of the new California design colony is that such cars are being imagined and prototypes built. After decades of nothing but uninspired nips and tucks, of corporate blandness, of timid styling, automobile designers are being allowed to design again. —*With reporting by Joe Sczensy/Detroit and Matt Rothman/Los Angeles*

AFTER YOU READ

Comprehension Questions

1. How many auto companies have opened offices in or near Los Angeles?
2. What are the advantages to having an office in L.A.?
3. What is the most highly respected design institute?
4. Which auto companies have used the work of their California designers the most?
5. According to the writer, what is the main reason for the success of the California design studios?

Discussion and Analysis Questions

1. Do you agree with the writer that the key to creative success is to be able to work undisturbed? Why or why not?
2. What might be a disadvantage in working so far from the central office of a company?
3. The fourth paragraph refers to California as an "unsurpassed multicultural proving ground." What does this phrase mean? Does the paragraph explain this idea? Given what you know about the United States and about California, is this description accurate?
4. Read the last sentence of the article. What negative words are used to describe the auto designs of past years? How do these negative terms help support the main idea of the article? Try to state the main idea of the article.

Group Activity

In groups of four or five, decide on ten ideal features of a car. Be specific. For example, instead of saying *safety,* you could say *ability to stop quickly in rain.* Then compare your group's list with those of the other groups. Which features do they have in common? Which features are unique?

Individual Work

Imagine that you need to create something (for example, draw a picture, compose a song, write an essay, or solve a problem). What is the ideal setting in which you can be creative? Write a half-page description of that setting. Be as specific as you can.

7 THE STRANGE BURDEN OF A NAME

BEFORE YOU READ

Preview

Names often reveal a lot about people's personalities and characters and the cultures in which they live.

Getting Started

In American culture, the family name (or last name) comes after the first and middle names (for example, Mary Kathleen Doyle). What is the order of names in your culture? Give examples.

Culture

bumper sticker ['bəmpɚ ˌstɪkɚ]   a small sign (often attached to a car's bumper) with a political, religious, or personal saying or message printed on it. The message may be serious or humorous.

evil eye ['ivəl 'aɪ]   a look or an eye believed to bring bad luck

feminism ['fɛməˌnɪzəm]   the movement that focuses on the social, political, and economic equality of the sexes

inauguration [ɪnˌɔg(j)ə'reʃən]   the ceremony that marks the beginning of a presidential term of office. Inauguration Day in the United States is January 20 following the national election that is held every four years.

preppie ['prɛpi]   a student at a private secondary school, often a boarding school; a person with the characteristics of a prep (preparatory) school student

Puritan ['pjɚəˌtən]   a member of the Protestant group that came to New England (the northeastern part of the United States) in the 17th century. Puritans led a very severe life.

Vocabulary

aura ['ɔrə]   an atmosphere; a distinctive surrounding air

(The) coast is clear. [ðə 'kost ɪz ˌklɪr]   There is no visible danger.

crack [kræk]   a joke; a sarcastic remark

down the road ['daʊn ðə ˌrod]   in the future; at a later time or date

(to) sail along ['sel ə'lɔŋ]   to move quickly and easily

solidarity [ˌsɑlə'dɛrəti]   oneness; unity; mutual support

stuck with ['stək 'wɪθ]   burdened with someone or something

(to) ward off ['word 'ɔf]   to protect from; to keep away

wilds [waɪldz]   dangerous or untamed areas

Culture and Vocabulary Activities

1. Does your culture have the concept of the "evil eye"? If so, do many people hold the belief?
2. Create several sentences for each of the following phrases: *down the road, to sail along,* and *to ward off.*

The Strange
Burden of a Name

A NAME IS SOMETIMES A RIDICULOUS FATE. FOR EXAMPLE, A MAN afflicted with the name of Kill Sin Pimple lived in Sussex, in 1609. In the spring of that year, the record shows, Kill Sin served on a jury with his Puritan neighbors, including Fly Debate Roberts, More Fruit Fowler, God Reward Smart, Be Faithful Joiner and Fight the Good Fight of Faith White. Poor men. At birth, their parents had turned them into religious bumper stickers.

Names may carry strange freights—perverse jokes, weird energies of inflicted embarrassment. Another 17th century Puritan child was condemned to bear the name of Flie Fornication Andrewes. Of course, it is also possible that Andrewes sailed along, calling himself by a jaunty, executive "F.F. Andrewes." Even the most humiliating name can sometimes be painted over or escaped altogether. Initials are invaluable: H.R. (Bob) Haldeman, of the Nixon White House, deftly suppressed Harry Robbins: "Harry Haldeman" might not have worked for him.

Names have an intricate life of their own. Where married women and power are concerned, the issue becomes poignant. The official elongation of the name of Hillary Rodham Clinton suggests some of the effects achieved when customs of naming drift into the dangerous atmospheres of politics and feminism.

The history of "Hillary Rodham Clinton" goes back in time, like a novel: at birth, Bill Clinton was William Jefferson Blythe, his father being a young salesman named William Jefferson Blythe 3rd, who died in a car accident before Bill was born. In a story now familiar, the 15-year-old future President legally changed his name to Bill Clinton in order to affirm family solidarity with his mother and stepfather, Roger Clinton. In 1975, when Bill Clinton got married, his new wife chose to keep the name Hillary Rodham. But five years later, Clinton was defeated in a run for re-election as Arkansas Governor, at which point, to assert a more conventional family image, Hillary Rodham started calling herself Hillary Clinton. But she was not exactly taking Bill's name either, since "Clinton" had not originally been Bill's. Bill was once removed from his own birth name, so now Hillary was, in a sense, twice removed.

A name may announce something—or conceal something. In some societies, the Arab or Chinese, for example, a beautiful child may be called by a depreciating name—"Dog," "Stupid," "Ugly," say—in order to ward off the evil eye. Hillary Rodham knew that in some parts of the political wilds, she attracted the evil eye to the 1992 Democratic ticket. So during her demure, cookie-baker phase, she was emphatically "Hillary Clinton," mute, nodding adorer and helpmate of Bill. She half-concealed herself in "Hillary Clinton" until the coast was clear. With the Inauguration, the formal, formidable triple name has lumbered into place like a convoy of armored cars: Hillary Rodham Clinton.

The name problem for married women is a clumsy mess. Married women have four or more choices. 1) Keep the last name they were given at birth. 2) Take the husband's last name. 3) Use three names, as in Hillary Rodham Clinton; or, as women did in the '70s, join the wife's birth name and the husband's birth name with a hyphen—a practice that in the third generation down the road would produce geometrically expanded multiple-hyphenated nightmares. 4) Use the unmarried name in most matters professional, and use the husband's name in at least some matters personal and domestic. Most men, if they were to wake up one morning and find themselves transformed into married women, would (rather huffily) choose Option No. 1.

Variations: one woman who has been married three times and divorced three times uses all four available last names, changing them as if she were changing outfits, according to mood or season. More commonly it happens that a woman has made her professional reputation, in her 20s and 30s, while using the name of her first husband, then gets divorced and possibly remarried, but remains stuck with the first husband's name in the middle of her three-name procession.

Names possess a peculiar indelible power—subversive, evocative, satirical, by turns. The name is an aura, a costume. Dickens knew how names proclaim character—although anyone named Lance is bound to hope that that is not always true. Democrats used to have fun with "George Herbert Walker Bush." The full inventory of the pedigree, formally decanted, produced a piled-on, Connecticut preppie-Little Lord Fauntleroy effect that went nicely with the populist crack that Bush "was born on third base and thought he had hit a triple."

How many names does a decent person need? For ordinary getting around, two, as a bird requires two wings. More than two, as a rule, is overweight. Only God should use fewer than two.

The words with which people and things are named have a changeful magic. Some cultures invent different names for people in different stages of life. In Chinese tradition a boy of school age would be given a "book name," to be used in arranging marriages and other official matters. A boy's book name might be "Worthy Prince" or "Spring Dragon" or "Celestial Emolument." (Does a father say, "Hello, have you met my boy, Celestial Emolument?")

Hillary Rodham Clinton may find her name changing still further as her White House power evolves. Perhaps by next year, she will be known as "H.R. Clinton." Maybe the year after that, she will be "H.R. (Bob) Clinton." ∎

AFTER YOU READ

Comprehension Questions

1. What is the history of Bill Clinton's name?
2. When did Hillary Rodham become Hillary Clinton? When did she become Hillary Rodham Clinton?
3. How many choices for names does a married woman in American culture have? What are they?
4. Some naming practices of Arab and Chinese cultures are mentioned in the article. What are they?

Discussion and Analysis Questions

1. Review your answer to Comprehension question 3. What does each choice imply about a woman's attitude?
2. What do you think the description "was born on third base and thought he had hit a triple" implies? What do you think the phrase "like a convoy of armored cars" implies? Are the phrases complimentary?
3. Reread the last three paragraphs of the article. What, do you think, is the writer's *tone* (attitude toward the topic)? Which words or phrases helped you decide?

Group Activities

1. In groups of four, discuss naming practices for married women in your home culture. Have these practices changed recently? Share your information with the class.
2. In American culture, nicknames (shortened versions of names) are used often. Below are common first names for men and women. In groups of four, try to decide what nickname is used for each.

William	Susan
Herbert	Elizabeth
Harold	Melissa
Robert	Sandra
Douglas	Rebecca
James	Melinda
Thomas	Kathleen
Richard	Margaret

Individual Work

Make a list of bumper stickers that you observe. Group them according to category (for example, political). Present examples to the class and, as a group, discuss their meanings.

INDEX OF CULTURE AND VOCABULARY TERMS

The following articles contain very minor editorial changes:

- "Ask a Satellite for Directions"
- "The Big Blowup—on Venus"
- "Breezing into the Future"
- "Do the Poor Deserve Bad Schools?"
- "Forget Verdi, Try Carmen"
- "Hot House of Champions"
- "Invasion of the Superbug"
- "Now Hear This—If You Can"
- "The State of Many Tongues"
- "The Tactics of Tantrums"
- "Why 180 Days Aren't Enough"

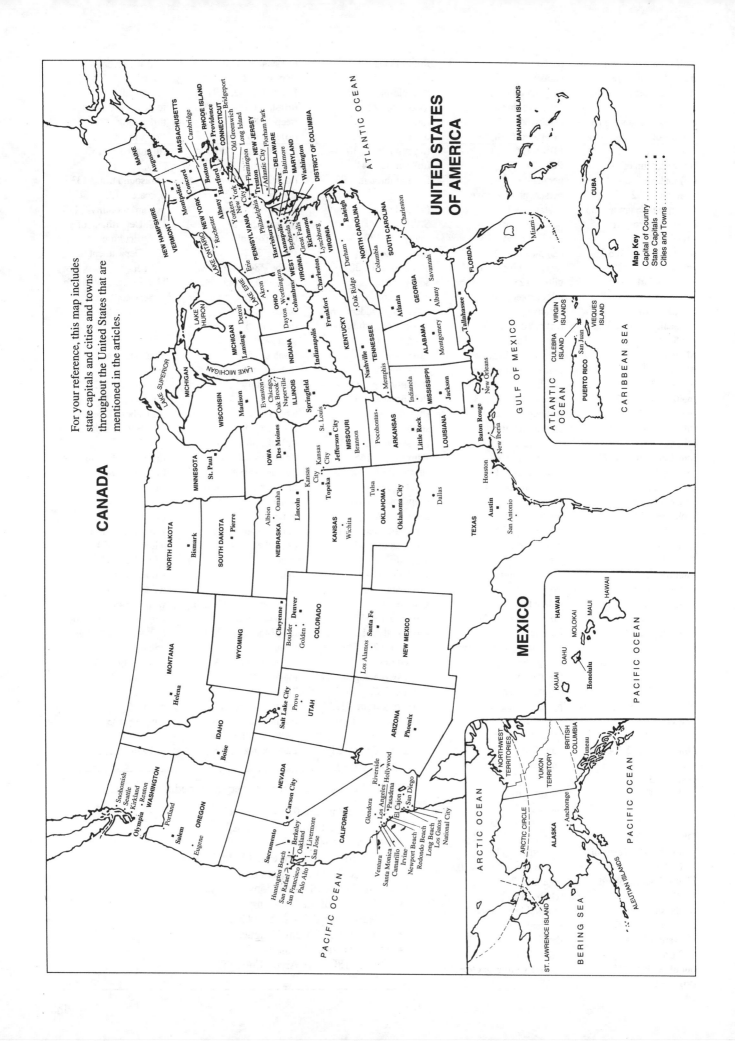

For your reference, this map includes state capitals and cities and towns throughout the United States that are mentioned in the articles.

UNITED STATES OF AMERICA

CANADA

MEXICO

Map Key

Capital of Country ....
State Capitals ....
Cities and Towns ....